Ideology and the International Economy

Also by Robert Leeson

A.W.H. PHILLIPS: Collected Works in Contemporary Perspective

THE ECLIPSE OF KEYNESIANISM: The Political Economy of the Chicago Counter-Revolution

ECONOMISTS AND EXPECTATIONS: From Microfoundations to Macroapplications

THE POLITICAL ECONOMY OF THE INFLATION–UNEMPLOYMENT TRADE-OFF

Ideology and the International Economy

The Decline and Fall of Bretton Woods

Robert Leeson
Associate Professor in Economics
Murdoch University
Australia

palgrave
macmillan

First published 2003 by
PALGRAVE MACMILLAN
Houndmills, Basingstoke, Hampshire RG21 6XS and
175 Fifth Avenue, New York, N.Y. 10010
Companies and representatives throughout the world

PALGRAVE MACMILLAN is the global academic imprint of the Palgrave Macmillan division of St. Martin's Press, LLC and of Palgrave Macmillan Ltd. Macmillan® is a registered trademark in the United States, United Kingdom and other countries. Palgrave is a registered trademark in the European Union and other countries.

ISBN 1–4039–0370–0

This book is printed on paper suitable for recycling and made from fully managed and sustained forest sources.

A catalogue record for this book is available from the British Library.

A catalog record for this book is available from the Library of Congress.

10 9 8 7 6 5 4 3 2 1
12 11 10 09 08 07 06 05 04 03

Printed and bound in Great Britain by
Antony Rowe Ltd, Chippenham and Eastbourne

Contents

Part IV Friedman and the Policy Revolution

Part V End Game

Acknowledgements

I am grateful (without implication) to Bob Coats, Graeme Dorrance, Stanley Fischer, Dan Hammond, Melanie Hearne, Robert Hetzel, David Laidler, Michael Parkin, Mark Perlman, James Powell, Pierre Rinfret, Don Walker, Richard Watson, John Williamson, Warren Young and participants at the June 2001 conference 'The Open Economy Macro-model: Past, Present and Future' and the July 2002 International Economic History Association Congress. Harold James very kindly read the manuscript and Jim Broughton made numerous helpful suggestions. As always, Milton Friedman was extremely generous with his time. Financial assistance from the Gerald R. Ford Presidential Library is gratefully acknowledged. Six groups of librarians – at the Inter Library Loan desk, Murdoch University (Doris McIntyre and Ida Bertolini), the Hoover Institution (the Friedman Archives), Duke University (the Don Patinkin Papers and the Homer Jones Papers), the Joseph Regenstein Library, at the University of Chicago (the George Stigler Papers), the Gerald R. Ford Presidential Library (the Arthur Burns Papers and William Simons Archives) and the IMF archives – were exceptionally helpful. I am grateful for their permission to cite from these archival sources and to Stephen Stigler for his permission to cite from the George Stigler Papers and to Milton Friedman for his permission to cite from his correspondence. I am most grateful to Philip Tye for editorial assistance in the production of this volume. One of the laws of the scholarly universe is that the singularity of curiosity is followed by the Big Bang of research projects expanding infinitely in all directions. Regrettably, I was unable to inspect the raw Nixon White House tapes (only the transcripts) which, for example, may have shed some light on the conflicting accounts of the 27 April 1970 Nixon–Friedman–Rinfret meeting.

1
Introduction

On the frontispiece of Alfred Marshall's *Principles of Economics* is the statement: *natura non facit saltum* ('nature does not proceed by sudden leaps'). Yet, in the early 1970s, after a quarter of a century of bureaucratically determined exchange rates, the world appeared to leap into a regime of market-determined exchange rates. In the previous decade, those who administered and policed the Bretton Woods international monetary system considered a variety of reforms but 'firmly and unanimously discarded at the very outset' the two reforms that were subsequently implemented: flexible exchange rates and flexible gold prices (Triffin 1968, 105; 1976, 49). The role played by academic economists in this international revolution has usually been relegated to minor proportions or ignored altogether. Yet, what appeared to be a sudden policy leap had been preceded by years of academic campaigning – a campaign that is documented and analysed in this study.

John Maynard Keynes shared with Karl Marx the belief that capitalism was inherently unstable. Keynes's (1936, 383) hope for a 'middle way' solution to the instability of the 1930s rested on the belief that the 'power of vested interests is vastly exaggerated compared with the gradual encroachment of ideas'. In Milton Friedman's (1967, 76) judgement, the debate over flexible exchange rates pitted private sector bankers with 'unlimited faith in the ability of government bureaucrats' against academics with faith in private market outcomes. This study documents the process by which the idea of allowing the price of foreign exchange to be determined largely by market forces rather than forces supervised by the International Monetary Fund (IMF) gradually encroached on the policy-making process. This free market idea was opposed by those who had a vested interest in the preservation of the writ of the IMF edict and who were haunted by the 'specter' of institutional impotence

(Southard 1979, 45). This vested interest intermingled with the understandable fear that floating exchange rates would unleash all the furies of the 1930s.

Paul Volcker described aspects of the 'intellectual and institutional base' for the Bretton Woods international order (Volcker and Gyohten 1992, 3). The advocates of floating exchange rates assaulted first the intellectual base and then the institutional base: a classic example of the gradual encroachment of ideas. But in 1968, Friedman presented the case so as to appeal to President-elect Richard Nixon's vested interest in being a two-term President. What Nixon (1980, 245) described as Friedman's 'escape' route began to appeal to those who were averse to the crises that appeared to be endemic to the Bretton Woods system. Simultaneously, Friedman's case for monetary targeting appealed to those who were grappling with the apparently intractable problems of restraining price and wage inflation and the associated industrial disputation.

After the Bretton Woods system collapsed, Friedman (1988a) wrote the introduction to an anthology for the American Coalition for Flexible Exchange Rates, which had been formed to prevent a return to exchange rate fixity (Melamed 1988a, xvi). Earlier, before the collapse of the par value system, academic economists behaved 'as if' they were members of a coordinated coalition pressing for flexible exchange rates. This study documents the process by which Friedman's case converted academic economists into what amounted to an organised pressure group (the first phase) and then permeated (marginally) into the international monetary bureaucracy (the second phase) and then penetrated (forcefully) into Nixon's White House (the third phase). The fourth phase, the establishment of a futures market in foreign exchange, was undertaken by the Chicago Mercantile Exchange as the Bretton Woods system was collapsing. The first and second processes were 'organised' by Fritz Machlup; the third stage was facilitated by US Treasury Secretaries David Kennedy, John Connally, George Shultz, William Simon and their deputies (including Paul Volcker) and to a lesser extent by Gottfried Haberler, Consultant to the US Treasury and chairman of President-elect Nixon's Task Force on the Balance of Payments. Friedman played an important role in all four stages.

This study therefore examines the interactions between three groups of agents in the international economic arena: academic economists, the Bretton Woods administrators and US policy makers. Part I examines the intellectual background: the combatants (Chapter 2), the relationship between fixed exchange rates and the two goals of full employment and free trade (Chapter 3), Friedman's case for flexible exchange rates (Chapter 4) and the characteristics of those who were determined to maintain the par value system (Chapter 5).

Part II describes the academic and intellectual process from the 1940s to the late 1960s, when Friedman was President of the American Economic Association (AEA) and Nixon was President of the United States: the early history of Friedman's case (Chapter 6), the emerging academic consensus (Chapter 7), four 1966 academic conferences (Chapter 8) and Friedman's 1967 debate with Robert Roosa, the President of the American Finance Association (Chapter 9).

Part III describes the policy process from Nixon's 1968 election victory to the August 1971 New Economic Policy (NEP) which introduced wage and price control and allowed the dollar to float. Both were designed to be temporary, although the par value system did not remain patched up for long. Chapter 10 describes the process by which the case for flexible exchange rates became influential in Washington. Chapter 11 outlines Friedman's attempt to persuade Nixon that flexible exchange rates were an ideal vehicle for his re-election.

From victory in Europe to defeat in Vietnam, Americans had been spared the choice of being for or against Nixon in only two national elections (1948 and 1964). When Connally wanted to 'hit Nixon right where he lived' he taunted him with the prospect of being the one-term Herbert Hoover of his time (Rather and Gates 1974, 279). Between Hoover's Presidency (1929–33) and the policy hegemony of the Hoover Institution economists (1981–89), Roosevelt was the perennial President and then Nixon was the perennial candidate.

Franklin Delano Roosevelt was elected US President not once but four times. At the start of his first term, Roosevelt suspended the internal convertibility of the dollar into gold (the nationalisation of gold). In August 1971, Nixon suspended the external convertibility of the dollar into gold (the demonetisation of gold). Chapter 12 describes Friedman's attempt to persuade Nixon to disburden himself of the 'cross of gold'. Chapter 13 describes the path towards the price and wage controls that were experimented with on both sides of the Atlantic in the early 1970s, experiments which coincided with the decontrol of exchange rates.

Part IV illustrates Friedman's interaction with the international monetary system. Chapter 14 discusses the nature of Friedman's influence. Some comparisons are drawn between Keynes and Friedman, and some of the associations formed at the University of Chicago are examined. Friedman's loyalty to the Chicago cause is examined, as is the loyalty of the Bretton Woods administrator to the system of fixed exchange rates.

The following six chapters (15–20) examine previously unreported correspondence to dissect Friedman's relationships with 16 (mostly highly important) players in debates about the international economy: five intellectuals, Lionel Robbins, Enoch Powell, John Kenneth Galbraith, Paul Samuelson and Charles Kindleberger, two US Senators, Paul Douglas and Barry Goldwater, the international policemen and especially Per Jacobsson of the IMF, the four US Treasury Secretaries of the era, David Kennedy, John Connally, George Shultz and William Simon, the two Federal Reserve Chairmen of the era, William McChesney Martin and Arthur Burns, plus a White House adviser, Pierre Rinfret, and Nixon. Of the intellectuals Robbins was a senior libertarian, Powell an aspiring British Prime Minister, Galbraith a leading Left Keynesian, Samuelson a leading Right Keynesian and Kindleberger a leading international economist and textbook writer. Rinfret competed with Friedman for Nixon's ear.

As the international monetary policemen struggled to patch up the fixed exchange rate system and began to consider placing more elastic bands around the par values, Nixon was consumed by Watergate and foreign policy (especially relations with China and the Soviet Union and the wars in Vietnam and the Middle East). His Treasury advisers wished to bury Bretton Woods: in international negotiations they offered 'faint praise' for a revised par value system while guaranteeing their right to let the dollar float. The system had been under strain throughout the 1960s, but the advice that Nixon received from his Task Force on the Balance of Payments and from his Treasury Secretaries differed from the advice that Presidents Lyndon B. Johnson, John F. Kennedy and Dwight D. Eisenhower had been offered. The crucial US participants in the efforts to patch up the system were motivated by a different perspective about the desirable end-state than were their predecessors.

Part V describes continues the narrative until the 1975–76 revision of the IMF Articles of Agreement which legitimised floating. Although the system of fixed exchange rates collapsed for a variety of reasons, efforts to revive the system were abandoned in large part because of the attitudes of those within the Nixon–Ford Treasury Departments. The success of their (and Friedman's) advocacy of a floating system was conditional on the attitude of 'benign neglect' that they encouraged Presidents Nixon and Gerald Ford to adopt. Chapters 21 and 22 analyse the final collapse of the par value system, during Shultz's and Simon's tenure as Treasury Secretaries. Concluding comments are provided in Chapter 23.

Part I

The Intellectual and Institutional Framework

2
The Combatants

This study is largely organised around the intellectual and institutional battles between the IMF and the influence of Milton Friedman. It focuses on the process by which the defenders of a par value system were confronted by an academic heretic who, having nailed his theses (first in Germany, just as a predecessor had done four and quarter centuries before) tenaciously pursued his heresy. Friedman's intellectual rebellion against 'papal' authority invoked the right of national economic sovereignty, and after almost '30 years' of intellectual and political schism, the 1976 'Treaty' of Jamaica resembled the 1648 Treaty of Westphalia in terms of the toleration offered to heretical floaters.

The IMF sat at the centre of the monetary universe until it was replaced by market forces in what the German central banker Otmar Emminger (1976, 13) described as 'a sort of "Copernican revolution"'. This international revolution facilitated the domestic monetarist counter-revolution – although Friedman was not impressed by the continued attempts to influence the value of the dollar (Friedman and Friedman 1980, 70). However, no account of the fall of the Bretton Woods system would be complete without an attempt to discuss the role of the IMF and the consequences of their 'undeviating' devotion to the par value system (Southard 1979, 23; de Vries 1985a, 105).

Contemporary history frequently generates considerable polemical heat, and few institutions have been as controversial as the IMF and the Chicago School of Economics. For example, mainstream economists, such as Rudiger Dornbusch (1993, 103) declared that 'When it counts, the IMF can be relied upon to be disappointing.' Others have been even more uncompromising. *The Case against the IMF* (McQuillan 2000) has been marshalled at the Hoover Institution (ideologically, a Chicago outpost). In *Who Needs the IMF* Shultz, Simon and James Wriston (1998) argued that the IMF was 'ineffective, unnecessary, and obsolete'. In his prestigious AEA Ely Lecture, Shultz (1995, 5) recommended that the IMF be abolished and a 'drastically' pruned institution be established by merging the IMF and the World Bank. Indeed, before the Senate Committee on Foreign Relations, Shultz gave the IMF an 'F': it was time 'to close the book on the IMF' (Hoover Digest 2000, no. 3).

Part of Shultz's reasoning was based on competence:

> The evidence is that the IMF's economic programs have often been wrong, so their competence in economics, their presumed area of expertise, must be questioned. But when they get into the business of prescribing policies that infringe on the politics of countries, they really don't know what they're doing.

This type of reasoning inevitably produces a defensive response from IMF economists, at least one of whom has detected in this volume a similar attempt to denigrate his institution. Therefore it should be made clear at the outset that this essay is part of no such preconceived agenda. Instead, it is an attempt to supplement the existing material by examining the intellectual and institutional campaign against the par value system.

The collapse of the patched up Bretton Woods system has usually been attributed to the failure to transcend national self-interest or, more often, to the insurmountable problems associated with maintaining exchange rate fixity after the oil price shocks of the 1970s. One historian asked why the outcome (the legitimisation of flexible exchange rates) differed 'so totally' from the original intentions of those who sought to save the system (Williamson 1987, 18). Events may have moved too fast to save the system (de Vries 1987, 96). But the world had also been turned intellectually upside down by the revolutionary advocacy of flexible exchange rates. Friedman's major co-author offered a four-word paragraph by way of explanation: 'Market forces had triumphed' (Schwartz 1987, 350). There was also, however, an intellectual and institutional triumph for those who advocated the ascendancy of market forces.

Certainly, the final outcome may well have been different had Nixon and Ford and their Treasury Secretaries been committed to a par value system. This has previously been acknowledged, as has the importance of 'key personalities' pressing for flexible exchange rates (Scammell 1983, 184; Williamson 1987, 19). But the intellectual and institutional dimensions of this policy volte-face have usually not been brought to the forefront. Friedman (1968a, 186) reflected about the 'extraordinary importance of accidents of personality' with respect to monetary outcomes; and both Shultz and Simon and their deputies were firm advocates of exchange rate flexibility. Nixon, under their influence, was also not inclined to defend the patched up Bretton Woods system. It is impossible to quantify these direct and indirect intellectual influences, but it is reasonable to conclude that such influences were highly significant and therefore worthy of detailed scrutiny.

IMF officials were apparently psychologically ill-prepared for the assault on the par value system. Their institution had been established to prevent a return to the dislocation of the 1930s. Until the 1960s, it was widely accepted both by academic and IMF economists that floating exchange rates were a species of law-breaking behaviour. For understandable reasons, this assumption became central to IMF thinking; their defence of civilisation became synonymous with their defence of the IMF. In a static or slowly changing world, collective institutional assumptions, like a common language, can reduce short-run communication costs. It is more costly to communicate with 'outsiders' who share neither language nor common assumptions. It appears that those who policed the Bretton Woods system regarded the benefits of communication with heretical 'outsiders' as usually being dwarfed by the costs.

Until the 1960s, the assumptions of the IMF held monopoly sway both at an intellectual and at an institutional level. But the Chicago counter-revolution was a coordinated and well-thought-out assault on orthodoxy. As international trading relations began to atrophy in the 1930s, Chicago graduate students were exposed to Jacob Viner's Economics 301, which produced what Friedman described as a 'revelation, a perspective that showed economic theory as a coherent and logical whole'.[1] The second-generation Chicago economists – especially George Stigler – constructed a theory of the sociology of knowledge which viewed the market for economics as a coherent and logical whole (Leeson 2000).

The par value system was destroyed both by market forces and by the weakened resolve to interfere with those market forces.[2] Friedman (and his associates) played the major role in the weakening of this resolve: he occupied, according to Stigler, the 'de facto presidency of the unorganised Friends of Private Enterprise'.[3] In *The Intellectual and the Market Place*, Stigler (1963, 42) noted that knowledge is produced under competitive conditions: 'confused' participants would 'watch their customers vanish, their best employees migrate, their assets dissipate'.

Moreover, a monopolist was 'overwhelmingly dominated by forces over which he had negligible control. This paradox that power deprives one of the certainty of success is partly verbal, as all good paradoxes are, but it contains an important truth.'

In *A Time for Truth*, William Simon (1978, 198) cited approvingly Friedman's view of monopoly: 'The major source of private monopoly has not been private collusion, it has been government activity. There is hardly a major monopoly in the United States that doesn't derive its power from government grants.' In the 1930s, the world had suffered from a lack of international leadership; the IMF had been established as a vehicle through which such leadership could be exercised. Institutionally, their monopoly power was limited only by intransigent national governments that sometimes resorted to currency floats, thus undermining the leadership of the IMF. In the 1960s, the IMF might legitimately have regarded their 'firm' as virtually the entire institutional 'industry'. However, they appeared not to fully appreciate the extent to which their institutional monopoly was conditional upon the support of the US Treasury.

Friedman's *academic* opponents became obsessed with his work: 'he controlled the Cambridge Universities and Yale. They were devoting much of their efforts to seeking to refute what he had most recently written' (Stigler 1988, 33–4). In contrast, the IMF was accustomed to consuming academic output as an intermediate good; they were not apparently willing to view themselves as operating in an intellectual duopoly. According to the IMF historians, the balance of payments difficulties that by the mid-1960s began to appear to be endemic to the Bretton Woods system, enabled floating rate advocates to 'muster additional adherents'. Yet their arguments were still regarded in official circles as 'untenable'. By 1969, the arguments of the Bretton Woods 'detractors' had spread outwards from academia to official circles and were being taken up by 'leading newspapers and public personalities' (de Vries and Horsefield 1969, 173; de Vries 1976a, 447–8, 501, 513; see also Williamson 1987, 85).

By the end of the 1960s the IMF had seen numerous academic reform proposals come and go. They had a double motive for wishing to let the floating option drift until it lost potency: not only did it represent an assault on the IMF creation mythology, it also threatened the existence of the institution. Thus when in September 1969, Paul Volcker, Nixon's Under-Secretary of Monetary Affairs at the Treasury (1969–74), raised both the issue of increasing exchange rate flexibility and of including 'outsiders' in what IMF officials regarded as the exclusive 'business of the Fund', they responded with incredulity. Perhaps in the expectation that this reform proposal would die if starved of bureaucratic oxygen, the IMF decided that this examination of flexibility 'should proceed at a slow pace' (see Chapter 5). But this sentence of death by bureaucratic inertia was both a miscalculation and an underestimation of Friedman's mission: to keep alive free market ideas until policy makers required solutions at a time of crisis (Friedman and Friedman 1998, 220).

With respect to policy outcomes, Friedman placed a great deal of emphasis on the qualities and attitudes of those who wield power. Friedman 'has long thought that [Shultz] would make a splendid president, if a non-career politician could conceivably get the nomination and win the election' (Friedman and Friedman 1998, 376). As the fate of the par value system hung in the balance, Friedman (6 November 1972) wrote to Treasury Secretary Shultz comparing him to Simon Newcomb's description of his nineteenth-century predecessor, Hugh McCulloch.[4] According to Newcomb, McCulloch displayed 'the highest administrative wisdom... [by making] a careful study of the prevailing conditions of public opinion, and of the means at his disposal for keeping the movement all things in the right direction... [and by] getting the best men in office'. Friedman added that McCulloch 'was a remarkable man' with an 'extraordinary similarity to your own characteristics'.[5]

Shultz displayed loyalty to Chicago principles and personnel. In 1962, W. Allen Wallis recruited Shultz to succeed him as Dean of the Graduate School of Business at the University of Chicago (Friedman and Friedman 1998, 132). In a section entitled 'Getting the Right People', Shultz (1993, 33–4) explained that upon becoming Ronald Reagan's Secretary of State in 1982 he recruited Wallis to be his Under-Secretary for Economic Affairs: 'Decisions might not go his way for political reasons, but as a forceful advocate of the free market, he never fails to leave his mark.' For his deputy he 'called Ken Dam right off... Ken had a brilliant mind, honed to a keen edge in the seminar rooms of Chicago'.[6] Shultz had recruited Arthur Laffer to Chicago and in 1970 took him to the Office of Management and Budget (OMB) as chief economist (Reeves 2001, 230; Blumenthal 1986, 177).[7] Shultz also persuaded Nixon to offer Stigler the position of foreign trade adviser to the President – an offer Stigler declined (Stigler 1988, 137).

One of Shultz's 'Right People' was William Simon. Although Simon (1978, 8, 50–1, 56) was appointed by Nixon to be the 'Albert Speer' of the energy problem, he also insisted on retaining his position as Shultz's Deputy Treasury Secretary. The 16 months he spent as Shultz's deputy were 'among the most rewarding periods of my life.... The greatest experience and the finest personal as well as intellectual, experience that any man could have. His brilliance, his analytical mind, his reasoning, his patience, his thoughtfulness were incomparable.' Simon found that his experiences as 'energy czar' illustrated 'a classic case out of a free market textbook'.

With a certain amount of hubris, the IMF Managing Director Per Jacobsson (1956–63) described his faith in a 'managed "invisible hand"' (Jacobsson 1979, 398, 401, 402). Simon (1978, 56, 76) sarcastically described his own efforts as overlord and overrider of the energy market as 'William E. Simon, Invisible Hand'. Shultz told him that 'I'm so glad it's *you* who's heading up the energy bureaucracy. That way it *will* go out of business, and you'll be able to keep the damage in check' [emphasis in original]. Nemesis came to the IMF system while Shultz headed up the Treasury (1972–74). The 'Right People' in the right place could, as if led by an invisible hand, promote an end that was no part of the intention of other players in the political market place. When this gradually became apparent to IMF officials they were forced to concede 'that the institution's future was uncertain' (de Vries 1987, 117).

Volcker initially regarded the Bretton Woods system as sacrosanct: 'all my life I have defended exchange rates' (cited by Safire 1975, 514, 518). Later he came to realise that those who supported par values had been 'trapped in channels that were far too conventional' (Volcker and Gyohten 1992, 115). Shultz agreed that the international monetary system 'had a life of its own'. He also reflected about the 'self-deception' of some key players (Shultz and Dam 1977a, 130).

At the end of the 1960s, few if any of those in official circles saw the collapse of the par value system as 'imminent' (de Vries 1976a, 447–8, 501, 513; Williamson 1987, 85). According to the IMF historian, at the end of the 1960s, the purely 'academic' issue of exchange rate flexibility became a 'live policy question' (de Vries 1987, 94). But with respect to exchange rate regimes the term 'academic' had pejorative connotations for those in the IMF. Within a short period of time, it was the IMF solutions which obviously had a 'distinct air of unreality or of having been an academic exercise' (de Vries 1985a, 140).

In June 1972, the IMF established a new Committee of the Board of Governors of the Fund on the Reform of the International Monetary System and Related Issues (the Committee of Twenty or C-20) to salvage the par value system. Even determined supporters of the par value system despaired about their lack of progress. As their system was being destroyed, Burns (1 February 1973) complained to President Nixon that the C-20 had 'made virtually no progress'.[8] When in September 1973, it was 'first surmised that the US authorities wanted "absolute freedom to float"...this came as a shock' (de Vries 1985a, 239). Henceforth the Committee were left to indulge themselves in 'a purely theoretical exercise without any practical meaning' (Emminger 1978a, 403). It was a 'very low point' when they realised the Shultz–Volcker position. Henceforth they realised it was 'pointless to keep on arguing' (de Vries 1985a, 239, 241).

Frank Southard (1979, 1), an IMF Deputy Managing Director, recalled that when the system that they were pledged to defend broke down, the IMF was 'shaken to its roots'. Jacobsson's successor, Pierre-Paul Schweitzer, was apparently placed on a Nixon administration enemies list and there was opposition to his continuation as IMF Managing Director (he was replaced by Johannes Witteveen in September 1973). Thus as their system collapsed, the IMF was saddled with a lame duck leadership (Coombs 1976, 220; de Vries 1985a, 118, 130, 150; Solomon 1982, 225, 228; James 1996, 244).

Lawrence Krause (1971, 50) concluded that 'ideological intransigence is more damaging to the [Bretton Woods] system than lack of foresight'. The Bretton Woods administrators appeared to suffer both handicaps. As their system was collapsing, the IMF instructed 'The Economic Counsellor', Jacques Polak, to provide a new and more lasting set of par values. When this abstract exercise was completed in December 1971, the IMF Research Department was 'euphoric' (de Vries 1976a, 524, 537–8; 1985a, 126; 1987, 93; James 1996, 223). Polak (1979, 39) later reflected on their 'lack of foresight' and also to the 'assumption' held until the early 1970s that 'fixed exchange rates would have to stay'. A second component of this ideological intransigence was the 'unthinkable' proposal to increase the price of gold. These orthodox views were, Polak thought, held by 'virtually everyone'. He discussed the forces which set certain 'limits to our ability to influence the system', but there was little apparent realisation of the intellectual dimension: the pressure exerted by economists from outside the banking fraternity.

This study examines the interactions between these combatants. It does not, however, attempt to adjudicate between fixed and floating diehards. Instead, it seeks to analyse the process by which Friedman's case for flexible exchange rates became fertile: by converting the academic community and then permeating influential sections of the US policy apparatus, and then by transforming the international monetary system.

In the process, Friedman was obliged to overcome the institutional influence of the person responsible for him pursuing an academic career, Arthur Burns. When Burns was appointed Chairman of the

Board of Governors of the Federal Reserve in 1970, John Davenport wrote a note in *Fortune* entitled 'Where Arthur Sits' which ended: 'It has been said that no matter what job Burns holds, "where Arthur sits, there is the head of the table".' Friedman concurred with this judgement about Burns's personality: he was also Friedman's 'surrogate father' (Friedman and Friedman 1998, xi, 30).

For Nixon (1962, 309–11) Burns was 'a good prophet' because he had predicted an increase of unemployment just before the 1960 US Presidential election (a prophecy made as immediate AEA past President). Just before the 1968 US Presidential election, Friedman (1968b) used neoclassical price theory in his AEA Presidential address to prophesy increasing unemployment (and inflation). After this highly visible AEA Presidential predicting of stagflation, Friedman acquired enormous academic credibility and political influence.

But Friedman had not wished to be AEA President at that time. On 3 January 1964, Friedman wrote to Stigler (AEA President and chairman of the AEA nominating committee):

> I do hope that you will not in any way try to push my nomination for the presidency. In view of our closeness, that would be embarrassing for both of us and demeaning for you...I have sufficient confidence to believe that they will come to me sooner or later + so far as I am concerned the later the better...I very much fear the drain of time and energy involved.[9]

Friedman's reprieve lasted only a year: in early 1965, he became AEA President-elect for 1966 and President for 1967. Had he been successful in delaying his Presidency he might have chosen a topic that would have associated Chicago economics with ridicule rather than superior predictive ability.

Simon (1978, 50, 82, 84) described the 'collective hysteria' which followed the October 1973 attempt by OPEC to exert the quasi-monopoly power of a cartel in the oil market. Friedman denounced the idea that only centralised state planning could solve the energy crisis as a 'monstrosity'. On 9 January 1974, Friedman used the platform of the University of Chicago annual Board of Trustees dinner for faculty to further illustrate the predictive power of neoclassical price theory. Had Friedman succeeded in delaying his AEA Presidency, he may well have used the platform of a Presidential address on 29 December 1973 to predict the demise of OPEC price fixing: 'The world crude oil price cannot stay at $10 a barrel; it will drop dramatically within the next six or nine months' (Friedman 1974a, 12). Friedman's prediction was out by over a decade. Had Chicago economics been associated with this predictive failure, policy makers might have looked elsewhere for scientifically reliable guidance.

But Nixon narrowly became President in 1969 (rather than Hubert Humphrey, whose advisers would presumably would have been less susceptible to a free market solution to the US balance of payments problem) and Friedman, by chance, delivered his AEA address at an opportune moment for Chicago predictions. As a result, monetary targeting acquired an increased appeal to policy makers struggling to contain both inflation and price and wage controls.

On 21 September 1974 the editor of *The Economist* noted that Friedman was 'taking Britain by storm' – an episode that has already been documented (see for example Keegan 1984; Smith 1987; Parsons 1989; Pepper and Oliver 2001). The process by which Friedman's case took the international monetary system by storm has not hitherto been systematically analysed.

Indeed, Friedman was not mentioned in the analysis of 'Fifty Years of Exchange Rate Research and Policy at the International Monetary Fund' (Polak 1995). His case was not mentioned in the 1946–65 volume of the official IMF history nor in *The IMF Experience* nor in *Economic Policy behind the Headlines* (Shultz and Dam 1977a) nor in *Closing the Gold Window: Domestic Politics and the End of Bretton Woods* (Gowa 1983). It was accorded three sentences in both the 1966–71 volume and the monumental National Bureau of Economic Research *Retrospective on the Bretton Woods System*; plus eight sentences in the official history of the 1972–78 period (Horsefield 1969a, b; de Vries and Horsefield 1969; de Vries 1976, 1985a, 1987; Bordo and Eichengreen 1993). In the study of *International Monetary Co-operation since Bretton Woods*, written 'with the full cooperation' of the IMF, Friedman was described, in passing, as someone who in the early 1970s was 'regarded as an eccentric outsider' (James 1996, v, 213, 101).[10] His case was allocated 16 sentences plus footnotes in L. Yeager's (1976) history and one sentence in Robert Solomon's (1982) history. This study therefore does not attempt to replace but rather to supplement the orthodox chronology and analysis.

3

Full Employment, Free Trade and Fixed Exchange Rates

From Adam Smith to Alfred Marshall (1926 [1903], 394) most respectable economic opinion accepted the 'simplicity and naturalness of Free Trade' over the corruption and 'moral harm' associated with protection. The 1944 Bretton Woods agreement was designed to provide the post-war international stability to facilitate the approach towards both free trade and full employment. Per Jacobsson (1959, 12, 14) and his associates who administered the par value system believed that they were providing a vital ingredient that relieved businesses of the uncertainty associated with exchange rate instability, thus lowering costs and contributing to the expansion of world trade. They also believed that the IMF was the institution which guaranteed exchange stability. They did 'not think that anyone would seriously dispute' the 'purposes' of the IMF in this regard. They believed that 'strengthening of the existing exchange structure' was 'in the general interest'.

The simultaneous pursuit of these three post-war policy objectives posed a dilemma. According to one influential Keynesian observer, it was 'hardly an exaggeration to say that instead of being on a Gold Standard we are on a Labour Standard' (Hicks 1959, 52–3, 55, 64, 88–9, 155). But Bretton Woods was a dollar standard (backed by gold) and the single instrument of monetary policy had to target the two objectives of maintaining a fixed exchange rate and low levels of unemployment. John Hicks noted that the international repercussions of these national labour standards were a 'very grave preoccupation'. This led to the conclusion 'from which we can hardly escape' that a second policy instrument was required: 'there really is something in the Employment argument for Protection'. Since fixing exchange rates in terms of gold was 'the best guarantee of solidity that mankind had yet discovered', this created 'a strong case for Import Restrictions, as a means of facilitating expansion without weakening the Balance of Payments'.

Friedman (1968b, 7–8) believed that underpinning these sentiments lay an undue emphasis on the short- rather than the long-run consequences of policy. Certainly, Robert Solow (1966a, 60–1), a leading advocate of full employment, favoured free trade, but 'elementary realism' led him to conclude that 'significant steps' towards free trade 'will come very slowly, if indeed they come at all...in the meantime the immediate problem remains'. Influential players in the political arena such as George Meany (1973, 3–15), the President of the American Federation of Labor and Congress of Industrial Organizations (AFL-CIO), calculated that between 1966 and 1971 'unfair' imports had cost 900,000 job opportunities for Americans. In 1971, the US Labor movement was actively campaigning for the Burke–Hartke Bill which sought to impose import quotas on a wide spectrum of goods (Shultz and Dam 1977a, 113). As full employment advocates went on the offensive, free trade advocates were 'on the defensive' (Irwin 1996, 206). Within Nixon's White House, the 1971 devaluation of the dollar was regarded as 'the strongest argument we had to repel protectionism' (Volcker 1978–79, 7).

Between Marshall and Friedman (a leading Marshallian) lay the evolving advocacy of John Maynard Keynes. The younger Keynes (1972–89, *Collected Writings,* hereafter referred to as JMK XVII [1923], 451) advocated that 'We should hold to Free Trade as a principle of international morals, and not merely as a doctrine of economic advantage.' Later, as part of his 'long struggle of escape' from his Marshallian heritage, Keynes (1936, Ch. 23; JMK IX [1931], 238–42) found wisdom in mercantilist writings. As Friedman (1968a, 2) noted, Keynes advocated a tariff in 1930–31 as a remedy for unemployment. In July 1930, Keynes (JMK XX 378, 488, 494–5) advised the Prime Minister that he had 'become reluctantly convinced that some protectionist measures should be introduced'. His advocacy of tariffs caused a sensation in Britain. Perceiving the choice to be between tariffs and exchange rate flexibility, Keynes explained,

> if I look into the bottom of my own heart, the feeling which I find there is...that a tariff is a crude departure from *laissez-faire,* which we have to adopt because we have at present no better weapon in our hands, but that it will be superseded in time, not by a return to *laissez-faire,* but by some more comprehensive scheme of national planning.

This was the antithesis of the Chicago view and had been directly assaulted by economists at the London School of Economics (Beveridge *et al.* 1932). When in 1941 the University of Chicago sought to confer an honorary degree on Keynes in celebration of its fiftieth anniversary, Frank Knight vehemently opposed the suggestion because of Keynes's 'neo-mercantilist position' (cited by Patinkin 1981, 301). Knight (1954–55, 264, n. 3) explained that laissez-faire was 'of course a synonym for freedom, used in the economic connection'. Henry Simons (1948 [1944], 123) saw the world as a Greek-style tragedy in which policy 'rules' were confronted by 'its nemesis...racketeering – tariffs, other subsidies and patronage dispensations generally and, outside of government, monopoly'. Friedman was a graduate student at Chicago in 1932–33 and 1934–35, and an early version of his case can be found in Simons's (1934, 53–4) 'Money and the New Deal'. Simultaneously, Frederick Soddy (1934, 131–2, 173, 201; 1943, 25) outlined a 4 per cent money growth rule (which he attributed to Gustav Cassel) and advocated freely floating exchange rates as a vehicle to facilitate free trade.

Simons (1962 [1936]) created what Richard Selden (1962, 323) described as the 'Rules Party' and was regarded by some as 'the real leader of the real Chicago School' (Albert Hart cited by Samuels and Medema 1990, 112). Simons (1948 [1942], 199) implicitly defined his opponents by referring disparagingly to 'Hansen and his school'. Alvin Hansen (regarded as the 'American Keynes') and Charles Kindleberger favoured a 'dynamic approach' which stood in contrast to the passive acceptance of

> the play of 'natural' forces...many economists are coming to think that action along these traditional lines would by itself be wholly inadequate. It is increasingly understood that the essential foundation upon which the international security of the future must be built is an economic order so managed and controlled that it will be capable of sustaining full employment.

Hansen and Kindleberger (1942, 467, 469) insisted that the 'elimination of large-scale unemployment must be undertaken through international collaboration' which would prohibit a country from 'forc[ing] exports into areas where that action would displace equally or more efficient labour engaged in making the same products'. The following year in an AEA discussion of 'International Economic Relations', Margaret Gordon (1943, 447) described Simons as representing 'one school which believes we must restore free trade and at the same time restore a maximum degree of freedom in the domestic economy'. In the same session, Henry Chambers (1943, 450–1) described Simons not as the leader of a school, but as a romantic and isolated mountain-climber trying to 'ascend to this economic "Shangri-La"... "free trade", "free and stable exchanges" and "antimonopoly"'.

According to Chambers, Simons ascended almost alone: 'How many economists would agree that the difficult problems of reconstruction, after the terrific disruptions of the war, can be solved by leaving them to the free play of the unrestrained forces of the market and to the aggregate profit-motive of various people and interests?' Later, Keynes's self-appointed bulldog offered what she believed to be a further debunking of the free trade 'façade of a dogma with solid interests behind it... the free-trade doctrine is just a more subtle form of mercantilism. It is believed only by those who gain an advantage from it' (Joan Robinson 1966, 6, 24).

These three revolutionary or reforming imperatives interacted uneasily. The free trade reforming cause dates from the Smith–Ricardo attacks on mercantilism; the full employment imperative dates from the Keynesian revolution of the 1930s. But the Bretton Woods 'founding fathers' were also revolutionaries. These 'zealots' had given institutional expression to the 'revolutionary ideas' of banishing the 'twin devils' of the 1930s: depression and beggar-thy-neighbour trade policy, involving competitive currency devaluation (Reisman 1996, 82; de Vries 1996, 129; Campos 1996, 99). Indeed, some, such as Fed Chairman William McChesney Martin (1970, 9–10, 12, 15–16), invoked the authority of Keynes to justify 'the restraining conscience' that they exerted on those who might be tempted to pursue full employment without an appropriate anti-inflationary discipline. It was necessary 'to pool some of our sovereignty', that is, to relinquish national power to the IMF, the institution that was evolving into a world central bank. The public servants who policed the international economy believed that before 'us' lay the deluge of competitive devaluations. They also assumed that after 'us' lay a similar fate: 'a path leading into unknown darkness' (Caves 1963, 129). In this sense, they displayed some of the characteristics of an *ancien régime*.

McChesney Martin's successor as Fed Chairman was also apocalyptical in his defence of the par value system. For Burns (1969 [1964], 234; [1968], 301, 318, 298), devaluation 'would unsettle commercial and financial markets throughout the world. It would leave a legacy of fear that could result in a lasting constriction of international trade and investment. Worse still, it might injure fatally our country's foreign prestige and, therefore, its capacity for political leadership of the Free World.' The deteriorating balance of payments position had led governments to impose 'disturbing' restrictions on the outflow of capital, 'an interference with private investment that is contrary to our national traditions.... The decline in economic freedom that we are experiencing may not stop with lending and investing. As you well know, control of foreign travel by Americans has been under active consideration recently.' For Burns (1969 [1967], 285) there was the 'basic truth' that 'we need to learn better' that stable prices were required not only for 'sustained prosperity' but also to 'maintain international confidence in the dollar'.

Fixed exchange rates and a fixed price of gold were the Newtonian certainties upon which the Bretton Woods system rested (Volcker and Gyohten 1992, 7). A League of Nations (1944, 118, 128, 137, 159, 210–11) publication, primarily written by Ragnar Nurkse, outlined the 'proved disadvantages of freely fluctuating exchanges.... If there is anything that inter-war experience has clearly demonstrated, it is that paper currency exchanges cannot be left free to fluctuate.' This system 'would almost certainly result in chaos'. The actual system adopted in the 1930s ('The Devaluation Cycle') was believed to be 'associated with disturbances not very different from those associated with freely fluctuating exchanges'. In addition to the 1930s analogy, apocryphal Swiss bankers were often conjured up to demonstrate the compelling nature of the case against floating rates. Galbraith's (1964, 117, n. 9) banker informed him that the Swiss response to a devaluation of the US dollar might be a competitive devaluation 'late the same afternoon'.

For Friedman (1968a, 30, 71, 182; 1972a, 54–5), the macroeconomic pursuit of full employment was 'a modern invention for producing inflation'. The system of extensive controls over foreign exchange transactions was 'one of the few really new economic inventions of modern times'. This system had been 'perfected' in 1934 by Hjalmar Schacht 'primarily in order to despoil the Jews'. Friedman advised an Israeli audience that 'As a Jew, rather than an economist, I say to you, why don't you get rid of the false appearance, why don't you abolish the exchange controls and make your practice conform to your values. Set your people free.' Friedman first formulated his case for flexible exchange rates in 1950 as part of his contribution to the rehabilitation of Germany. His memo (dated 22 December 1950) formed the basis of his famous 1953 case which transformed academic perceptions and which helped to undermine the Bretton Woods system.

Friedman (1967, 17–18, 117–19, 183) argued that one of the major advantages of flexible rates was that 'it makes it so much easier for the layman to understand the merits of Free Trade'. This debate over the relative merits of the price mechanism as a social organiser involved two rival perceptions of what constituted the authentic American tradition. The Chicago view was that liberalised international trade, capitalism and therefore liberty were being undermined by the Frankensteins of trading blocks and the state. Friedman's (1962a, 2) *Capitalism and Freedom* was organised around the theme 'How can we keep the government we create from becoming a Frankenstein that will destroy the very freedom we establish it to protect?'

In the post-war period closer and closer approximations to full employment were visibly associated with higher and higher rates of open wage and price inflation. Some national policy makers wanted the discretion to pursue full employment, but since adverse inflation differentials were usually inconsistent with the maintenance of a fixed exchange rate (the 'sacred' symbol of national strength), price and wage inflation had to be suppressed through *Exhortation and Controls* (Goodwin 1975).

By 1965, moral suasion in the US had been supplemented by guidelines: specific numbers attached to targeted productivity gains and tolerable wage settlements. Also in 1965, foreign trade and investment guidelines (including tariffs and import quotas) were extended and a 15–20 per cent improvement in the US balance of payments was specified (Shultz and Aliber 1966, 294, 333, 340). Chicago economists opposed these controls. But according to the 1965 Council of Economic Advisers (CEA) Report, the guidelines were 'in the tradition of America, asking those to whom the society has entrusted economic power to exercise it in ways consistent with the national interest' (cited by Shultz and Aliber 1966, 312–13). CEA Chairman, Gardiner Ackley (1966, 73), explained that the guidelines attempted to 'harness this sense of social responsibility to the national interest in price stability or balance of payments equilibrium'.

It was thus becoming increasingly clear that fixed exchange rates, the pursuit of full employment and the absence of exchange controls were three sides of a triangle, only two of which could be connected by the same straight line. Typically, politicians 'solved' the problem by trampling on the free trade tradition by imposing import surcharges and capital controls (thus maintaining reforming credentials and electoral respectability with respect to the pursuit of full employment). In May 1971, at least one long-term IMF Governor (and, simultaneously, Governor of the Bank of Norway) argued that in the face of the threat of a German float, the par value system had to be preserved by controlling capital movements: 'The remedy was to reduce that freedom.'[1]

The policy responses to the adjustment crises experienced by the three dominant parties at the Bretton Woods conference raised the spectre of the protectionist solution of the 1930s. In the late 1950s, high unemployment led the Canadian authorities to seek a competitive advantage by depreciating their dollar while the Governor of the Bank of Canada advocated import controls (Marsh 1970, 341). In 1964, the British Labour government imposed a 15 per cent import surcharge: protection to defend a fixed exchange rate. In August 1971, President Nixon imposed a 10 per cent import surcharge to make certain 'that American products will not be at a disadvantage because of unfair exchange rates'. Samuelson (1974 [1971], 433) warned that this import surcharge might 'feed the fires of protectionism…we are playing with dynamite in terms of certain sentiments that run very deep in American life'. The internal aim of Nixon's New Economic Policy (NEP) was to reduce both inflation and unemployment; the external aim looked suspiciously similar to the protectionist sentiments that spawned the 1930 Smoot–Hawley tariffs (Plumptre 1977, 251).

Much of the literature on Bretton Woods has been organised around the 'holy trinity' of adjustment, liquidity and confidence (Eichengreen 1993, 621). Yet there was another holy trinity: the three apparently inconsistent post-war policy objectives of full employment, free trade and fixed exchange rates. Friedman's counter-revolution has been described as the 'monism of monetarists' (Sargent and Wallace 1976, 171). Yet Friedman raised the standard of revolt against both the labour standard and the Bretton Woods standard of fixed exchange rates. The fulfilment of the second (international) objective was a necessary though not sufficient condition for the achievement of the first (domestic) objective. Indeed, some of Friedman's domestic proposals were designed to facilitate the introduction of flexible exchange rates. For example, there was no *x* per cent money growth rule in the 'Monetary and Fiscal Framework for Economic Stability' because the money supply had been 'select[ed]' for counter-cyclical 'domestic stability'. It was therefore also incapable of defending a fixed exchange rate. But Friedman (1953 [1948], 142, n. 13) noted that 'it would be equally appropriate to present the proposed domestic framework as a means of implementing flexible exchange rates'.[2]

Friedman (1968c) believed that fixed exchange rates led to suppressed inflation, which subverted the price mechanism and opened the door for protection. Floating exchange rates would stimulate international trade and capital flows because they were 'a substitute for present or prospective restrictions'. Friedman (1968b, 14–15) supplemented the case for free trade with the notion that there was a 'natural' end-point for the macroeconomic pursuit of full employment: using monetary policy to target unemployment was akin to 'a space vehicle that has taken a fix on the wrong star'. Removing 'restrictions' or 'imperfections' at both the international and the *micro*economic level would produce better inflation–unemployment outcomes. The *macro*economic pursuit of full employment would be defeated by *micro*economic reality (the short-run Phillips curve would shift outwards in an adverse direction). The Chicago view was that the tariff was 'the mother of all trusts' and that free trade was required to permanently shift the Phillips curve downwards (Gideonse 1937, 111; Shultz and Aliber 1966, 3–4, 13). Thus policy activism at a microeconomic and international level would produce better outcomes than macroeconomic discretion.

The Chicago choice lay between a permanent shift of the Phillips curve (a) in a beneficial direction through free trade and microeconomic reform or (b) in an adverse direction following the macroeconomic pursuit of full employment (through the operation of the forces expressed by neoclassical price theory). In contrast, Friedman's Keynesian opponents hoped that price and wage control would allow *macro*economic policy to produce better inflation–unemployment outcomes (by interfering with the allocative mechanism of neoclassical price theory).

In his AEA Presidential address, Friedman (1968b, 4) referred to an AEA 'official attempt to codify the state of economic thought of the time' edited by Howard Ellis (1948). Ellis (1949, 437) specifically discussed the constraint imposed by the IMF commitment to 'exchange rate revisions only at infrequent intervals' and asked: 'What is going to give? Does not full employment achieved under a system of rigid prices almost inevitably imply...the outright control of international trade?' Since the choice for many Keynesians lay between full employment plus some form of incomes policy (which displaced the economy in a downwards vertical direction away from a Phillips curve), or abandoning full employment (disinflation which shifted the economy downwards and outwards along a Phillips curve), the first alternative was regarded as a 'bargain' (Solow 1970, 314).[3] As Paul McCracken, Nixon's CEA Chairman put it, a 'social bargain or compact' could be a crucial 'ingredient' in the fight against inflation ([1970] cited by De Marchi 1975, 348–9). Indeed, Joan Robinson (1969, xii) argued that prices and incomes policies were the logical applied corollary of Keynes's theory of prices, which the authorities had been obliged to accept for analogous reasons for the acceptance of full employment: the pressure of events and public opinion.

For Friedman any short-run benefits from this Faustian 'bargain' were countered by the long-run threat it posed to free trade (the revolutionary imperative with the longest lineage). He sought to undermine two of the three pillars of the post-war order, in part because they had combined to subvert the third. Those who argued for fixed exchange rates were guilty of the same perverted logic as the military strategists whose televised exploits in Vietnam were traumatising the world: 'It was necessary to destroy the city to save it' (Friedman 1972b, 104).[4]

A campaign was conducted to convert economists, bureaucrats and politicians. In 1960, Presidential candidate John Kennedy declared both his unalterable commitment to defend the dollar and his opposition to monetary policy as the 'sole means' of controlling inflation (Roosa 1967a, 269). Yet, the two years or so straddling Nixon's resignation (1973–75) witnessed the 'Transition from Fixed Exchange Rates to Money Supply Targets'. Two 'sacred' symbols (full employment and the Bretton Woods system) were jettisoned and replaced by another 'sacred' symbol: monetary targeting (Parkin 1977).

4

Friedman's Case for Flexible Exchange Rates

Friedman advanced floating exchange rates as the only reliable method of facilitating free trade, about which 'there has been virtual unanimity among economists'. In this way 'international cartels would disappear' and the US 'could come close to eliminating any danger of significant internal monopolies' (Friedman and Friedman 1980, 60–1, 76–7). Friedman (1953, 158, 164–5, 167, 171, 187, 197) took 'unrestricted multilateral trade' as an axiomatic objective: 'the fundamental requirement is that governments not use restrictions on trade of any kind to protect exchange rates'. The 'absence of flexible exchange rates is almost certain to be incompatible with unrestricted multilateral trade'.

According to Friedman (1962a, 40–2, 57, 71), the 'liberal's dilemma: a stable monetary framework without the danger of the irresponsible exercise of monetary powers' could be solved by an 'honest-to-goodness gold standard'. But such arrangements had never existed and 'certainly the situation is now more extreme as a result of the adoption by country after country of the view that government has responsibility for "Full Employment"'. The liberal's nightmare was that 'we shall be led to adopt far-reaching economic controls in order to "solve" balance of payments problems...there are few interferences which are capable of spreading so far and ultimately being so destructive of free enterprise'. Government price control was 'inconsistent with a free economy'; flexible exchange rates were the antidote to the 'never ending spiral' of increasing government intervention. Such a system 'would solve the balance of payments problem once and for all.... So long as we are firmly committed to the straight jacket of fixed exchange rates, we cannot move definitively to Free Trade.'

Friedman (1953, 165, 195; see also 1967, 12) opposed fixed exchange rates partly because of

> the inflexibility of [internal] prices, or different degrees of flexibility.... The adjustment [to changes in external conditions] takes the form primarily of price changes in some sectors, primarily of output changes in others.... The consequent decline in real income...is clearly a highly inefficient method of adjusting to external changes...the adjustment will not have been completed until the deflation has run its sorry course.

It was the strong commitment to 'a full employment policy which greatly limits the possibility of using changes in the internal price and wage structure as a means of adjusting to changes in internal conditions'.

The solution, Friedman (1953, 173) argued, was to 'Let the government simply stay out of the picture.' Restraining prices occupied an enormous amount of bureaucratic effort: the argument for flexible exchange rates was

> very nearly identical with the argument for daylight saving time. Isn't it absurd to change the clock in summer when exactly the same result could be achieved by having each individual change his habits?... The situation is exactly the same in the exchange market. It is far simpler to allow one price to change, namely the price of foreign exchange, than to rely upon changes in the multitude of prices that constitute the internal price structure.

The 'widespread emphasis on Full Employment' and the emergence of 'independence of internal monetary policy as a major policy goal' undermined the case for changes in internal prices or income as adjustment mechanisms: 'after the Great Depression completed the elevation of full employment to the primary goal of economic policy, nations have been unwilling to allow deficits to exert any deflationary effect'. Friedman (1953, 181; 1967, 137–8) thought that influential people needed to be 'educated on this issue'; the 'alternatives have not been made clear'. After being informed of the alternatives, nobody would choose 'a substantial recession or depression' over a 'slight fluctuation' in exchange rates. Given that the commitment to full employment was a constraint, the limited remaining adjustment capacity should not be 'fritter[ed] away on forcing prices up and down, on introducing exchange controls or capital controls'.

The linchpin of Friedman's (1953, 200; 1967, 17) argument was that removing the fixed exchange rate constraint allowed each country to pick a combination of inflation and unemployment 'according to its own lights...flexible exchange rates are a means of combining interdependence among countries through trade with a maximum of internal monetary independence'. Friedman (1953, 177–8, 199; 1967, 21–2) dismissed the argument that the exchange rate was a potent national symbol and a superior mobiliser of anti-inflationary forces. If, under a flexible rate system, 'any one country inflates, the primary effect is a deterioration of the exchange rate'. But 'public recognition that a substantial decline in the exchange rate is a symptom of or portends internal inflation is by no means an unmixed evil. It means that a flexible exchange rate would provide something of a barrier to a highly inflationary domestic policy.' Because foreign trade was a small part of total trade, the idea that removing the discipline of fixed rates would 'open the door to irresponsible inflationary policy...has negligible merits for the United States'.

Friedman objected to 'administrative rather than market control' over exchange rates: 'we have been driven as if by an invisible hand' to employ all the other expedients such as trade restrictions. One of the arguments against these expedients was that 'they are politically degrading and demeaning. We are a great and wealthy nation.' Flexible exchange rates would allow us to 'again become masters in our own house...the monetary authorities could concentrate on domestic prices and employment'. According to Friedman (1962a, 66; 1974b [1963], 394–5; see also 1967, 11), fixed exchange rates prevented the USA from having a 'healthy' expansion of the money supply.

It was fear of an inflation–devaluation spiral which underpinned part of the opposition to flexible exchange rates expressed by Robert Roosa (1967b, 47) and Lionel Robbins (1967, 11). Friedman (1953, 180–1) argued that the standard inflation–depreciation argument was defective: if 'the monetary authorities are ready to [increase the money supply] to validate any rise in particular prices or wages, then the situation is fundamentally unstable'. He disputed the argument that 'this innate instability is held in check by some sort of political compromise and that this compromise would be disturbed by the change in the exchange rate'. The 'wage–price spiral' was a 'crucial fallacy...a term that is impressive enough to conceal the emptiness of the argument that it generally adorns'. The depreciation-induced rise in the price of foreign goods increased the cost of living and generated the demand for wage increases, but this

> does not in and of itself provide the economic conditions for a wage rise – or, at any rate, for a wage rise without unemployment.

> A general wage rise – or a general rise in domestic prices – becomes possible only if the monetary authorities create the additional money to finance the higher level of prices.

The 'Chicago position today' is that 'what is interpreted as cost push is…the delayed impact of earlier demand pull inflation' (Friedman 1974c [1971], 375).

5
The Bretton Woods Establishment

The first two IMF Managing Directors, Camille Gutt and Ivar Rooth, both independently described their experiences as 'the worst years' of their lives. There was a perception that the Fund was ill suited to the post-war environment and had become a 'white elephant' and a 'bank without clients' (James 1996, 83–4, 91, 102). In the early years, there had been several devaluations and several renegade currencies floating. But after 1957, the IMF was pleased to report a reversal of these tendencies. The return of the prodigal Italian, Greek and Canadian currencies was especially welcomed: these experiences reinforced IMF prejudices against fluctuating rates (de Vries 1969, 164). In December 1958, Jacobsson negotiated with the French to establish a par value with the IMF for the first time since 1946 (James 1996, 106–7). Afterwards, to preserve the par value system, the international policemen began insisting that exchange rate adjustment could only be considered under very exceptional conditions (Machlup 1966a, 65). Thus the IMF was regarded as having come of age at this time (Krause 1971, 14).

In the early 1960s 'a second great period of international institution building took place, all with the purpose of defending and supporting the Bretton Woods system'. These institutions included the Group of Ten (G-10), various IMF committees and Working Party No. 3 (WP3) of the Economic Policy Committee of the OECD (Volcker and Gyohten 1992, 27). Behind these efforts apparently lay the final objective of 'a world central bank [which] is the ultimate to which all efforts towards international cooperation tend'. The 'scattered limbs' of a world central bank already existed in the guise of the IMF, the OECD and the Bank for International Settlement (Morse 1972, 78–9). It is important to explain why fixed exchange rates were embraced with such determination and why the solutions proposed by par value advocates later became 'swamped and lost to sight' (Fleming 1974, 3).

In the immediate post-war period, American support for the Bretton Woods agreement derived from the desire to avoid 'another world war'. Treasury Secretary John Synder exclaimed that 'we cannot permit economic warfare to weaken the bonds which hold the United Nations together' (Gardner 1956, 288). IMF officials viewed their activities as 'the key to securing world peace' (de Vries 1985a, xvi). Their failure to preserve their system cannot be attributed to a lack of responsibility. For many this devotion to the par value system was presumably influenced by personal experiences of the pre-Bretton Woods era.

For example, Schweitzer, the IMF Managing Director and Chairman of the Board of Directors who presided involuntarily over the demise of their system, was a war hero of considerable dimensions. He was wounded in the German invasion of France, escaped captivity and became a leader in the Resistance. Captured again by the Nazis, he was tortured and, after a failed suicide attempt, interned in the Buchenwald concentration camp. He was later awarded the Croix de Guerre and the Medal of Resistance. It is not difficult to imagine that he saw in the IMF an opportunity to prevent the slide back to the economic conditions of the 1930s.

According to McChesney Martin (1970, 11), the 'art' of central banking was 'one of the keystones in the arch of our civilisation'. This civilisation had been challenged in the 1930s by the 'economic barbarism' associated with floating exchange rates (Coombs 1976, 4). The history of the IMF was 'the record of one of the ways in which that challenge was met' (Horsefield 1969a, 5). But the IMF historians who chronicled the response to that challenge barely mentioned the intellectual forces that undermined the Bretton Woods system. Fixed exchange rates were the 'central core of the new international cooperation' and the IMF 'opposed all suggestions' which resembled the system that prevailed after 1973 (de Vries 1969, 40, 152). This was both 'the critical fact' and the critical weakness of the position taken by the international policemen (de Vries 1987, 91). Even in March 1973, as their system was irretrievably breaking down, they continued to be haunted – unnecessarily as it turned out – by the spectre of the 1930s. As a *Washington Post* columnist noted, 'floating still conjures up a fear of total instability, and is regarded with horror in many high places, including the IMF, the Federal Reserve System (notably the conservative and influential New York Fed) and by the Government of France' (Rowen 1973).

Shultz highlighted the dangers of 'the growing net of relationships' associated with government officials operating through 'an informal consultative process.... What arrangements are being worked out behind closed doors? What anticompetitive tendencies are implicitly condoned if not encouraged? And, as Harry Johnson says, the procedure itself has the characteristics of movement towards a corporate state' (Shultz and Aliber 1966, 11).

Johnson (1970, 43) became an influential Chicago advocate of floating. He regarded the proponents of exchange rate fixity as being doomed to play the role of the monstrous 'Cerberus-like' dog preventing re-entry into the mythological hell of the 1930s. This artificially constructed body began to associate its own prestige with the health of the world economy. Perceived national self-interest had to be constrained by the obligation to abstain from any policy discretion that might break the 'rules' of their membership and to respond to the disciplinary alarm bells of an outflow of gold and foreign exchange reserves. The Fund imposed a 'Code of Conduct' on the world: exchange rates were 'at the heart of the code' (Gold 1969, 564).

According to Johnson (1969, 25; 1970, 45–6, 48), the obsession with the 1930s was based on a misconception about the realities of the world economy: they were 'guarding the gates of hell rather than guarding legitimate business'. The 'old central bank devil' tended to 'believe that they know better than the market does'. Academic economists, therefore, had to provide an 'educational process' for the bankers. The international policemen responded to this educational process by initially dismissing it, then confronting it and then being defeated by it.

Some critics have detected faith and mythology at the heart of both the Chicago and IMF views of the world. According to Kindleberger (1976, 29), flexible exchange rates were synonymous for Chicago economists with 'God', although Johnson, not Friedman, was the Archbishop of Canterbury. Others thought that under a floating system, it would not be 'God or his angels – that is to say the economists' who would determine when central banks would intervene. Vested interest groups, it was believed, would capture that power (Triffin 1970, 57).

In the alternative, Chicago view, the IMF was an integral part of the post-war planning system which sought to override market forces. In Johnson's judgement, this IMF system 'rested on a foundation of mythological belief and conventional assumption'. Fixed exchange rates delivered power and prestige to those who administered the system, and 'practical' bankers found it impossible to comprehend how a floating rate system would work. Johnson, therefore, invoked economic sociology and 'institutionalism' as appropriate vehicles to explain international monetary arrangements (1969, 12; 1976, 414, 416; 1977, 261; see also Caves 1963, 129).

Observers detected in the official world a 'theological aversion to exchange rate flexibility' (Williamson 1978, 162). Prior to the advent of the IMF, there were believed to be 'no rules of the game except the devil take the hindmost'. Under the IMF system, 'the cardinal rule of the game was consultation' (Coombs 1976, 2–3). Southard (1979, 14) described how those who flaunted the IMF rules were abandoned to the Soviet 'devil'. In 1953–54, the IMF decided that a variety of deviations, including an unauthorised change in the par value of the Czechoslovakian koruna, transformed that country into 'a sheep so black that it should not be allowed to run with the flock'. The offending country was informed that it could retain IMF membership only if it 'confessed' its 'sin' and 'purged itself of the charges', which it refused to do.

There were clearly a variety of motives behind the decision to withdraw Czechoslovakia from IMF membership. But several points are revealed by an examination of this episode. First, for 16 months, IMF officials discussed the question of the par value of the koruna 'ad nauseam'.[1] At an Executive Board meeting, Southard stated that 'every country in the world would like to have immunity in par value matters. That's something that no one around this table I'm sure or no one in the staff would question for a moment.' A fundamental disequilibrium must be demonstrated before a change in the exchange rate could be contemplated: 'we must not yield that point'.[2]

In their defence of civilisation, the IMF played the role of policemen, prosecutor, judge, jury and executioner. Heretics were examined through a procedure that resembled an Inquisition. Thus in 1954, the Czech representative was grilled and informed that 'We are a technical organization. We have nothing to do with politics.'[3] These sentiments were clearly in tune with the methodological chapter of Friedman's 1953 *Essays in Positive Economics*; but were also the antithesis of the chapter on flexible exchange rates. Within two decades, the IMF Managing Director acknowledged that the survival of the system 'often raises problems of a political as well as purely economic nature' (Schweitzer 1971).[4] It was political forces within Nixon's Treasury Department which turned against the IMF system and destroyed it.

As the par value system finally collapsed, IMF officials were acutely aware that 'funeral orations' were being preached over their 'casket' (Southard 1979, 1). Friedman (1975 [1973], 178) was delighted to see 'another nail in the coffin'. The IMF historians (unintentionally perhaps) conjured up the image of a living organism equipped with head, heart, backbone and self-interest. With the inauguration of the fixed exchange rate system, the 'world consciously took control of the international monetary system' (Gold 1969, 513).

The Bretton Woods founding fathers intended that within this world currency bloc, 'fundamental disequilibrium' could also be corrected by changes in exchange rates. One of the IMF historians thought that it was 'so enlightened' to leave undefined this crucial concept of 'fundamental disequilibrium' (Gold 1969, 581). Others were concerned about the dangers associated with rates being too rigid (Hawtrey 1946, 4; Graham 1940; 1954, 10). Neither issue worried Jacobsson, who exclaimed that he could no more define equilibrium than he could define 'a pretty girl, but you can recognise one when you meet one' (cited by Volcker and Ghoyten 1992, 14). The 'consensus' coagulated around the need to prevent the par value system from being undermined.

But the Articles had a 'protean quality' and the IMF sought to be 'mistress in her own house'. According to Jacobsson, the IMF Charter was 'a living tree capable of growth and expansion within its natural limits' over which they had the authority to adopt 'final' interpretations. Officials apparently reached decisions about what was in the interest of the world and then searched for a legal authority on which to base a pronouncement (Gold 1969, 574). It was envisaged that the power of this body would relentlessly expand until it became 'an International Federal Reserve System' (Roosa 1962, 346). In 1947, the policemen decided that 'jurisdiction over rates of exchange is at the heart of the Fund's function and that constriction of that jurisdiction could maim the Fund's authority' (Gold 1969, 548, 567, 571–3). As the international monetary system was collapsing, the IMF Managing Director reassured the Governors that the Fund was still 'at the heart of the system' (de Vries 1976a, 483–4).

The dollar was regarded as the 'backbone' of the IMF system (Blessing 1970, 35). But for the dollar to provide the backbone for this living organism to flourish required the willing cooperation of US officials. The bankers were very protective towards their creature: par value changes were regarded as 'comparable to major surgery on a human patient...inherently dangerous' (Coombs 1976, x). But this supposedly benign Frankenstein could not withstand the attitude of 'benign neglect' on the part of US Treasury Secretaries and Gottfried Haberler, the Chairman of Nixon's Task Force on the Balance of Payments. When in early 1970 the policemen first heard mention of the policy of 'benign neglect' the reaction was 'overwhelmingly critical, the expressions of disapproval ranging from sadness and astonishment to anguish and horror' (Haberler (1974 [1971], 411).

The *Annex Prepared by Deputies* (published in August 1964) 'explicitly ruled out' flexible exchange rates (de Vries 1969, 50; Solomon 1982, 42, 65–7). The 1964 IMF *Annual Report* (1964, 27–8, 117) advocated 'less expansionary policies than they would otherwise prefer' as the antidote to persistent deficits. The need to adjust par values 'should arise less frequently to the extent that the policies described above are followed'. By the end of 1965, the IMF Board had not even discussed the general role of exchange rates in the adjustment mechanism (de Vries 1969, 116).

On 24 September 1969, Volcker (Nixon's Under-Secretary for Monetary Affairs) raised the issue of exchange rate flexibility in what, in retrospect, was a portentous meeting with IMF officials. Schweitzer said that he would make 'a brief reference to the matter' in his speech to the 1969 IMF annual meeting, explaining that he would 'give emphasis to the need to preserve the integrity of the par value system' and that the Executive Directors would 'study the matter further'. Volcker 'then raised the issue of the way in which the study should be handled. Mr. Schweitzer said this was the business of the Fund and repeated that the Executive Directors intended to study it and were fully equipped to do so.' The IMF officials appeared to regard Volcker's questions as impertinent: 'Mr. Volcker asked how this would be handled in the Fund. Mr. Schweitzer replied that it would be handled in the usual way; the staff would prepare memoranda and the Board would discuss them.'

Volcker then foreshadowed the removal of the IMF from the centre of the exchange rate system: 'Mr. Volcker then said – not very clearly – that there were people who felt that handing the matter over solely to the Fund would not assure decisive or definitive action… [and] raised the possibility of some sort of special group which might be appointed by G-10.' The notes appear to reflect incredulity about the possibility of 'outsiders' being included: 'At one point he suggested that this group could include… outsiders.… He was never specific about this, including the level or status of such persons. Mr. Schweitzer resolutely opposed any such new *ad hoc* working party.'

The notes of the meeting were taken by Frank Southard, IMF Deputy Managing Director (1962–74) who for 25 years had 'facilitated the transitions from one Managing Director to another' (de Vries 1976a, 636). But neither Southard nor Schweitzer were prepared to facilitate the transition from the IMF system to a system of floating exchange rates. The notes continued: Volcker 'kept pressing the point.... Mr. Schweitzer finally said that he saw no need for any new study arrangement and would oppose it.' Volcker then hinted that the US Governor might raise the issue in his speech to the annual meeting: 'Mr. Schweitzer and the staff members expressed dismay that there would be any statement by the US Governor which would seem to reflect lack of confidence in the Fund. At this point the discussion was terminated.'[5]

As a result, the IMF Executive Board were 'instructed, under American pressure' to review exchange rate regimes (Williamson 1977, 7; Solomon 1982, 59, 167–70). Under this obligation, the IMF continued to insist that 'The fulfilment of national needs demands the protection of international safeguards', the abandonment of which would pose 'grave risks' (de Vries 1976b, 275, 324). Thus fixed exchange rates allowed the international Leviathan to impose an almost Hobbesian contract by asserting (in the words contained in the Annual Address of the IMF Managing Director) 'the primacy of the general interest in a matter which concerns the welfare of all' (Witteveen 1975, 262).

When the IMF review was complete, Schweitzer reported that after two years of intensive study, the Executive Directors had concluded that 'the basic principles of the Bretton Woods system are sound and should be maintained and strengthened'. A wider band of allowable movement was acceptable; but there were 'grave risks' associated with the 'abandonment of the safeguards of the par value system'. National exchange rate policies must continue to be influenced by 'international opinion'; it was not wise to 'leave a vacuum' in this area (IMF 1970, 30, 42, 67). This August 1970 report was interpreted as a eulogy to the par value system. Soon afterwards, the international policemen appeared utterly confused by the 'collapse of the old order' (de Vries 1976a, 650).

IMF officials were contemptuous of their opponents who, they thought, were offering 'some "gadget" that can free them from the impact of balance of payments considerations' (Jacobsson 1979, 361). The Canadian authorities were informed that they had set 'an extremely bad precedent' by allowing their dollar to float in May 1970. The IMF refused to consider that the Canadian float was anything other than 'transitional' and pressed strongly for a return to the fold 'at the earliest possible date'. The IMF dispatched a mission to Ottawa – but their report was not even discussed by the Executive Directors because by the time it was ready the Bretton Woods system had collapsed (de Vries 1976a, 478, 481, 519).

The slow pace with which the IMF responded to US pressure to review exchange rate regimes returned to haunt them in the months prior to the NEP. At a crisis meeting of the IMF Executive Directors on 5 May 1971 to discuss the impending float of the mark, Schweitzer reiterated that 'I think we would all agree that our first objective must be to preserve the par value system and to make all efforts to avoid measures which might risk permanent damage to that system'. Schweitzer continued: it had been 'generally agreed after the last [1970] Annual Meeting that [the flexibility] exercise should proceed at a slow pace. It was in this vein that we decided to focus our attention this year primarily on technical aspects and not on the merits or demerits of particular changes in the system.' The French Executive Director, Marc Vienot, complained that it would be administratively inconvenient to speed up this process: 'Mr Vienot recalled that the Fund's future program of work had been agreed upon after lengthy discussion and a certain amount of compromise.... He was, therefore, not in favor of speeding up studies of exchange rate flexibility which, in his view, would represent a major change in that program of work.'[6]

An Alternative Executive Director, G.P.C. de Kock, found it 'depressing' that the international monetary system had been diverted onto a trajectory which rendered previous IMF deliberations worthless:

> it should be recalled that the staff had produced an excellent report on the subject [of exchange rate flexibility] and that the Board had spent a great deal of time in discussing it and on reaching certain conclusions. To suggest, on the basis of the events of the last few days, that those conclusions were no longer valid, that more weight should be given to changing the exchange rate system was rather disheartening.[7]

The ponderous and leisurely IMF approach to flexibility had been overtaken by events. Apparently horrified by the suggestion that 'outsiders' be involved in the exclusive 'business of the Fund', IMF officials may have calculated that this delaying tactic would serve to secure their position. As it turned out, it left them unprepared for the crisis that unfolded.

The Bretton Woods establishment regarded themselves as members of a 'club' who policed the international monetary order (Jacobsson 1979, 95). Roosa, a prominent member of the club, described their activities in terms of 'military doctrine: rings of outer and inner defenses for the defense of the dollar and for the system' (Volcker and Gyohten 1992, 32). They regarded themselves as pugilists going into combat against any undisciplined or self-interested national economic policy which might deliver a price of foreign currency different from that which the policemen had decreed.

But as Burns (1969 [1967], 284) reflected, 'Economic generals, not unlike their military counterparts, sometimes forget which war they are fighting, nor do they always know which war to fight.' Nixon (1987, 25) recalled that one of Burns's wars involved a 'titanic' rearguard action to preserve the par value system. As their system entered the 'iceberg years', the official IMF historian recounts that they literally rearranged their chairs so as to pretend that it was not the Executive Directors who were discussing 'limited' flexibility of exchange rates. Moreover, 'there was stress on the word "limited".... Pointedly, they did not discuss regimes which were inconsistent with the par value system.'

These 'fourth floor' deliberations, which took place during the first nine months of the first Nixon administration, reinforced their view that they should maintain their course (de Vries 1976a, 501–2; McChesney Martin 1970, 21). Within the first two months of the second Nixon administration these prizefighters were forced to 'throw in the towel' (Emminger 1978a, 401). They 'seemed to be more buffeted than in control of events' (de Vries 1985a, 118). Speculation about a return to a par value system soon came to be regarded as a 'consolation for traditionalists sick with nostalgia' (Machlup 1976, 33). As Southard (1979, 21) later reflected, 'A policeman's lot is not a happy one.'

Part II

The Academic Process: from the 1940s to the Friedman and Nixon Presidencies

6
The Early History of the Case for Floating Exchange Rates

Friedman was neither the first nor the only economist to make the case for flexible exchange rates (Machlup 1964, 79–80).[1] Roy Harrod (1933, 102–3, 137–40, 173–5, 180–1), for example, described '*The New Freedom*.... When the Gold Standard is Abandoned.... The *only* well-tried expedient is *laissez-faire*; most of the authorities, who think about the matter at all, probably hope that the old expedient will still serve. Their hope is not likely to be realized' [emphases in original]. Harrod advocated 'international co-operation' through an 'international committee' so that exchange rates could be changed (by a maximum of 2 per cent per annum) in a 'regular and orderly manner'. Harrod also conceded that his analysis of world monetary reform could be 'condemned as merely academic'. But he added that 'The present generation of politicians and bankers will pass away. They will endeavour to hand on their stock of clichés to those who succeed them. But even clichés pass out of fashion in time.'

Harrod exerted an influence on Haberler (Young 1998), and there are distinct similarities between the policy of 'benign neglect' that Haberler advocated for the Nixon administration and the 'policy of the ostrich' that Harrod (1933, 140) described. Haberler consistently analysed floating exchange rates in a more sympathetic manner than did most of his contemporaries (Bordo and James 2002). By the time of the Nixon administration, Haberler (1969c, 359) found it 'exceedingly difficult to think of valid objections to flexible exchange rates'. But in June 1945, Haberler (1945, 308, 311) described an exchange rate determined in a free market as 'the ultimate ideal, which cannot be realized at once. *All experts* [emphasis added] agree that in most countries more or less stringent controls of the foreign exchange market will have to be maintained for some time after the war.' Thus a system of freely floating exchange rates was 'hardly acceptable'.

James Meade (1948a, 109; 1948b, 12) also suggested that the IMF system could make greater use of exchange rate flexibility. But the IMF 'rules of the game' had to be strictly adhered to so as to prevent competitive devaluations. Meade specifically prefaced his reformist remarks by distancing himself from the possibility that the price mechanism might deliver a blow to British post-war pride: 'Let me make one thing clear at the outset. I am not advocating that here and now the pound sterling should be devalued. Far from it.' Meade (1949, 101, 4) patiently spelt out the limitations which might prevent the price mechanism from working effectively with respect to exchange rates.[2]

In the early 1950s, there was a group within the British Treasury, with some support from the Bank of England, who favoured a floating pound (Brittan 1964, 173–7). But at the end of decade, Meade was the only witness to appear before the Radcliffe Committee who 'entertained the idea' of floating rates. Thus the Committee felt confident to conclude 'strongly in favour' of a fixed parity for sterling rather than the 'desperate expedient' of a system of fluctuating rates (HMSO 1959, paras 719, 722, 721; Middleton 2002). Indeed, Meade (1963, 311, 316) described his preference for increased flexibility as 'an academic exercise…frankly utopian in form'. The 'dangers' of flexibility were 'real possibilities. For this reason the authorities of the Western countries are extremely unlikely to adopt an uncontrolled system of freely floating exchange rates.'

Meade's (1967, 122–3; 1966, 10, 15) 'case' could hardly be described as advocacy at all: 'I am not absolutely convinced myself that fluctuating exchange rates necessarily lead to inflation.' Fears of an inflation–devaluation spiral were not 'wholly imaginary'. Indeed, 'life in this wicked world is a choice of evils' and it was important to 'search for the snags' of 'increased flexibility' (see also Haberler 1949, 213–14). Likewise, as Michael Bordo and Harold James (2002) point out, Haberler was 'an analyst not an advocate' who was 'a captive of the contemporary perception' of the 1930s. It took 'Haberler 40 years to fully make the case for floating exchange rates as the cure for the "bacillus" of the international spread of depressions that his analysis in *Prosperity and Depression* [1937] suggested'. In contrast, Friedman's case, while cautious about the possibilities of persuading policy makers, contained no such self-disparaging caveats and was by far the most influential in the debates that followed.

In September 1946, Friedman returned to the University of Chicago. He dates the beginning of his 'active involvement in the political process' to the founding meeting of the libertarian Mont Pelerin Society in April 1947. Describing himself as a 'young, naïve provincial American' on his first trip outside the US, Friedman found that the Mont Pelerin reformers were 'all beleaguered in their own countries'. He observed that in post-war England 'price, wage and exchange controls were extensive and rigid' (Friedman and Friedman 1998, 159). Shortly afterwards, the Bretton Woods system faced one of its earliest crises, and Friedman played an important role in persuading one of the founders of the post-war international monetary system to float their exchange rate.

On 17 November 1947, Canada imposed what Donald Gordon (1948, 22), the Deputy Governor of the Bank of Canada, described as 'drastic limitations' on imports so as to preserve the fixed external value of the Canadian dollar. On 17 April 1948, Friedman made the case for floating the Canadian dollar to Gordon, prior to a University of Chicago Round Table radio broadcast the following day. Friedman formed the distinct impression that Gordon had never properly encountered the argument before (Friedman and Friedman 1998, 189). In the broadcast, Gordon emphasised that Canadian policy was driven, in part, by the desire to prevent 'the spread of communism'. Unfortunately, these responsibilities had generated inflation. Friedman (1948, 22) replied that 'direct controls through rationing and price controls' were 'bad ways of fighting inflation'. Friedman then outlined the policy agenda to which he devoted his professional life: 'the most effective and efficient way of solving problems is by using the traditional mechanism of a free price system and the general mechanism of broad credit control, foreign exchange rate change'.

Gordon's (1948, 22) initial response to Friedman was to draw the same distinction that Solow (1966a, 60–1) later made between long-run objectives and short-run possibilities. Gordon also remarked that Canadians had to 'keep in mind our obligations under the International Monetary Fund'. Friedman (1948, 22) replied that he welcomed the attachment to the 'long-run virtues' of relying on the price mechanism, but 'heartily' disagreed with the view that controls were required to 'solve the short-run problem'.

Galbraith's (1981, 164, n. 1) efforts to control wartime prices in the United States were redoubled as a result of an envious glance north at the apparent successes achieved by the Canadian Wartime Prices and Trade Board, which had been directed first by James Coyne and then by Gordon. Coyne (1949, 1), a future and highly controversial Bank Governor, was the apparent author of a Bank memorandum dated 31 January 1949 and labelled 'SECRET' which advocated that the Canadian dollar should be free to find its 'natural rate'. In September

1950, the Canadian dollar was allowed to float and one of the sponsors of the Bretton Woods system was perceived by an IMF official to be 'embarking on a piratical pursuit' (Muirhead 1999, 137, 141, 145). At the same time, the remaining restrictions on imports imposed in November 1947 were lifted (Powell 1999, 37).

The early post-war academic consensus favoured the view that fluctuating exchange rates were an obstacle to free international trade (e.g. Nurkse 1945, 3; Hawtrey 1946, 99). According to Robert Triffin (1948, 413), until a decade or so before, most experts on international disequilibrium

> could dismiss the whole problem summarily with the observation that exchange control is the most harmful of all interferences with freedom of trade.... Lesser writers would be carried further by their arguments and demonstrate easily the superiority of free and stable exchanges over any system of exchange control.

Likewise, doubts expressed by Hansen (1948, 379)[3] and Samuelson about the 'equilibrating efficiency of exchange rate variations' were widely held in the academic community. Samuelson (1948, 398) concluded that 'the strong burden of proof must be thrown onto any doctrine that favors an extreme, and generally unpopular, departure from the prevailing state'.

That was exactly what Friedman set out to do. He spent autumn 1950 in Europe as Special Representative attached to the Organisation for European Economic Cooperation (OEEC). One of his assignments was to analyse the proposal to establish a European Coal and Steel Community, the precursor to the European Economic Community (EEC). Another was to find a solution to the German balance-of-payments problem. He concluded that he had provided 'dramatic' evidence of the superiority of a flexible exchange rate to other currently available devices; but he could 'elicit no sympathy whatsoever' for his recommendation to allow the mark to float (Friedman and Friedman 1998, 156, 159, 182).

Friedman's advocacy may have made more of an impression in Germany than he realised (see section 18.2). His memorandum on 'Flexible Exchange Rates as a Solution to the German Exchange Crisis' formed the basis of his 1953 case. He was led to write the memorandum after 'contemplation of the problem of...a common market.... In the absence of political unification, the only alternative that will permit a true common market – in fact and all the time, not on paper and from time to time – is flexible exchange rates among the member countries' (Friedman 1969a, 16).

Friedman had three academic obstacles to overcome. First, he had to construct a compelling Chicago case for flexible exchange rates. *Dollars and Deficits* was dedicated to Friedman's (1968a, iv) 'teachers and colleagues at the University of Chicago who kept alive a tradition and a body of thought that nearly expired in the rest of the academic world'. One of his teachers, Lloyd Mints, had constructed a previous Chicago case. However, despite an acknowledged input from Friedman it remained somewhat hesitant: 'it must be conceded that there would be [costs of exchange fluctuation] and that they would have some influence in the direction of reducing the volume of international trade' (Mints 1950, vii, 94; see also Simons 1948 [1944], 265).

Viner (1964, 12–13, 19, 32–3), who also taught Friedman at Chicago in the 1930s, was 'a believer in a free market and in the useful function of flexible prices. That is where my biases lie.' But Viner declared that aversion to devaluation was the 'only one rock of any solidity that stands against a fairly serious degree of inflation engineered or at least unrestrained by government'. The fixed exchange rate, 'cult, myth, rigidity, illogicality though it be – is in many countries the sole surviving barrier to almost unrestrained inflation'. The US and other countries 'are not to be safely trusted with a floating exchange rate'. Viner, a Canadian, also noted that the demise of the Canadian float had been 'bemoaned by many economists'.

Secondly, Friedman had to find a publishing outlet for his essay. Friedman (15 January 1951) returned to Chicago, telling Stigler that 'Europe was fine, except for one thing: I had to put in too many hours at the office for appearances sake. I can't say I did anything worthwhile. I wrote a bunch of memoranda to be neglected.'[4] Friedman's memorandum on floating exchange rates was left 'lying around' for a year or so until Friedman began an exchange with Lionel Robbins (see section 15.1). The day after his first letter to Robbins, Friedman (22 January 1952) offered his 'case' to John Davenport at *Fortune*:

> The problem has recently become again highly topical and I feel more strongly than ever that the single most urgent step in international affairs is the establishment of a system of flexible exchange rates; that this was done, the results on an international level would be nearly as striking as the results on a national level for the German monetary reform; that if it is not done, there is no chance at all the real liberalisation of trade, economic integration of Europe, or any of the other noble objectives towards which our external policy has supposedly been directed.

Davenport replied (21 February 1952) that the essay was far too technical for *Fortune* readers: 'I don't think we have a thousand readers who could manage it.'[5] It therefore appeared the following year in Friedman's (1953) *Essays in Positive Economics* and became one of the most influential essays of all time.[6]

The third obstacle was expressed by Seymour Harris (1948a, 483, 378): 'Unfortunately, the theorist is able to give the practical man only limited help.' There were 'so many economists' addressing the problem of international disequilibrium and the 'practitioner who seeks advice from the economist will find support' for a variety of solutions: 'How much reliance should be put upon one or the other will be the difficult problem.'

Had practitioners looked to academics for guidance about the stability properties of floating rates they would have discovered, in the early 1960s, intense scholarly disagreement. Egon Sohmen (1961a, 426) elaborated on Friedman's argument about stability: 'my primary purpose [Sohmen 1957] was to destroy the generally accepted notion that a system of *freely floating* rates might conceivably break down because of static instability' [emphasis in original]. Jaglish Bhagwati and Harry Johnson (1960; 1961) disputed the validity of this proposition. Johnson was a leading trade theorist; shortly after writing the first of these two essays, Johnson migrated from the University of Manchester to Chicago.

According to Polak (2002), Johnson's discovery of the monetary approach to the balance of payments around this time 'seemed to have the liberating force of an epiphany'. In this 'new gospel', the 'mantra' of money entered the analysis as 'a kind of anti-Keynesian manifesto'. According to Kindleberger (1976, 29), Johnson became the leader of a religious cult organised around the need for flexible exchange rates.

But by the mid-1960s, this diversity of academic advice was replaced by an academic consensus around the need for increased, if not complete, flexibility of exchange rates. Friedman recalled that flexible exchange rates were 'the most continually debated topic' at successive Mont Pelerin meetings (Nash 1976, 419, n. 197). In addition to Stigler (who organised an important 1966 Chicago conference) two other fellow Mont Pelerin reformers, Haberler and Machlup, played important supporting roles.[7] They 'mobilised' the academic consensus that began to operate 'as if' they were a pressure group.[8]

7
An Emerging Academic Consensus

In the 1960s, there were tensions within the White House about international monetary reform. Douglas Dillon, President Kennedy's Treasury Secretary, had been Under-Secretary of State during the Eisenhower administration and was an 'elegantly tailored, handsome man…with the quiet assurance of someone having just achieved a pinnacle of personal success'. When Charles Coombs (1976, 16–17, 20), the senior Vice President in charge of the foreign exchange desk at the New York Fed, 'watched [Dillon] at international gatherings I could not help feeling a certain national pride'. Coombs recalled Kennedy insisting that the gold–dollar price was 'immutable'. The idea of altering either of these prices was 'not a respectable matter for discussion in the halls of the Treasury' (Volcker and Gyohten 1992, 20, 22, 25).

Academics such as James Tobin indignantly believed that international financial policy was too important to be left to financiers. The crisis managers were, he believed, obsessed with their virtuosity as net-less tightrope walkers to the detriment of the performance of the American economy. When it came to fiscal policy, Dillon was regarded as the first Treasury Secretary to accept the neo-Keynesian principle of deficit financing (Kraft 1962, 12). But when reforming ideas about the international monetary system were presented, Dillon 'regularly and gracefully shot them down' (Schlesinger 1965, 515–17).[1]

Triffin (1957, 137) argued that the IMF was structurally defective and had failed in its mission. James Angell (1961, 691, 699, 707–8) of Columbia University suggested that it had become increasingly recognised that 'an extensive and even drastic reorganization of our present international monetary arrangement is both imperative and urgent.… The present IMF should be completely reorganized, along somewhat the same general lines as those proposed by Triffin.' Angell added: 'To date, however, few responsible officials have shown much desire to put Triffin's proposals into effect.'

Jacobsson informed Dillon that 'we could not do all that some professors proposed'; to which Dillon agreed: 'that would not be the way' (Jacobsson 1979, 360–1). Dillon, with his eight years of international diplomatic experience, appeared to insult academic economists at the October 1963 IMF meeting by ruling out their involvement in the discussions about the future of the international monetary system. Academic economists were portrayed as being 'so much in disagreement with one another that their advice was practically useless to those in charge of decision-making'. Secret deliberations by responsible officials were required. Three academic economists (Machlup, Triffin and William Fellner) present at the IMF meeting as guests decided 'on the spot' to organise a response (Machlup, Malkeil *et al.* 1964, 5–6, 9; Malkeil 1978, 17; Triffin 1978, 147).[2] The 'organised' case for flexible exchange rates was about to enter a new phase.

Between December 1963 and June 1964, the insulted economists held four conferences and a report was placed in the hands of the printers. One of the selection criteria for attendance was to capture 'the notorious divergence' of views held on international monetary reform. (Government economists, however, were specifically excluded.) The report's publication coincided with the publication of the *Annex Prepared by Deputies* and the 1964 IMF *Annual Report* which were, by design, released to the public on 10 August 1964 (de Vries 1976a, 36). The conclusions of the economists' report contrasted sharply with those of the bureaucrats. Although 'it was regarded as a miracle', through an elaborate questionnaire system with drafting committees working late into the night, an academic consensus had emerged 'on the importance of exchange-rate change as a method of adjustment' (Machlup, Malkeil *et al.* 1964, 9, 14, 20, 97, 104, 106).

This consensus was in sharp contrast to the plethora of proposals that had surfaced just immediately before. Between the first and second editions (May 1962–October 1963) of Machlup's *Plans for the Reform of the International Monetary System* there had been 37 new 'pronouncements' about how to patch up the Bretton Woods system: 'spawned at an extraordinary rate' (Machlup 1964, preface). These academic exercises were uncoordinated and often contradicted each other. For example, Herb Gruebel's (1963) *World Monetary Reform Plans and Issues* contained 24 separately drafted proposals or comments. There were a smorgasbord of plans on offer (Jacobsson, Rooth, Poole, Harrod, Stamp, Bernstein, Lutz, Zolotas, Postuma, Triffin, Rueff, Maudling, Barber, Volcker, Angell,

Day, etc.) plus Roosa bonds, the GAB (general agreement to borrow), CRUs (collective reserve units), gold tranches, rings of swaps, etc.

There was another issue complicating this 'apparently unbridgeable gulf' between the attitudes of economists and bankers (Halm 1965, preface). When WP3 was formed, Jacobsson stressed that those in the Fund 'talked over problems in a friendly manner'. With his faith in a 'managed "invisible hand"' and 'intelligent planning' he forged 'a remarkable degree of consensus…not to rock the international system' (Jacobsson 1979, 398, 401, 402). Not only were academic economists 'rocking the boat', but their rhetoric and models could hardly be described as banker-friendly. Embarrassment-averse central bankers were often seen as a constraint and the choice between fixed or floating rates often involved a 'comparative embarrassment analysis' about whether a loss of reserves or a fall in the value of the currency was 'the greater embarrassment to the central banker' (Machlup 1964, 82). Triffin (1963, 438–9) also provocatively asserted that the strengthening of the international monetary structure 'of the West, and indeed of the world itself' was being inhibited by 'the enormous inertia of timorous, tradition-bound bureaucrats' who always opposed changes to the 'modes of thought to which they are accustomed'.

After Nixon's first Presidential election victory, it was IMF officials who felt they were being insulted – by Dillon's successors and their deputies in the US Treasury. They responded by deliberately imparting inertia into their study of exchange rate flexibility. On 15 August 1971, Treasury Secretary Connally responded by marginalising the IMF from decisions about the future of the international monetary system – an insult that was followed in March 1973 by the collapse of the par value system.

8
1966: Four Conferences

8.1 Princeton

After the publication of the two competing reports in August 1964, a series of joint bureaucrat–academic conferences were held. The first was at Princeton in April 1966. Fellner (1966, 112, 122) presented a statement signed by an impressive array of economists including Friedman, Johnson, Meade, Hansen and Jan Tinbergen complaining (among other things) that exchange rate flexibility had 'received little attention in official circles'.[1] Haberler (1966, 128, 134) complained that those involved in 'practical discussions' often tacitly assumed that wages and prices were entirely flexible. In reality, wages were rigid downwards and contraction would violate 'the modern view, to which almost everyone subscribes, that, in principle, unemployment must be avoided. To that extent everybody is a Keynesian now.' Haberler pressed for exchange rate variations as 'the only alternative to more and more controls'. Tibor Scitovsky (1966, 197) complained that exchange rate adjustment was regarded as 'an extreme emergency measure'. This contrasted with the 'greater faith – or hopes…of most of the academic specialists today – towards greater exchange rate flexibility' as opposed to selective restrictions and controls which were 'counsels of despair' (Fellner, Machlup and Triffin 1966, 5–6). The choice was perceived to be between exchange rate or aggregate demand adjustment and direct controls. Many economists had 'deep-seated aversions to direct controls' which, in any case, were 'no solution to the problem'. To use controls instead of floating rates was 'either a thoughtless perversion of thought or a disingenuous use of a pretext for a concealed real purpose of the restrictions'. An increase in exchange rate flexibility was 'the only genuine alternative' (Machlup 1966a, 63, 71, 73).

Having been apparently dismissed as irrelevant by Secretary Dillon less than two and a half years before, the academic economists had mobilised themselves and were making an impression on the bureaucracy. WP3 chairman, Jonkheer Lennep (1966, v–vi), politely thought the conferences had been illuminating: 'The mixture of theorists and practitioners turned out to be a most productive one.' But within the IMF, a less welcoming attitude was taken. The debates were described as 'heated' and as emanating largely from 'academic circles'. In any event, they were perceived as having lapsed into insignificance as the Bretton Woods system reached maturity. The IMF rejoiced that between 1954 and 1965 the proportion of Fund members with fixed or very 'stable' rates had increased from 59 to 86 per cent, representing the 'effective attainment of the par value system' (de Vries 1969, 48–9).

8.2 Chicago

Stigler organised an April 1966 Chicago conference on 'Policy Choices in a Full Employment Economy'. Stigler (1966a, 278) was

> interested in how weak the criticisms of flexible exchange rates were . . . the opposition is inarticulate and unrationalised. . . . From this, I deduce that the opposition to flexible exchange rates is not based upon analytically defensible criticisms of how the economy would behave. Rather the opposition rests upon an instinctive and possibly atavistic belief, on the century-old history of the gold standard, that a fixed price of gold serves to discipline dangerous fiscal and monetary tendencies.

In the opening conference paper, Friedman (1966, 18, 22, 31–2, 34–6, 39) disparaged 'the gospel according to the Council of Economic Advisers'.[2] In reality, Friedman argued, 'inflation was always and everywhere a monetary phenomenon'; the popularity of the cost-push explanation resulted from 'the desire of government authorities to shift the blame for inflation'. The Kennedy–Johnson Guidelines were a 'foretaste of what suppressed inflation implies . . . disquieting harbingers of what currently looks like the wave of the future'. Suppressing inflation was like breaking a thermometer: 'it simply adds to our ignorance', it destroyed political freedom and created a collectivist economy. The price system was 'the only technique that has so far been discovered or invented for efficiently allocating resources'. The only substitute was 'some kind of clumsy physical control. A striking example is provided by India...the pegging of the exchange rate is the key to India's economic failure.... As in India, the pegging of exchange rates is the most conspicuous example of the suppression of inflation in the United States.' Moderate and steady inflation was moderately harmful but '*so long as prices are free to move* [emphasis in text], the extremely flexible private enterprise system will adapt to it, take it in its stride and continue to operate efficiently'. Friedman predicted that (in the absence of a major war) inflation would continue in the moderate range of 3–10 per cent. This would not be 'disastrous. The greatest harm will continue to be done by the measures taken to peg exchange rates.'

Solow (1966b, 42–5, 50, 63–5) responded in 'The Case against the Case against the Guideposts'. The Phillips curve was the 'dilemma' for public policy: movement up the Phillips curve was constrained by the fact that 'in our rather international trading world, governments may not be able to...acquiesce in an inflationary spiral'. One solution was 'to accept the universe' and live with the unemployment and output costs of zero inflation, estimated by Solow to be an annual loss of $10 billion of output at 1965 prices. The alternative was 'to accept some inflation' and rely on 'an informed and mobilized public opinion' to modify the inflationary costs of rising up the Phillips curve. This was a 'far cry from wage and price control'. Solow's attempted rebuttal stimulated Friedman (1966, 60) to formalise the natural-rate expectations augmented Phillips curve which undermined the theoretical legitimacy of the macroeconomic pursuit of full employment.

Gardiner Ackley (1966, 68, 72–3, 74, 78), Johnson's CEA Chairman, dismissed Friedman's monetary explanation of inflation as a 'doctrinal matter...of limited importance to this discussion'. The Guideposts made a 'modest but significant contribution to price stability' by checking 'premature inflation'. Corporations were prepared to accept their social responsibility with respect to inflation and balance of payments outcomes; the threat that education and social responsibility would lead to the corporate state was 'hardly supported by history'. The guidelines were aimed at the '*real*' problem of the existence of the Phillips curve: but 'All of us in government will appreciate your participation in helping to find...alternatives which are constructive and superior.'

8.3 Princeton

In May 1966, immediately following his Chicago experiences, Solow (1966a, 57, 59, 61, 73) appeared to be somewhat on the defensive: 'It begins to seem as if I am the only respectable economist, not in the employ of Lyndon Johnson, who is willing to say anything good about the wage–price guideposts.' The existence of the Phillips curve was a 'discouraging fact' and a 'genuine dilemma' and the guidelines deserved to be 'kept alive' and used in the battle to 'keep inflationary expectations from hardening'. An 'educated and mobilized public opinion may be able to exert some pressure in the right direction'. Solow (1966a, 57, 58) repeated his objections to what he saw as the role of 'automatic ideology' in the case against the guidelines and dismissed W. Allen Wallis's advocacy of the 'simple' Chicago proposition that monetary policy was the sole cause of, and sole solution to, inflation as being unworthy of consideration. Solow simply 'presume[d]' that 'not many' would like to see unemployment above current levels of 3.75 per cent.

But the tide was turning with respect to the pursuit of full employment. Publicly, Friedman (1967, 91) stated that 'in the present situation you have relatively Full Employment and I trust you will continue to'. Confidentially, Friedman (1988b [1968], 433) informed President-elect Nixon that 'Today, the worldwide problem is over-employment.'

8.4 Chicago

Valéry Giscard d'Estaing was chosen to open a second 1966 Chicago conference (in September, five months after the first). The previous year, Giscard d'Estaing had made it clear to the British Chancellor that he believed that the gold exchange standard was doomed (Callaghan 1987, 185). In opening the Chicago conference Giscard d'Estaing (1969, 13–14) complained that 'exchange rates are fixed much too firmly'. He rallied the conference by stating that this 'fetish... must be combated'. When Giscard d'Estaing first proposed reform in 1963, he had violated the unwritten code of the international policemen who remained 'friendly' with each other by ignoring such suggestions and agreeing 'not to raise too complicated or too violent questions'. He explained that the Chicago organisers had invited him to provide inside information about 'the attitude and position of various parties in the present action for international monetary reform'.

The conference organisers sought to 'mobilize our intellectual resources to make a frontal assault on scientific problems that have thus far resisted solution' (Mundell 1969, 3). The conference began with a 'commercial from Chicago', which stated that the bureaucrats' 'easy panacea' of controls had been framed in ignorance of the long-term consequences: 'the deeper destruction of the legal and moral values [which] make the system worthwhile' (Mundell 1969, 5). There were 'tactical' discussions of where 'to concentrate propaganda for reform of the international monetary system' and references to 'disguises' being 'effective' or not. If the 'disguise is too thin: it will not deceive anybody and the resistance will be just as strong as against the real thing' (Haberler 1969a, 179). As Robert Mundell (1969, 4), one of the conference organisers, put it, economists had 'to put Humpty Dumpty together again'.

9

1967: the AEA President versus the AFA President

An editor of *Fortune* magazine described the May 1967 Friedman–Roosa debate about exchange rates as 'the most important money debate' he had ever heard.[1] Roosa, the current President of the American Finance Association (AFA), was regarded as 'the foremost American expert on international monetary affairs' (Volcker and Gyohten 1992, 21). The 49-year-old Roosa (1961, 125) was the quintessential 'Best and Brightest'. Friedman, the current AEA President, had been '*persona non grata* in the Federal Reserve Board' (Wallis 1976 [1964], 102). He continued to demonstrate to the satisfaction of increasing numbers of academic observers that his solution to the US balance of payments problem could achieve what all the king's men could not.

Roosa (1967a, 10, 169–70) had been chairman of the group of deputies of the Ministers and Governors of the G-10 who had been commissioned to undertake a thorough examination of the functioning of the international monetary system. Through 'multilateral surveillance', the international monetary policemen had 'provided a tight ring of defences around the world's leading currencies'. The 1966 WP3 Report on *The Balance of Payments Adjustment Process* (1966, 18, 27) established an early warning system to alert the international community to impending national problems and recommended the speedier dissemination of improved balance of payments statistics. Only the traditional solutions were canvassed; there was almost no discussion of the 'distasteful' subject of changing exchange rates (Williamson 1987, 84). There was an awareness of the existence of a potential shortage of liquidity: 'a crack in the structure that could require its abandonment'. But Roosa (1967a, 189; 1967b, 32) believed that the crack could be patched over not by Friedman's solution of flexible exchange rates but by an international version of his domestic proposal to expand the supply of money by *x* per cent per year. IMF credit facilities had (in quantity theory terms) 'added to the M′ and the V′ of the world's monetary system'.

Roosa (1961, 125) was associated with the view that 'money really matters' and regarded the search for a stable volume of international liquidity as a desirable international form of the monetarism that Friedman was preaching at a domestic level. Roosa (1967a, 8, 26, 28–9; 1967b, 28, 46) recalled that there was little sympathy for 'supposed shortcuts to "balance of payments independence"'.[2] The received view was that any suggestion of US willingness to 'scrap important pieces of the existing system...would have brought a deluge of new problems'.

The banker's view of international competition corresponded more closely to Marxian analysis than to the view prevalent in Chicago.[3] The 'real world' was 'a world of red bloodied competition' and 'mutual combativeness' in which, without fixed rates, 'each successive episode of internal domestic difficulty' would lead to cumulative depreciations 'to gain a momentary trade advantage' which would reinforce 'potential inflationary developments' (Roosa 1967b, 50–1, 67, 82, 85, 87, 90, 98). The linchpin of Roosa's argument was that the alternative to Bretton Woods was 'the anarchy of an entire world on flexible exchange rates, or (and this would be the more probable) the protectionism and economic autarchy of the sort of currency blocs that prevailed in the 1930s'. The choice was not fixed or floating but stable or unstable rates.

Roosa (1967a, 166; 1967b, 167) regarded the Bretton Woods system of fixed exchange rates as the peace treaty or 'armed truce' that prevented a return to the 'anarchy' of the competitive devaluations of the 1930s, an experience that was 'all too searing still in our memories to forget'. Flexible exchange rates were both 'defensive wall[s]' and aggressive instruments of 'open economic warfare' – in effect, the captured creatures of the tradable goods sector. Canada, he argued, the only major floating country, had responded to excess unemployment in 1961–62 by attempting to engineer a 1930s-style beggar-thy-neighbour depreciation. In the 1960s, slightly wider (but still constrained) bands of permissible par adjustments were entertained as a superior domestic adjustment mechanism; but removing the internationally agreed constraints on further flexibility was regarded as a species of mutually assured destruction.

The central bankers and officials responsible for patching up the Bretton Woods system sought to perform 'modern alchemy...the world's first effort to create...a money that can be universally acceptable among the central banks of the world'. With a banker's mentality, they assumed that confidence in the system would be best maintained through stability: that is, if changes in exchange rates were viewed as the 'last resort'. They believed that they had considered the proposals of even the 'most extreme critics' of their evolutionary approach. But until just before the system collapsed they apparently excluded from serious discussion any detailed consideration of the system that 'they' would be replaced by, namely, flexible exchange rates (Roosa 1967a, 4, 29, 261, 268; 1967b, 87, 90, 98). There was no reference to Friedman and only brief dismissive references to the case for flexible exchange rates in Roosa's *The Dollar and World Liquidity*. Instead, Roosa wrote of his preference for the 'secrecy and aloofness' of the central banker and he disclosed that the White House bureaucrats sought to 'establish a very tight control over matters that were being considered'.

According to Roosa (1967b, 61, 82–3, 85–6, 176), if the Bretton Woods system was abandoned, the world would slide down into the abyss of bartering trading blocks. The high employment domestic 'truce' required anti-inflationary guidelines for wages and prices; without the international guidelines of fixed exchange rates 'the whole system...would break down into a sequence of competitive devaluations which would create the conditions of bilateralism'. If the exchange rate was free to fall, this would increase import prices and 'an all-round sequence of other internal cost and wage increases, and the initiation of internal inflationary pressures'. Roosa feared that governments, if let loose, would not follow a consistent policy of internal stability. Roosa acknowledged that there had been a 'regrettable trend' towards increased capital controls, but 'we are fighting a war' in Vietnam.

Friedman considered both the strengths and weaknesses of his opponents' arguments and the likely persuasiveness of his assault on orthodoxy. His analysis was mixed with sociological observations about the nature of knowledge construction and destruction in the marketplace for economic ideas and policy advice. Friedman (1953, 203, 198) noted that the case for flexible exchange rates had been dismissed 'partly because of a questionable interpretation of limited historical evidence'.[4] Flexible exchange rates had been ruled out as a result of an intellectual agreement between 'a curious coalition of the most unreconstructed believers in the price system, in all its other roles, and its most extreme opponents': the 'traditionalists' for whom internal policy was determined by the discipline of the gold standard and 'the dominant strain of reformers, who distrusted the price mechanism in all its manifestations'. The 'political reluctance to use changes in exchange rates...reflects a cultural lag...it is a consequence of tradition and lack of understanding'.

Roosa (1967b, 30) thought that fixed rates provided 'the most hospitable environment for encouraging market-orientated adjustments within and among nations'. For Friedman (1967, 4, 13–14, 17–18, 117–19, 183) the 'truth' was simple: 'Let the fixed price differ from the price that would clear the market and it will take herculean efforts to hold it.... Fix prices – and the problem will multiply; let prices find their own level in free markets – and the problem will disappear.' Controls, Friedman argued, were 'congealing the blood of capitalism'; it was fixed rates which 'keeps forcing more and more quotas, more and more restrictions upon us'.

Friedman appeared to suggest that import quotas were impossible under floating rates: 'Why should [other countries] impose import quotas? They can't – under floating rates they can only import more from us if they export more to us.' With floating rates, 'we could behave in foreign trade like a great nation, not like a mendicant, by unilaterally moving towards freer trade without having to be concerned about our balance-of-payments problems'. A reduction in tariffs simultaneously increases imports and exports (via a rise in the price of foreign exchange): 'There is not even a temporary importation of unemployment.'

The 'administrative freezing' of exchange rates led to crises which ensured 'a maximum of destabilising speculation...the worst of two worlds'. When Friedman (1967, 20–1) first began campaigning for flexible rates, he took seriously the fear of destabilising speculation. The post-war experience led him to dismiss this objection: 'it is time therefore that this bug-a-boo is given a decent burial – at least until someone can come along with some real evidence that it is more than a bug-a-boo'.

Friedman (1953, 180–1; 1967) denied that Bretton Woods was a successful peace treaty or 'armed truce'. With respect to the domestic 'truce', he denied that there was any truth in the argument that 'this innate instability is held in check by some sort of political compromise and that this compromise would be disturbed by the change in the exchange rate'. The 'wage–price spiral' was a 'crucial fallacy'. The standard argument about an inflation–depreciation spiral was defective. Moreover, the par value system was throttling the quest for freer trade: the 'absence of flexible exchange rates is almost certain to be incompatible with unrestricted multilateral trade'.

Friedman (1967, 14–16, 22, 72–4, 79; 1969a, 4) jangled the nerves of those involved in patching up the Bretton Woods system at a time when the patching up was as unglamorous and as unsuccessful as attempts to control domestic wage and price increases. The orthodox pursuit of greater international liquidity was 'the standard answer of the man who cannot manage his affairs'. Friedman mocked the Bretton Woods 'veterans' who undertook the 'herculean' labour of restraining market forces, and sarcastically referred to the 'grave problems' and 'frantic scurrying of high government officials from capital to capital...one of the major sources of the opposition to floating exchange rates [is that] the people engaged in these activities are important people and they are all persuaded that they are engaged in important activities'. With flexible exchange rates, the international jetsetters who 'man the emergency phones...could be released to do some truly productive work'. Friedman taunted these jet-setters with the jibe that it was simply the 'tyranny of the status quo' and their emotional attachment to the Bretton Woods system which were the real reasons that it was 'very likely' that floating rates would be eschewed. Friedman found in his opponents only 'bland faith' and a determination to avoid reality by discussing 'a glittering gold man with only an occasional side glance at reality it conceals...I rubbed my eyes as I read all of this'. His opponents were setting up 'a straw man, a scarecrow of shreds and patches to frighten children with'.

Roosa had been Kennedy's Under-Secretary of the Treasury for Monetary Affairs at a time when it was expected that those in Camelot could override market force. In July 1962, for example, President Kennedy had broken the upward pressure on the price of gold by stating on an internationally televised broadcast that 'The United States will not devalue its dollar.' This statement 'changed world history. At least that was what Pierre Salinger thought. The only thing he could compare it to was the first atomic bomb.... Ten seconds of the man live on television had changed the value of money in most of the world' (Reeves 1993, 328–9).

Roosa was a Rhodes Scholar and a partner of Brown Brothers Harriman, a leading Wall Street bank (Galbraith 1971, 80). He joined the Fed in 1946 and had recently been Vice President of the Federal Reserve Bank of New York. He was highly regarded by both Samuelson and Dillon; Jacobsson ranked him second only to McChesney Martin 'in quality of judgment' (Schlesinger 1965, 136, 515; Coombs 1976, 16; Jacobsson 1979, 320).

Jacobsson repeatedly stated that those who advocated altering either the value of the dollar or the dollar price of gold 'knew nothing about exchange markets' (Jacobsson 1979, 320, 324). Friedman (1967, 95) deferred to Roosa's superior knowledge about the day-to-day operations of the foreign exchange market, but was incredulous when Roosa denied that a market in foreign exchange would actually exist without fixed rates: 'because there isn't a real going and lasting market, the relationship that will begin to develop will be the kind which will lead to the creation of the bloc system...fixed rates within each bloc and barter among them' (Roosa 1967b, 185; see also Robbins 1967, 11).[5] Roosa (1967b, 53) predicted that foreign exchange traders would not wish to be

> crushed between the pressures generated by central bank giants in a free-for-all...I am not trying to confront Professor Friedman with an organised strike of my fellow traders in the foreign exchange markets of the world...[but] there would surely...be no little recruiting problem in getting the trading desks capably manned for the launching of his system.

Friedman had found a weak link in his opponent's argument. Roosa (1967b, 189–90, 192) acknowledged that Friedman's 'most telling thrust' had isolated 'a fundamental defect' of the Bretton Woods system: the asymmetry of the adjustment burden with respect to deficit as opposed to surplus countries. Roosa left his debate with Friedman with 'even more respect, if that's possible, for [Friedman's] capacity for making any case plausible and persuasive and I will undertake to study a little further the offer that you have given me to find the conditions under which a flexible exchange rate could possibly be considered'. Roosa's parting words were 'there has to be a presumption, I confess, that such a brilliant jockey could not have chosen a horse as poor as the one I think I see'. Within months, the Bretton Woods 'horse' was on its last legs.

The immediate response of some of the bankers to the Friedman–Roosa debate was contemptuous. Dr G. Carli (1967, 56), Governor of the Bank of Italy, issued a statement which was printed in *Banking* alongside a report of the debate:

> When economists without operational responsibilities discuss this matter, they sometimes put forward alternatives which imply the abandonment of some cardinal point in today's economic order. This applies in particular to the adoption of flexible exchange rates.... This proposal ought to be rejected. Not that the existing structure of parities is sacrosanct, but to give up the system of fixed exchange rates would mean taking a decisive step back.

Within a decade, Roosa (1976, 43–4) was obliged to describe the agreement that legitimised floating exchange rates as a move 'forward' for the international monetary system.

Part III

The Policy Process: 1968–71

10
From Academia to Washington

In 1945, 90 per cent of AEA economists polled favoured the adoption of the Bretton Woods agreement (Meier 1982, 52). Eli Shapiro (1970, 84) doubted that 1 per cent of post-war monetary economists would have predicted the extent of Friedman's 'Plaguing of the Central Bankers'. But in the 15 years from his seminal 1953 essay to his occupancy of the AEA Presidency, Friedman's case was transformed from minority to majority academic position. Friedman (1967, 133–4) estimated that in this period, the proportion of academic economists favouring increased flexibility of exchange rates had risen from less than 5 per cent to greater than 75 per cent.[1] Others thought that towards the end, at least 90 per cent of academic economists accepted the theoretical soundness of the case for floating rates (Roosa 1967b, 177; Fellner *et al.* 1966, 5–6; Sohmen 1961b, xi; Halm 1970, vi–vii; Laffer 1973, 25). Friedman (1975, 162, 166, 178) modestly downplayed his own 'powers of persuasion', but noted that his 'fellow believers' in flexible exchange rates had grown from 'a meagre platoon to an army'. Some of his opponents (such as Burns and Roosa) maintained their faith in a par value system. But within a remarkably short space of time they had been relegated to 'the fringes of debate' (Volcker and Gyohten 1992, 136, 154).

Machlup (11 October 1968) wrote to Friedman explaining that he was

> about to form another group. The time has come, we think, to make a more aggressive push towards greater flexibility of exchange rates. I believe that an increasing number of people in Congress and in the Treasury would like to give more favourable consideration to 'band proposal'. I know, this is a compromise, but it is probably the only strategy towards recognition of the

> advantages of flexible rates. I have even gotten Bob Roosa to help in an objective study...the nice thing about this plan is that the officials of the Group of Ten know of the project and have given us their tacit blessing.[2]

Friedman (23 October 1968) replied that he was

> delighted to hear that you are pushing on for greater flexibility of exchange rates. You may be right that the 'band proposal' is the only effective strategy. It probably is at a time when you do not have a crisis. I am still of the opinion that the way flexible exchange rates will in fact be most likely to be adopted is as a result of a widespread international liquidity crisis which leaves that as the only alternative open to the authorities.[3]

The week before Friedman (15 October) reconstructed his 'case' with the intention of presenting it to Nixon (Friedman and Friedman 1998, 376). On the same day, Peter Jay, writing in the London *Times*, referred to 'the increasingly impressive analytical and predictive results of the Chicago School of monetary economists'. A leader in *The Times* on 'Understanding the Role of the Money Supply' revealed the growing sympathy of the paper for monetarist ideas (Parsons 1989, 181; Congdon 1978, 14, n. 6).[4]

Even after Nixon's election victory on 5 November 1968, some of Friedman's critics failed to see the persuasive power of these straws in the wind. In his Harvard Godkin lectures on *New Dimensions in Political Economy*, Walter Heller (1967, 9) asserted that 'conceptual advances and quantitative research in economics are replacing emotion with reason'. One of these advances was acceptance of the Keynesian model and the Hansenian strategy for the pursuit of full employment: 'When Milton Friedman, the chief guardian of the *laissez faire* tradition in American economics, said not long ago, "We are all Keynesians now" the profession said "Amen".' On 14 November 1968, Heller (1969, 27) assured an academic audience that 'floating exchange rates are not just around the corner...Milton and the monetarists are quite safe. Their theory and policy prescriptions won't be put to the test of application, so there will be no chance to disprove them.'

Further academic conferences were held in Burgenstock,[5] Madrid[6] and elsewhere. At the 1969 Federal Reserve Bank of Boston conference, Sir Maurice Parsons (1970, 42–3), the Deputy Governor of the Bank of England, highlighted the bankers' framework of perceived choice: either

(a) a fully fledged gold standard, or (b) siege economies with some barter, or (c) the 'disastrous' regime of floating exchange rates which, he was 'afraid' commanded support 'in some quarters'. Since all three were defective, the ideal 'compromise' was the existing Bretton Woods system.

11
Flexible Exchange Rates as a Vehicle for Nixon's Re-election

With a witch-hunting reputation to live down, Nixon's chances of winning in 1968 were regarded as 'dim'. Both Edward Kennedy and Hubert Humphrey were in favour of the draft and Nixon's narrow victory has been partly attributed to Nixon's conversion to Friedman's long-held advocacy of an all-volunteer army. This was the marriage of ideas and vested interests, transmitted to Nixon via the head of his research department, Martin Anderson (Anderson 1993, 173–4; Friedman 1977, 12; Friedman and Friedman 1998, 377–81; Safire 1975, 77). Shortly after taking office, Nixon was again exposed to Friedman's proposal to take the wind out of the anti-Vietnam war rhetoric by announcing a timetable for the phasing out of conscription. Defense Secretary Melvin Laird was an advocate of Friedman's position. Nixon scribbled: 'Get Laird's comment on this intriguing proposal' (cited by Reeves 2001, 51, 77).

Nixon had lost in 1960 and won in 1968 by the slightest of majorities, and 1972 was expected to be just as close (Safire 1975, 273). Nixon never needed any encouragement to consider his own political self-interest, and after the 1968 election Friedman framed his exchange rate proposal as a mechanism by which Nixon could achieve a second term.

Although Nixon was not the first President to wish for a second term, it was the excessive activities of the Committee to Re-elect the President (CREEP) and the attempted cover-up which finally drove him from office. Friedman (1967, 114–15) calculated that in the absence of a major crisis, the only way to achieve flexible rates was to persuade an incoming government of the merits of the case within two weeks of coming to power and before they had committed themselves to defending the Bretton Woods system. For Nixon the international monetary system only figured as an unwanted constraint that must not be allowed to impede his determination to be a great foreign policy president: 'We cannot afford a system that almost every year presents a new invitation to a monetary crisis' (Nixon 1972, 3; see also Volcker and Gyohten 1992, 104).

After the election, all the members of the task forces met with President-elect Nixon to present their conclusions. The Task Force on US Balance of Payments Policy was divided, with two members, Walter Hoadley and Tilford Gaines, issuing a dissenting statement to an early draft of the report which declared that 'the suspension of convertibility early in the new Administration would be a major threat to world stability'.[1] Friedman was not a member of this task force but nevertheless pursued Nixon on his own initiative.

Peter Flanigan (9 May 1968), the moderator of the Nixon Advisory Group on the Economy, informed Friedman that the value of any proposal would 'ultimately be determined by its political usefulness during the coming campaign'.[2] On 15 October 1968 Friedman (1988b [1968]) completed the second draft of a 'CONFIDENTIAL' memorandum entitled 'A Proposal for Resolving US Balance of Payments Problems'. On 5 December Friedman sent his memorandum to Bryce Harlow to 'show the kind of rhetoric that can be marshalled in favor of the proposal to set the dollar free'. Friedman requested a meeting with President-elect Nixon 'sometime in the next month...I shall be glad to come to New York or anywhere else for that purpose at your or his command. There is no other economic issue on which I feel that prompt courageous action could contribute so much to the cause we both serve.'[3] Shortly afterwards, Friedman presented his memorandum to Nixon in person (Friedman and Friedman 1998, 376).

Friedman's (1988b [1968], 429–30) advocacy of flexible exchange rates pandered both to Nixon's interconnected desires for re-election and for a crisis-free system. He informed Nixon that 'On one Sunday afternoon in 1948, Ludwig Erhard abolished price controls, setting the mark free.... He therefore unleashed the German economic miracle and assured the Christian Democratic Party unquestioned political dominance for several decades.' Friedman compared Erhard's political longevity to Harold Wilson's

> gruesome cautionary tale.... If he had floated the pound on first gaining office, putting all the blame, as he could then have done, on the alleged 'irresponsible policies of the prior Tory government', it is very likely that he would still be firmly in the saddle, and that

> the Labour Party would hold unquestioned political power. His failure to take this step forced on him one unpopular expedient after another – and did not even prevent later devaluation.

Friedman (1967, 15) had publicly asked: 'Why not have the dog wag the tail, instead of the tail wag the dog...a system of flexible exchange rates completely eliminates the balance of payments problem.' Friedman (1988b [1968], 429–33, 437–8) confidentially recommended to Nixon that he acquire the 'courage and wisdom to cut off the dog's tail in one stroke'. Freeing the dollar would cause a temporary depreciation which might 'momentarily' set 'off a trade war'. But for a trade war to 'spread and last is equivalent to water flowing uphill'. Friedman informed Nixon that 'on the economic front, there appear to be only gains and no costs' from floating the dollar:

> there is probably no other economic measure that the new administration will have the power to take that can contribute anything like so much simultaneously to greater freedom of US citizens from government control, increased economic prosperity, liberalization of international trade, and the freedom of manoeuvre of the US government in foreign affairs.

Although economists as policy advisers sometimes act as salesmen, they do not usually offer unsolicited advice about timing and covering rhetoric. But this is precisely what Friedman (1988b [1968], 430–1) offered Nixon: a draft speech announcing the end of the Bretton Woods system. On the second or third Friday evening or Saturday after his inauguration, Nixon should announce that he was

> shocked at the state in which the preceding administration had left the balance of payments...the measures taken by the Johnson Administration have so distorted the situation that it is impossible to know what the appropriate rates of exchange are. The new administration therefore proposes to put its faith in the strength of the economy and its free enterprise system, not in a growing network of bureaucratic controls.

The gold standard had been the institutional arrangement for Pax Britannica; Bretton Woods performed a similar function for Pax Americana. Successive Presidents had been inculcated with the belief that national strength was synonymous with the strength of the dollar.

President-elect Kennedy had been advised by the authors (including Roosa) of his Task Force Report on the Balance of Payments that the 'first task of economic statesmanship' was to 'dispel fears about the value of the dollar…a cornerstone of our banking responsibility'. The post-war international monetary arrangements had been 'slowly and laboriously built up', and what was required was 'quiet negotiation' and 'frequent consultation between financial authorities' (Roosa 1967a, 285, 287, 291, 307; Schlesinger 1965, 140). The official US position was that any discussion of flexible exchange rates or a change in the official price of gold was 'off limits' (Emminger 1978b, 176). Kennedy was obliged to promise that 'If elected, I shall not devalue the dollar' (cited by Volcker and Gyohten 1992, 21). Fed Chairman McChesney Martin told President Johnson that defeat in Vietnam was preferable to the financial defeat of devaluation, which no President could politically survive (Brandon 1973, 218). In contrast, Friedman (1988b [1968], 436) associated greatness with *not* having to negotiate within the Bretton Woods system: 'We are a great nation. The dollar is the leading currency in the world. We should behave like a great nation, not engage in demeaning and niggling negotiations to get other countries to agree to "let" us depreciate by x per cent vis-à-vis this currency, by y per cent vis-à-vis that currency.'

The Nixon Task Force Report on International Economic Policy was not made public, but those who had helped to write the report had no doubt about its strategic importance (Volcker and Gyothen 1992, 65). The final product was believed to have been 'greatly influenced' by Friedman, although Haberler was the major author (Mayer 1981, 151). One of its members, Hendrik Houthakker (1978, 51), recalled that the policy recommended by the task force was to curtail or prevent the conversion of surplus dollars into gold so as to force a devaluation of the dollar.[4]

An early version of the report also concluded that 'a solution along these lines may prove impossible to attain. A perhaps more promising avenue for bringing about exchange rate adjustment would be to work towards introducing greater exchange flexibility into the Bretton Woods system.' Also canvassed was the proposal that

> inconvertibility could be adopted not just temporarily. Decisions on the price of gold and on exchange rates could be postponed indefinitely. This would allow other countries to decide whether they want to peg to the dollar or allow it to float. In fact, suspension of convertibility, if coupled with reasonable monetary and fiscal

> policies on the part of the United States and close international consultation and cooperation, might prove a viable long-run system under which most countries would continue pegging their currencies to the dollar.
>
> (Report of the Task Force on US Balance of Payments Policies 1968a, 2–3).

In the final version of the report, Nixon was warned that he would face impeachment proceedings initiated by Representative Henry Reuss if he increased the dollar price of gold without Congressional approval. Nixon was also advised that it was 'essential that the political element in exchange-rate decisions be de-emphasised' and that limited exchange rate flexibility 'would be an adequate remedy' (Report of the Task Force on US Balance of Payments Policies 1968b, 2, 26, 32).

The Nixon Task Force on Inflation recommended that

> monetary policy be the primary tool of an anti-inflation program.... For the immediate future the Federal Reserve must be prevailed upon to use its monetary and other powers to achieve stabilisation objectives...[and] should place primary emphasis, as a guide to monetary policy, on the growth rate of the monetary base.

They recommended that inflation be moderated in a *'gradual and systematic manner rather than stopping inflation abruptly'* [emphasis in original]. They recognised that

> this recommendation has important implications for our balance of payments under the present system of fixed exchange rates because it means effective control of domestic prices and purchasing power for balance of payments purposes becomes largely inoperative due to the priority given to domestic employment considerations. Hence, we are led to a collateral set of balance of payments recommendations that entail important modifications of the links between the dollar and gold, and of the current fixed exchange rate system.[5]

Simultaneously, Haberler (1969b, 11, 12, 25, 41–2, 47–8; 1969c, 359) publicly assaulted the analysis provided by the officials responsible for monetary policy who 'still cling' to the system of fixed rates and who represented a minority opinion among economists. Dillon's advice was discounted, as were other 'wild exaggerations' underpinning the case for Bretton Woods. Open inflation was preferable to suppressed inflation because of the tendency to resort to 'controllitis': an 'Ersatz' change in the exchange rate through dishonest exchange controls. Haberler found it 'exceedingly difficult to think of valid objections to flexible exchange rates'.

The Cross of Gold

Appropriately for a story about revolution, the ghost of Lenin began to haunt deliberations. The IMF officials appeared to regard themselves as a politburo established to defend the Bretton Woods revolution. They were confronted by a counter-revolutionary who was aware of Keynes's (probably fictitious) reference to Lenin's dictum about debauching a currency as a prelude to revolution (Friedman 1968a, 174). Friedman (1988a, xix, xxiv) regarded the NEP as 'a sharp break in the monetary regime adopted by the major Western countries'. But the NEPers were apparently unaware that they were rhetorically the heirs of Lenin.[1] The first NEP was Lenin's attempt to reach a temporary compromise with the domestic forces of capitalism; Nixon's NEP fatally compromised the Bretton Woods system (Friedman 1972a [1971], 426). As frantic efforts were being made to revive the Bretton Woods system, Friedman advanced the prospects for international monetary revolution by pressing Nixon to debauch still further the currency of the Bretton Woods system, not through inflation but by undermining the role of gold.

Friedman reflected on the process by which 'economists like me exercise influence...we exert influence by keeping options available when something has to be done at a time of crisis' (Friedman and Friedman 1998, 220). Friedman (1967, 115) estimated that major international crises only happened every 20–30 years. The crisis that led to the NEP also led Friedman to offer Nixon again his 'option': 'as I predicted, the pressure of events forced the president to take essentially the same measures on August 15, 1971' (Friedman and Friedman 1998, 377).

In 1945, the US owned over half the world's stock of official gold (Volcker and Gyohten 1992, 12). Between 1946 and 1951, the IMF had sought to enforce a restriction in the price of gold; from 1951 to 1960 it relied on moral suasion (Horsefield 1969a, 598; 1969b, 225, 310). On 20 October 1960, during the Nixon–Kennedy Presidential election campaign, the 'London gold rush' drove the dollar price of gold towards $40 per ounce. The Gold Pool (a 'gentleman's agreement' between certain European central banks and the New York Fed) was formed to prevent fluctuation in the price of gold in the free market 'such as might undermine the stability of exchanges'. The IMF (1964, 131–2) believed that this selling consortium and buying syndicate helped to 'maintain confidence in the existing international monetary structure'. But the gold outflow continued: in early 1971, Washington's gold holdings had dropped from their 1960 level of $17.8 billion to $10.7 billion. By 1970, US official reserves (monetary gold, reserve currencies and IMF reserves) had fallen to 15.7 per cent of the world's total (Eckes 1975, 238, 255). By 15 August 1971, foreign official holdings of dollars were more than three times greater than US gold holdings when valued at $35 per ounce (Shultz and Dam 1977a, 114).

Yet as the system collapsed it commanded an almost mystical confidence. Kennedy's 1963 Message to Congress had referred to the fixed price of gold as the 'foundation stone of the free world's trade and payments system' (Mayer 1981, 75). After the 1964 annual IMF meeting in Tokyo, a group of officials visited an ornamental Zen Buddhist garden in which 15 stones were arranged so that the viewer could never see more than 14 stones at any one time. Roosa (1967a, 187–8) reflected that 'It went without saying at Tokyo that the price of gold, having been fixed at $35 per ounce, is now taken as the cornerstone of the international monetary system…as certain and secure as the fifteenth stone.'[2] Friedman (1968a, 244) believed that such phrases were 'ritual incantations to conceal the emptiness of thought'.

In March 1968, less than four years after Roosa's semi-mystical insight, the Gold Pool collapsed and the link between the official and the private gold market was severed. The Gold Pool had lost $2.75 billion; the cost to the US Treasury alone was over $1 billion (Scammell 1983, 123; de Vries 1976a, 403). Henceforth, the price of gold fluctuated freely in the private market, although central banks continued to trade gold among themselves at $35 per ounce (Haberler and Willett 1971, 1). The IMF had always been 'apprehensive' about the consequences for fixed exchange rates of a rise in the price of gold (Horsefield 1969a, 598, 614). At the 1968 IMF annual meeting (just before Nixon was elected), the US Governor reaffirmed the 'vital stake' of the international community in maintaining a fixed price of official gold which should not be demonetised (de Vries 1969, 407–8). However, gold was ceasing to be the 'firm anchor' of the international monetary system.

A former member of Nixon's CEA noted that there was 'as yet little public knowledge of what exactly led to the President's decision to suspend the convertibility of the dollar into gold' (Houthakker cited by Brandon 1973, 225). It is now clear that Friedman played an important role in the removal of the fifteenth stone. Part of Friedman's (1953, 192) case for flexible exchange rates involved the institution of a free gold market. At the Chicago conference, one of the 'alternatives' was to replace the fixed relationship between gold and the dollar with more flexible exchange rates: 'No one cited a cross of gold speech but the idea is very much alive' (Shultz and Aliber 1966, 3–4, 13).

Within the Fed arguments were being marshalled to oppose this threat to 'the cornerstone of the IMF'. Coombs (13 August 1971) sent Burns a memorandum: 'Advocates of closing the gold window seem to be overlooking at least one disastrous consequence of such action. This would be the massive destruction of international liquidity that would inexorably follow.' Coombs informed Burns that the scenario was part of the accepted fabric of central banking thought: 'On numerous occasions in the past, individual central bank officials have predicted to me precisely such a sequence of policy actions abroad.' If the dollar were allowed to float and the gold window were closed, 'trade within the Common Market and with adjoining countries would suffer a catastrophic decline' forcing the establishment of 'a monetary block among themselves'. Thus 'closure of the gold window would pull out the cornerstone of the IMF and immediately paralyse any lending by that institution'.[3]

Friedman (1988b [1968], 430, 438) had advised President-elect Nixon that pegging the price of gold had put a 'loaded gun' in the hands of other countries; the new administration should therefore abstain from further gold transactions. At the Camp David weekend (13–15 August 1971) Nixon instructed Shultz to attempt to gain Friedman's sympathy for the NEP (Reeves 2001, 364–5). Certainly, Shultz asked Friedman for advice – apparently on how to end the wage and price freeze. Friedman (21 August 1971) replied: 'On the key question of how to end the freeze with the least damage, I must confess that I am still bereft of any good ideas.' Friedman suggested to Shultz that the administration should 'end the prohibition on the ownership, purchase, and sale of gold by private individuals.... This action would appeal to many of Mr Nixon's conservative supporters.'[4]

Thus Friedman reformulated his proposals for gold and presented them to Nixon (via Shultz) as a vehicle for the President's political advancement. H.R. Haldeman's 'Action Paper' explained that Nixon was

> very much interested.... Friedman's point was that this is a move that would very much please the Conservatives, would be a very big marker with them and would have no appreciable significant effects otherwise. The point is that FDR took away the right for Americans to own gold and Richard Nixon could get the credit for getting it back. Friedman suggested this to Shultz. The President would like the research done on it and a proposal in to him as quickly as possible.
>
> (Oudes 1989, 312)[5]

13
Price and Wage Regulation, Exchange Rate Deregulation

Burns (1969 [1967], 263) noted that 'practice' could often turn out to be 'less orthodox' than 'rhetoric'.[1] Indeed, alongside free market rhetoric there was also the rhetoric of 'a social bargain or compact' (De Marchi 1975, 348). On both sides of the Atlantic, support for price and wage controls was gaining ground. In Britain for example, there were rhetorical similarities between the rhetoric of the Conservative Party election manifestos of June 1970 and May 1979. After Friedman's September 1970 Wincott Lecture, the Institute of Economic Affairs arranged for him to be 'discreetly ushered in' to see Edward Heath, the newly elected Prime Minister, for an hour's talk.[2] Friedman (19 September 1970) told Stigler that 'Heath impressed me very favorably.... What he wanted to talk to me about was (1) floating exchange rate; (2) monetary policies for fighting inflation.' Friedman reported that Heath indicated 'a lack of interest in wage + price controls or guidelines or incomes policy'.[3]

Academically, the establishment of the Manchester University Inflation Workshop in July 1971 (funded by the Social Science Research Council) also contributed to the monetarist explanation of inflation (Congdon 1978, 20). But despite the free market rhetoric of 'Selsdon Man', by mid-1971 it was clear that the new British government was increasing both the money supply and public expenditure. In early 1972, Alan Walters (1989, 22) a part-time Cabinet Office adviser, offered a monetarist critique of this policy and was relieved of his position. On 2 November 1972, a group of monetarists (self-styled 'Economic Radicals'), including Walters and Harry Johnson, published a *Memorial to the Prime Minister* arguing that the rate of growth of the money supply needed to be reduced to restrain inflation (Smith 1987, 50; Keegan 1984, 44). According to Tim Congdon (1978, 5) the *Memorial* was in effect 'a charter of incorporation of the new [British monetarist] school'.

But on Guy Fawkes Day (5 November 1972), Heath appointed Geoffrey Howe (1991, 94) to the Cabinet as the 'Minister for Keeping Down Prices'. The following day, a 90-day freeze of wages, prices, rents and dividends was imposed. The government 'threw' themselves into price control 'with enthusiasm'. Heath explained that his government was 'determined to sail through the whirlpool' (Howe 1991, 94; Cockett 1995, 100, 203–9).

On the other side of the Atlantic, Stigler (1967, 356, 361) complained (before Nixon's victory) that confidence in the working of competition was 'at a low level... [and] the majority of economists have lost much of their faith.... The only effective challenge to generous opportunism is a trenchant ideology, and that is precisely what we no longer have.' The following year Friedman (1968a, 19) predicted that price controls would be 'resuscitated' in the near future. Just before Burns's appointment as Fed Chairman, Roosa called for a six-month moratorium on wages, prices and dividends (De Marchi 1975, 317). In the *New York Times Magazine*, Galbraith (1971 [7 June 1970], 80–1) applauded Roosa's proposal, adding: 'Controls are not a temporary expedient. There must, alas, be a permanent system of restraint.'

The Swan diagram, an influential macroeconomic model of the period, also stressed the importance of wages policy in the simultaneous pursuit of internal and external balance. Trevor Swan (1963 [1955], 391–2, 394) concluded that 'effective short-run control of Real expenditure (E) and effective long-run adjustments of the Cost Ratio (R) are both necessary to reconcile full employment with long-run external balance. The cost adjustments required are essentially adjustments of real wage rates.' Successful real wage resistance to a devaluation of the currency would require import restrictions to become 'a permanent feature of the economy'. Therefore, if real wages could not be directly controlled, they would have to be indirectly controlled by targeting the 'lower limit' of the 'full employment' range. In other words, higher levels of unemployment would have to be tolerated.

Faced with this choice, Nixon could be expected to favour a direct assault on wages. Burns played an important role in the 1960 'Scholars for Nixon and Lodge' organisation (Wells 1994, 17). Privately, Burns warned Nixon (1962, 309–11) of an impending economic downturn which would reach its nadir in October 1960, just before the election. Burns recommended 'decisive government action' to head off this threat to Nixon's election campaign. Nixon reflected that Burns was 'a good prophet'. Unemployment increased to 452,000 in October 1960: 'All the speeches, television broadcasts and precinct work in the world could not counter that one hard fact.' Nixon attributed his defeat by Kennedy to an insufficient degree of political sensitivity within Eisenhower's Cabinet with respect to the forthcoming election. The first time he met Herbert Stein (1995, 96) in December 1968, he asked what Stein assessed to be the nation's biggest economic problem. Stein replied with some discussion of inflation, but soon realised that 'unemployment was very much on his mind and would remain so throughout his administration'.

In October 1968, candidate Nixon had promised that the way to stop inflation was to 'reverse the irresponsible fiscal policies which produce it' (cited by Goulden 1972, 421). With respect to domestic policy, Nixon's attitude was that 'We'll take inflation if necessary, but we can't take unemployment' (cited by Ehrlichman 1982, 254). However, the *Washington Evening Star* (11 October 1968) reported that Alan Greenspan, Nixon's chief economic adviser, had stated that 'Guideposts fight the symptoms of inflation, not the causes.'[4] Greenspan suggested that Nixon would allow the economy to slide down a Phillips curve to defeat inflation (*Washington Evening Star,* 11 October 1968). The following day Greenspan was philosophical: 'The carefully thought-through decisions can always be changed; it's the arbitrary decisions that can't be changed' (cited by Safire 1975, 76). The Nixon advisers were not inclined to be philosophical about such a sensitive issue. The idea that Nixon would tolerate more unemployment was regarded as 'Greenspan's blunder' which Burns was asked to correct in an address to the AFL-CIO.[5]

Shortly after the inauguration, Nixon's CEA Chairman, McCracken, made a similar blunder, by suggesting that inflation would have to be curbed by an increase in unemployment. Labour leader George Meany did not accept that unemployment had to be increased to reduce inflation: what was required was the implementation of the 1946 Full Employment Act which, he thought, would simultaneously solve the inflation problem. Nixon sent 'a squad' of senior Labor Department officials, led by Shultz, to the February 1969 AFL-CIO Council as a peace gesture. Shultz handed Meany a letter from the President which appeared to contradict and overrule McCracken (Robinson 1981, 281).

During the 1968 campaign, Nixon often instructed his staff to 'Check it out with Arthur' (Malkin 1971, 264). Nixon (1978, 342, 519) was keen to appoint Burns as Fed Chairman, but McChesney Martin refused to leave before his contract expired. Nixon therefore created a special interim position for Burns as Counselor to the President. On the fourth day of his Presidency he issued an order to his closest staff: 'P[resident] ordered all of us to read Burns' book tonight. Very determined to get things moving – wants action.' Haldeman (1994, 21) reflected, 'Burns is great, has good effect on P[resident].'

Within two months, Burns was 'worn to a frazzle' and had fallen out with Nixon's Germanic White House mafia: 'E[hrlichman] and I had a knockdown with Arthur Burns at lunch. Pretty bitter discussion, still didn't settle the problem of getting a domestic program. Burns determined to run the show, but it's obvious he can't manage' (Haldeman 1994 [28 March 1969], 43). Nixon was getting bored with Burns's didactic style and by April 1969, Haldeman was physically blocking Burns's access to the Oval Office (Reeves 2001, 57, 71). Burns threatened to resign: 'Feels if he can't get in when he wants to he'll have to quit. No more need for him' (Haldeman 1994 [7 May 1969], 54).

Nixon claimed that he always gave 'great weight to Burns' opinions'. However at Burns's swearing-in ceremony as Fed Chairman, Nixon interpreted the applause as 'a standing vote of appreciation in advance for lower interest rates and more money'. Nixon added that he hoped that 'independently [Burns] will conclude that my views are the ones that should be followed'.[6] Subsequently, Nixon bluntly instructed Burns: 'You see to it: no recession' (cited by Wells 1994, 42).

On 3 April 1969, the Treasury consultants discussed a paper on inflation by David Meiselman and co-authors. They were told, 'This paper is administratively confidential and must in no way be allowed to become public.' Wallich summarised the discussion for Secretary Kennedy:

> A fair proportion of the consultants were mildly sceptical of the Administration's gradualist approach to the control of inflation, preferring stronger measures.... There seemed to be agreement that 4–4.5 percent unemployment was consistent with stable prices, although the historical evidence supporting this assumption is not strong.[7]

Secretary Kennedy (11 June 1969) publicly suggested that the country was on the brink of a 'runaway inflation' (Evans and Novak 1971, 189). Burns (29 June 1969) 'flatly' stated that there would be no price and wage control.[8] Burns was quoted in the *US News and World Report* (14 July 1969) as saying the inflation was 'the nation's biggest danger.... What happened in Hitler's Germany is a story that all of us know.'[9] On 25 July 1969, Burns received a Treasury memo which explained that 'This Phillips curve relation for the US economy in the 1960s shown in Chart

1 indicates how close the relationship is.' The commentary suggested a 'rather gloomy' conclusion. Moreover, this Phillips curve was noticeably worse than the implicit Phillips curve agreed upon by the Treasury consultants: with unemployment between 4 and 4.5 per cent inflation would still be over 1.25 per cent.[10]

Shultz's views on anti-inflation policy 'carried considerable weight' within the White House (De Marchi 1975, 320–3). On 15 February 1970, Haldeman (1994, 127) had a 'Long chat' with Nixon 'about recession-minded Cabinet members, like those of DDE[isenhower]'s in '57 and '58'. Prior to the 1960 election, it was Burns who tried to save him from defeat; now it was Shultz: 'P[resident] more inclined to follow Shultz as only really knowledgeable economist.'

At a Cabinet meeting three days later, Nixon 'launched into his antirecession pitch'. George Romney, the Secretary of Housing and Urban Development (HUD),

> was not supposed to get into his wage-price-policy pitch but did. P[resident] really whapped him by saying wage-price-policy had never worked.... Pretty sharp alignment...against the Shultz–McCracken view, which is to handle things by fiscal and monetary policy. P[resident] had Shultz and me in after meeting, and covered the subject further, trying to lock up George's view, which made George fear that P[resident] thought he was a wild man on the subject.

But it was Romney who became a marked man in Nixon's imagination. On 21 May 1970, he planned to bring Rumsfeld to OMB and then after the mid-term election 'clean out Cabinet, especially...Romney and Kennedy'. A few days later, Nixon (6 June) successfully gave Shultz 'a *great* pitch' about becoming Director of a new and more powerful OMB. Nixon boasted to the press about the intellectual brilliance and high IQs of Shultz and his other advisers (Haldeman 1994, 128, 168, 172, 228).

Shultz's influence can be detected in the administration's series of 'inflation alerts' (7 August 1970, 1 December 1970, 13 April 1971) as the acceptable limits of such anti-inflation supplements to fiscal and monetary policy (De Marchi 1975, 320–3). While some economists sought to break out of the dilemma by abandoning the fixed exchange rate system, Burns looked to other policy tools.

In August 1969 Burns, increasingly dissatisfied with the administration's use of fiscal policy to restrain inflation, was 'jolted by the excessive wage settlements in construction'. In conversations with the President and in Cabinet meetings he began canvassing the possibility of a return to jawboning or an incomes policy. On 11 September, he informed the President 'It's heresy but I'm even thinking about wage and price controls' (cited by Reeves 2001, 216). In that month, Nixon responded to these pressures by announcing the creation of a tripartite Construction Industry Collective Bargaining Commission with powers to intervene in labour disputes (De Marchi 1975, 310–11). Burns (1978 [1970], 114–15, [1977], 471) argued that stagflation undermined 'the classical remedies' which required other tools 'to bring an end to the pressure of costs on prices'. High on his list was the development of 'a social consensus that leads to responsible price and wage behaviour by private parties'.

In preparation for the 1970 campaign, Nixon gave a precise instruction: 'don't get into the drawn-out business about the trade-off about price stability and unemployment' (cited by Safire 1975, 319). But the Republican defeats in the 1970 elections reinforced demands for a more forceful assault on stagflation (De Marchi 1975, 308, 325, 328, 336; Evans and Novak 1971, 193). Secretary Kennedy informed Nixon that the IMF had 'very forcibly' stressed that the US Phillips curve trade-off had deteriorated. Thus Kennedy concluded that the 'institution of a direct wage–price policy can serve as a "shield" for a more expansionary thrust from our conventional economic policies, without fomenting new inflationary expectations'.[11]

The *Washington Post* (15 November 1970) reported 'Burns Pressing Hard for "Incomes Policy"'. Economists from the Brookings Institution – described as 'the home away from home for Democrats out of office' (Friedman and Friedman 1998, 93) – circulated estimates that the money supply had to grow by 10–11 per cent per annum to get unemployment down to an electorally acceptable level of 4 per cent by 1972 (Rowen 1970). On 19 November 1970, Shultz brought Friedman into the Oval Office to 'try to straighten out the President's ideological spine' on the question of price and wage controls. Nixon told Ehrlichman that 'I really want the economy to boom beginning July 1972' (Reeves 2001, 264, 287, 637, n. 287).

Nixon was pleased with his meeting with Friedman. Haldeman (1994, 212) reported,

> Apparently had a good talk with (economist) Milton Friedman, and said after it was nice to have someone say we're doing things right. Friedman urges we stay on present course. Says we're in good shape if we stay with it. P[resident] still concerned about '72. Can't afford to risk a downtrend, no matter how much inflation.

The following day, Nixon again urged Burns to expand the money supply at a faster rate. Burns reiterated that some form of incomes policy was required (Evans and Novak 1971, 370).

On the same day, a strictly confidential 'Incomes Policy Strategy' was outlined which suggested the establishment of a three-person Wage, Price and Productivity Board with independent status to establish voluntary 'guidelines' to restrict wage and price increases. This proposed 'new economic initiative' eschewed price and wage controls. The document suggested that Shultz and the OMB should play a role in the strategy by monitoring 'the price implications of Government policies'.[12] On 7 December 1970, Burns publicly argued for an incomes policy in a speech at Pepperdine College and Nixon began to appeal to labour and management to 'start help fighting inflation'.[13]

Richard Whalen warned Burns that 'the knives are out these days'.[14] Burns needed no warning: within the Nixon administration the knives had been sharpened against him for some time. On 14 December 1970, Nixon announced that the dynamic John Connally would be his new Treasury Secretary. Nixon made a note to himself about the administration's image of 'competent gray men' which he now wished to change. The following day, he met with Burns ('one of the grayest') and instructed him to 'Err towards inflation' (Reeves 2001, 286).

On 21 December 1970, Herbert Stein, of the CEA, wrote a memorandum for Kennedy, McCracken and Shultz which found its way to Burns. In this 5-page document on 'Economic Situation and Policy' 16 lines were highlighted and 3 phrases underlined – presumably by Burns. Stein called for an 8 per cent annual expansion of the money supply, adding:

> The Federal reserve should be informed clearly of our desires. There is no reason to expect the Fed will agree, but they should not be able to say we never asked them. Also we should find out whether their cooperation *can be bought* [Burns's emphasis] with 'incomes policy'. If it can be, I think we should *pay the price* [Burns's emphasis]. If the Federal Reserve *cannot be persuaded or bribed* [Burns's emphasis] we have two alternatives: a. Try and pump the economy up by fiscal policy, or b. Try to force the hand of the Fed. I would be reluctant to go down the first route because I don't think it would work without the cooperation of the Fed and I think we might face the issue of who is running the country. Therefore, I would favor an open attack on the question of the relation between the Administration and the Fed. In that case we should have to prepare ourselves for battle, and thus

would raise the question whether we would be better off if it did not appear that only our stubbornness about incomes policy was standing in the way of expansion.[15]

Burns's 7 December 1970 speech would 'live in infamy' for some Chicago economists. Shultz believed that talk of controls would stimulate pre-control price increases, and was opposed to a reversion to guidelines. Burns (4 January 1971) wrote to Shultz indicating that he objected to being harassed on the issue: 'I have made just two public pronouncements on incomes policy.' Burns then added: 'a brief telephone conversation, originating for an altogether different purpose, is hardly the best medium for exchanging views on basic economic policy'.[16]

When Shultz became OMB Director, he echoed Friedman's critique of Fed policy and was 'the first in the administration to call publicly for an easing of monetary restraint' (De Marchi 1975, 308, 325, 328, 336; Evans and Novak 1971, 193). But Burns had indicated that monetary policy was not going to be available in the run-up to the 1972 Presidential election. This led Nixon's advisers to consider whether fiscal deficits could be temporarily enlisted (despite the fact that Republicans were traditionally in favour of balanced budgets). But Burns reiterated to Nixon that a balanced budget was a prerequisite for a 'serious fight against inflation'.[17]

Shultz advocated the notion of a full employment balanced budget, which legitimised deficit spending in the presence of less than full employment which had an obvious appeal to Nixon. At a meeting (5 May 1970) between Nixon and his 'top economic types' (Shultz, Kennedy, McCracken, Peter Flannigan and Robert Mayo) a decision was made 'not to hold to balanced budget in '70 and '71.... P[resident] much more concerned with upgoing economy in fall because he feels that's the only chance to make gains in the election' (Haldeman 1994, 160).

Nixon (7 January 1971) spoke in favour of such an expansionary unbalanced budget in an ABC television interview. Off air he quipped, 'I am now a Keynesian in economics' (Reeves 2001, 286–7, 295). On 31 January 1971 in an NBC television interview, Burns explained that 'one reason I keep cool is, that I expect this country will move into a vigorous price–wage policy. We have been moving in that direction. I think we need it.'[18]

On 19 February 1971, Burns testified that the current unemployment was not caused by monetary policy but by a lack of confidence. When they saw the press reports the following day, Nixon and his advisers were furious with the implication that Burns

> didn't have confidence in the P[resident]'s policies. The P[resident] was really upset about this. Arthur was trying to call him during the day, and the P[resident] said he would not take the call.... The P[resident] has the strong feeling that we've got to really put the screws onto Arthur and that he is not showing the proper gratitude or appreciation for the P[resident]'s having put him where he is. (Haldeman 1994 [20 February 1970], 249)

The following day, the *Washington Post* reported that Shultz blamed the ex-Fed Chairman McChesney Martin for the much of the current unemployment (Krause 1971). In Shultz's judgement, the Fed Chairman was the 'unsung villain' of the unemployment problem (Malkin 1971, 260). Shultz also asserted that wage and price guidelines 'don't seem to work' (cited by Krause 1971). The *Washington Post* (7 March 1971) reported that Burns found fault in Shultz's 'theological' opposition to his proposal of a Wage and Price Review Board (Rowen 1971).

Walter Heller (11 March 1971) wrote a confidential memo for Bob Brimberg explaining that he had 'heard repeatedly' from the press that 'the Burns–Shultz feud *is* getting personal'.[19] On 19 March 1971, Shultz tried another channel to influence Burns – over lunch. But Shultz's attempt to raise questions about monetary policy was curtailed by Burns who informed him that if anyone from the White House raised the matter with him again, he would 'throw him out bodily' (cited by Woolley 1984, 158).

Nixon (21 March 1971) told his Cabinet that he would not move halfway on wage and price controls: 'If and when we do it we're gonna leapfrog 'em all' (Safire 1975, 101, 587). On 17 May 1971, Burns received a report regarding the 'current status of planning for direct controls over prices, wages and salaries and rents' which indicated that the Office of Emergency Preparation was preparing new regulations which would be available by the end of June.[20] In June 1971, Nixon unsuccessfully attempted to persuade Friedman to urge Burns to accelerate the increase in the money supply prior to the 1972 election (Friedman and Friedman 1998, 386). Burns (22 June 1971) wrote to the President calling for 'a major shift in economic policy...a strong price and wage policy' with the possibility of 'a six-month wage and price freeze'.[21]

Gallup polls were revealing a low approval rating for the President. On 20 July, Nixon briefed Republican leaders on China and then 'had Shultz cover the economy. Apparently didn't go too well, especially the economy part. The P[resident] was really fed up with the attitude of the leaders' (Haldeman 1994, 221, 322). Three days later, Burns (1978, 121, 127) informed the Joint Economic Committee of the US Congress that cost-push inflation required 'a more effective incomes policy'. Ominously, from a Chicago perspective, Burns suggested that in the judgement of the Federal Reserve Board existing efforts in this direction needed to be 'carried further – perhaps much further'.

Burns was initially regarded as Nixon's 'man' at the Fed (Malkin 1971, 148). But as early as 13 April 1970, Shultz warned Nixon that Burns was hijacking his Presidency: 'Arthur has a way of holding the money supply as a hostage – saying that "if you don't behave, I'll tighten up on money" and in that way he's trying to run the whole executive branch with the Federal Reserve.' Nixon snapped: 'With that, the President slammed his hand on the table and said: "When we get through, this Fed won't be independent if it's the only thing I do in this office"' (Reeves 2001, 187).

This reluctance to engineer a boom before the 1972 election elevated Burns onto a formal or informal list of White House enemies. The formal list had been drawn up by mid-June 1971 by Charles Colson, a lawyer, who had been recruited because of his ability to 'chew some people up' (Reeves 2001, 129–30). A variety of vehicles for revenge were planned, including some covertly administered LSD (Summers 2001, 375, 407). Because Burns was regarded as having 'ratted' on Nixon, 'a vendetta of sorts among White House staff' developed against him (Malkin 1971, 264; Volcker and Gyohten 1992, 117; Safire 1975, 492–6).

On 3 July 1971, the Bureau of Labor Statistics (BLS) announced that unemployment had gone down from 6.2 to 5.6 per cent, but Harold Goldstein, its Assistant Commissioner, added that it was in part a seasonal statistical aberration. Nixon exploded: 'Washington is full of Jews.... Most Jews are disloyal.' Colson added: 'You just have to go down the goddamned list and you know they are out to kill us.' They discovered that 13 out of 35 BLS employees were Jewish. This number was reduced to 12 when Goldstein was removed (Reeves 2001, 343–4; Ambrose 1989, 457; Woodward and Bernstein 1976, 185). Haldeman (1994 [5 July 1971], 314) recorded in his diary that Nixon told him that 'we're going to have to start playing a harder game with Arthur, and we've really got to put the screws on the bad guys at the Bureau of Labor Statistics. He's talked to Colson....'

In that month, Nixon ordered Colson (1976, 68, 203–4) to leak to United Press International and the *Wall Street Journal* the false information that Burns had attempted to increase his own salary by almost 50 per cent while pressing for wage controls for everyone else.[22] White

House sources also hinted that the Fed was going to be brought under White House control. Haldeman (1994 [28 July 1971], 331–2) noted in his diary, 'We had a pretty good flap on Arthur Burns last night and this morning as a result of leaking some stories.... This got Arthur pretty upset, as it was intended that he would.'

The 'flap' backfired, evoking comparisons with Roosevelt's 1937 attempt to 'pack' the Supreme Court (Silberman 1971, 14). At the end of July 1971, NBC News reported that Wall Street had been shaken by the administration's attempts to use Burns as 'a scapegoat'.[23] The *Inside Washington* television programme reported (13 August) that there was 'growing talk' that Nixon was beginning to appear as economically incompetent as Herbert Hoover. One-third of Republican Senators publicly denounced Nixon's economic policy; one Senator suggested he was listening to 'bum advice'.[24]

Nixon regarded himself as a foreign policy President. On 15 July 1971, he appeared to cut one of the Gordian knots by accepting an invitation to visit Beijing (De Marchi 1975, 346). Connally (25 July 1971) told the CBS *Face the Nation* programme that he took 'exception' to Burns's suggestion that 'we've made no progress on inflation'. Connally said that a President who was prepared to be bold on China 'is going to exercise that same boldness and that same courage on the domestic and on the economic front. Now, it's just a question of what triggers it.'[25]

Nixon told his economic group that 'the decisions on the economy are final, we will not have a wage price board'. The following day he told his Cabinet that 'there will be no wage–price controls' (Haldeman 1994 [28–29 June 1971], 308, 310). At an impromptu press conference, Nixon declared that he was 'unalterably opposed... to the Galbraithian scheme... of permanent price and wage controls... the extremists on the left of the economy spectrum have always favored a totally government controlled economy' (Diamond 1972 [4 August 1971], 150, 152). He doubted that a wage and price review board could work without a 'new bureaucracy with enormous criminal powers, to fasten itself on the American economy' (cited by De Marchi 1975, 344).

But 11 days later, the administration embraced the 'Nixon shock' (Safire 1975, 527). In two Monday night sessions (2 and 9 August), Nixon, with Shultz and Connally, designed the NEP which both introduced a wage and price freeze and allowed the dollar to float (De Marchi 1975, 345). Nixon's strategy appeared to the 1972 AEA President as evidence of the bankruptcy of neoclassical economics (Galbraith 1973, 4). In reality, as Friedman recognised, it was the death rattle for the Bretton Woods system.

Burns (1978 [1 November 1971], 131) declared that 'more and more thoughtful citizens' had become convinced of the need for an incomes policy and so were 'in a mood to respond favourably' to the NEP. In contrast, some aspects of the NEP about-face horrified the Chicagoans: the 'jerry-built freeze' and the controls were 'deeply and inherently immoral... [they] threaten the very foundations of a free society'. If the USA 'becomes a collectivist society it will not be because the socialists win any arguments; it will be via permanent wage and price controls' (Friedman 1972d, 75; 1975, 126, 129). Shultz (1993, 176, 819–20) thought that they were 'an inexorable spiral of escalating disaster'.

Shultz therefore attempted to minimise their real as opposed to their rhetorical impact. After the NEP was announced, he was concerned that 'we're moving to an extensive control system and that the planners are working on the assumptions that the P[resident] has implied in his speeches'. As a result, 'we squeezed in a meeting with Shultz [and Nixon] in the middle of a fantastically loaded schedule today' (Haldeman 1994 [30 September 1971], 360).

Other aspects of the NEP were more congenial to the Chicago cause. Shultz had been forewarned by Nixon to be ready for the crisis weekend of 13–15 August, and he arrived with 5–7 billion of prepared budget cuts (Safire 1975, 509, 515, 521; Weinberger 1990, 40).[26] Friedman (1974c [1971], 366) 'applaud[ed]' these cuts.

The press wondered whether Burns was 'in the same boat' as the White House on monetary policy.[27] Haldeman and Erlichman summoned Chuck Partee, the Director of the Fed Division of Research and Statistics, to the White House and instructed him: 'don't you ever leave your office without asking what you have done to increase the money supply today?' Burns telephoned Nixon to protest against these political attempts to undermine the independence of the Federal Reserve (Mayer 1999, 69). By 16 August 1971, 'The Battle of the Economy' reached *Time*'s front page with a cartoon of Burns and Shultz in gladiatorial combat.

Their primary conflict related to the future of the par value system. In a letter to Homer Jones, Friedman (10 September 1971) wrote,

> The one element of brightness I see in the picture on the international front, we have made a greater movement towards floating exchange rates in the past few weeks than for many years. In addition, I am hopeful that now that the gold window is closed we will also get rid of the various forms of exchange control that have developed in the past few years.[28]

In contrast, Burns' major disagreement with the NEP was the 'gold move' (Safire 1975, 519; Volcker and Gyohten 1992, 113; de Vries 1985a, 134).

Burns (1979, 6) favoured fixed exchange rates as the exercise of the 'the rule of law' in international monetary affairs. He believed that 'floating would surely bring misery to mankind' (Volcker and Gyohten 1992, 130). He tried to pull rank with Nixon as a central banker with inside information:

> I get reports from the central banks the world over, every day. If we take the domestic steps, they'll applaud it, and they won't hit the dollar.... Once the dollar floats, the trade basis will change. The risk to world trade would be much greater. The profit margin in world trade, which is already very narrow, will vanish.... We release forces that don't need to be released. (Haldeman 1994 [13 August 1971], 342–3)

Shultz approved of some of these forces: 'He thinks the P[resident] has unleashed a lot of new forces...there are a lot of deep currents beginning to flow now, that we have cut a lot of our basic moorings and we don't know exactly where we're headed' (Haldeman 1994 [1 November 1971], 369). At the end of the 13 August session, Burns attempted a rearguard action and 'stayed afterwards to make a personal pitch against floating the dollar, and asked for a private session with the P[resident] later, which the P[resident] hedged' (Haldeman 1994, 344).

But Nixon (1978, 519–20) overrode Burns's advice: 'This was one of the few cases in which I did not follow his recommendations. I decided to close the gold window and let the dollar float...the best thing that came out of the whole economic program that I announced on August 15, 1971.' Burns had cautioned Nixon (1978, 519) against such a move on the grounds that '*Pravda* would write that this was a sign of the collapse of capitalism'. In contrast, Nixon and Volcker believed that they were ending an eight-year-long period of American 'feebleness' (James 1996, 221).

Part IV

Friedman and the Policy Revolution

14
The Nature and Origins of Friedman's Influence

Since the death of Keynes, no economist has exerted a comparable influence to that of Friedman. He influenced economists' methodology before he influenced their policy prescriptions: positive economics was the antidote to the use of 'arbitrary' principles such as Occam's razor which sought to discriminate between 'formal models of imaginary worlds' (Friedman 1953, 283). As a policy analyst, Friedman displayed 'inventiveness' (Stigler 1998, 155). His advocacy of flexible exchange rates is a classic illustration of the process by which academic ideas become fertile.

Giscard d'Estaing (1969, 13) described international monetary reform as 'a race that is being run on three tracks at once'. Adapting this analogy, Friedman's influence can be attributed to his determination to influence three marketplaces simultaneously: the academic, the political and the popular.[1] He influenced public opinion through *Capitalism and Freedom* (1962a), *Free to Choose* (Friedman and Friedman 1980) and his *Newsweek* column. He also influenced American Presidents, especially Nixon (born 1914), Ford (born 1913) and Reagan (born 1911). Along with Senator Goldwater (born 1909), Friedman (born 1912) was an almost exact contemporary of these men. Nixon, Reagan and Friedman all rose from modest social origins to positions of power and influence.

Reagan was caught surreptitiously reading *Capitalism and Freedom* during his first (1966) gubernatorial challenge in California (Friedman and Friedman 1998, 388–9). Friedman reflected that 'I was one of the people who talked to Reagan and there's no question that Reagan understood the relation between the quantity of money and inflation. It was very clear, and he was willing to take the heat' (cited by Taylor 2000, 108). Martin Anderson (1990, 172) recalled that President Reagan 'just could not resist Friedman's infectious enthusiasm and Reagan's eyes sparkled with delight every time he engaged in a dialogue with him'. Friedman was 'a ball of controlled energy' with an 'extraordinary personality'.

Nixon informed a television audience that he had 'great respect' for Friedman (Friedman and Friedman 1998, 370, 375–6, 382). In turn, Friedman reflected that 'My principles were Nixon's prejudices' (cited by Reichley 1981, 206). Ford (1979, 154) also 'wholeheartedly' agreed with Friedman about the need to reassert the power of the market relative to the control exerted by government.

Friedman hoped for (and maybe even angled for) a fourth President to continue the Chicago influence. World history, he argued, would have been profoundly altered had Reagan chosen Donald Rumsfeld as his Vice Presidential candidate in 1980 instead of George Bush: 'the worst decision not only of his campaign but also of his presidency'. Rumsfeld would have succeeded Reagan as President and 'the sorry Bush–Clinton period would never have occurred'.

In the late 1970s, Rumsfeld was one of 'the few' who publicly 'denounced' President Jimmy Carter's wage and price controls (Friedman and Friedman 1980, 92). In 2001, Rumsfeld explained that he was planning to use 'incentives, through the great principles of University of Chicago economics' to persuade Afghanis to provide information which would lead to the capture of Osama Bin Laden.[2] Galbraith (1987, 271) referred to the process by which for economists 'the age of John Maynard Keynes gave way to the age of Milton Friedman'. A two-term Rumsfeld Presidency would have provided Friedman with an unparalleled outside influence on the White House between 1969 and 1997.

There are several similarities and contrasts between Keynes and Friedman. Both asserted that they were the beneficiaries of a quantity theory oral tradition (JMK 1983, 11 [1911], 375–6; Friedman 2003a [1956]). In 'Keynesian Economics versus the Quantity Theory', Don Patinkin (1971, 14) accused Friedman of playing the role of Allah in propagating his revolution. In the 1930s, Schumpeter made an identical complaint about Keynes (Galbraith 1996, 137).

Both Keynes and Friedman brought intense evangelical passion to their work. Keynes's reaction to the treatment of the Germans at the 1919 Paris Peace Conference was as intense as Friedman's 1950 reaction to aspects of its consequences. Keynes told Margot Asquith it 'had made him morally, spiritually and physically *ill*. He had resigned out of protest.' Keynes wrote *The Economic Consequences of the Peace* to defend 'civilization'. He began writing on 23 June 1919, it was published less than six months later and within months it became an international best-seller (Skidelsky 1983, 166, 175, 378). Friedman's (1953, 157–203) critique of the post-Second World War economic settlement was as powerful as Keynes's critique had been of the first.

Post-Nazi Germany left its mark on the Friedmans. Those members of Rose Friedman's family who had not left their homeland 'all died in the Holocaust. We have never learned where or how.' In autumn 1950, as Milton worked in Germany for the OEEC, Rose apprehensively guarded their two children: 'Of course I knew there were no Nazis in the park but somehow there was always in my subconsciousness those terrible stories about what happened to Jewish children during the Nazi era. That trip to Germany haunted me for many years' (Friedman and Friedman 1998, 3, 180). Friedman (6 November 1950) wrote to Patinkin (his Israeli ex-Chicago colleague), about his experiences:

> on coming into Germany, Rose and I had a tremendous feeling of revulsion, the hatred of years came to the surface + we saw a Nazi in every German face. That softened a bit but did not disappear in a few days.... Industrially, Europe is a mess. By comparison, the US is the purest of pure competitive economies. Everything here is rigid + controlled and competition almost nonexistent. God knows what can be done about it.[3]

Friedman's work on flexible exchange rates was, in effect, an essay on the consequences of the economic peace. On his return to Chicago, Friedman (15 January 1951) wrote to George Stigler that with all the European 'disunity and defeatism', he expected (with a 50–50 probability) a Soviet invasion of Europe in spring 1951:

> The only hope is that the atom bomb will be enough to deter them.... Politics aside, the things that impressed us about Europe were the high income inequalities of income and the (related) terrific rigidity in the economic structure, the concept of free enterprise as freedom for everyone to protect his particular vested interest of the moment. By comparison, America is perfectly competitive – you don't need to measure the degree of monopoly; it's zero. Apparently the evil effects of the status economy and the rigidities were formerly much mitigated by international trade. The enormous extent of direct controls over international trade now has the opposite effect. Our efforts to liberalize trade have had some success but on the

> whole a relatively minor one. An absolute precondition for their being more effective is I think a system of flexible exchange rates.[4]

Keynes's (1883–1946) self-confidence has been attributed to the English upper-middle-class 'presuppositions of Harvey Road' (Harrod 1951, 4). He was 'part of the elite of each establishment of which he was a member' (Skidelsky 1983, 1). His father, John Neville Keynes, published *The Scope and Method of Political Economy* in 1891 – a book which had an important influence on Friedman's (1953, 3) methodology.[5] In 1894–95, Keynes considered and rejected an offer made by J. Laurence Laughlin, the founding chairman of the University of Chicago Economics Department and the founding editor of the *Journal of Political Economy,* to accept a chair at Chicago (Skidelsky 1983, 65; Moggridge 1992, 16).

John Maynard Keynes 'was not predisposed to admire the American way of life'; his preferred style of 'cultured' civilisation required 'ample domestic service' (Harrod 1951, 4–5). Friedman originated from a very different social background. In 1894–95 (as the Keynes were deciding to stay permanently in Cambridge), Friedman's parents migrated (separately) to the United States: his mother worked as a seamstress in a 'sweatshop', his father worked as 'a jobber. I do not know what that meant. The one thing I do know is that he never made much money' (Friedman and Friedman 1998, 20–1).

Keynes thought that staying in Cambridge would be 'death'. In 1906, at the age of 23, he began his Whitehall career before moving to the Treasury in 1915 at the age of 32 (Skidelsky 1983, 166). On 5 June 1934, during a visit to Columbia University, Keynes observed that the atmosphere in New Deal Washington 'reminded him of Whitehall in the early days of the war, with youth being given its head' (Skidelsky 1992, 507). Friedman had initially intended to become an actuary but the excitement generated by his Rutgers University teachers, Arthur Burns and Homer Jones, persuaded him to go to graduate school: Chicago (1932–33 and 1934–35) and Columbia (1933–34). Anti-Semitism made an academic career appear unlikely, and so on 19 August 1935, a few days after his twenty-third birthday, Friedman left Chicago to go to 'New Deal Washington...a wonderful place for a young economist'. Before his thirtieth birthday he had risen to a senior position in the Treasury (Friedman and Friedman 1998, 58–60).

In September 1931 (shortly after a visit to Chicago), Keynes (JMK IX [1931], xvii, xix, 245) celebrated 'The End of the Gold Standard'. Keynes 'rejoice[d].... The main point is that we have regained our freedom of choice.' For the 12 years prior to 'the national crisis', Keynes believed that he had been 'croaking' Cassandra-like against 'the overwhelming weight of contemporary sentiment and opinion'. Keynes (JMK IX [1931], 249) was optimistic about the possibilities for 'a new chapter in the world's monetary history' but noted that 'the magic spell of immobility which has been cast over the White House seems still unbroken'.

Friedman (2000) described a pegged exchange rate as 'a ticking bomb'. As the Gold Standard was abandoned, Keynes was observed 'chuckling like a boy who has just exploded a firework under someone he doesn't like' (Graham Hutton cited by Skidelsky 1992, 397, 400–1). Just previously, Keynes (JMK IX [1931], 157–8) had complained that

> the bankers of the world are bent on suicide.... It is necessarily part of the business of a banker to maintain appearances and to profess a conventional respectability which is more than human. Lifelong practices of this kind make them the most romantic and least realistic of men. It is so much their stock-in-trade that their position should not be questioned, that they do not even question it themselves until it is too late.

Friedman also campaigned to end the par value system in the face of the opposition of the overwhelming weight of contemporary banking sentiment. He wrote to the Fed Chairman about the 'central bank virus' (see section 19.2). He was 'appalled' at the 'intellectual homogeneity' and 'smug self-satisfaction' of the East Coast elite.[6] Friedman (1968a, 181–2, 241, 238; 1972b, 99) also detected behind the central bankers' benevolent veneer a contempt for democracy combined with 'dictatorial and totalitarian' sentiments. These 'small number of public officials' who were like 'modern King Canutes...commanding the tide not to rise – and are apparently determined to continue until we are engulfed by it'. They needed to 'examine their clichés'.

During the 1968 US Presidential election campaign, Nixon inveighed 'daily against the financial incompetence which had allowed a steady erosion of the dollar's value and pledged to do something about it'. But five months into his Presidency, the *Financial Times* reported that he was hemmed in by the constraints of unsatisfactory inflation and unemployment outcomes and faced 'an urgent need for powerful magic' (Graham 1969). A little over two years later, as Shultz had predicted, the White House succumbed to price and wage controls: an extension of the 'magic wand' of guidelines induced by a 'national crisis' (Shultz and Aliber 1966, 12).

Later, Nixon (1980, 238–9, 245) reflected that to those 'chafing under controls' and to policy makers 'resistant to the constraints that the balance of payments seemed to place on their domestic economic goals', Friedman's 'magic' solution of floating exchange rates 'offered an appealing escape'. In *Free to Choose*, the Friedmans (1980, 69, 354) argued that the price of foreign exchange was, like all prices, in need of the constitutional protection of an economic counterpart to the First Amendment because 'prices in a free market are a form of free speech'. In early 1973, the magic spell of immobility ('benign neglect') which has been cast over the White House, ended the regime of fixed exchange rates and opened a new chapter in the world's monetary history.

For 12 years, from the publication of *Studies in the Quantity Theory of Money* (1956) to the prediction of stagflation in his AEA Presidential address, Friedman (1968b, 2) believed that he confronted an environment in which 'monetary policy was believed by all but a few reactionary souls to have been rendered obsolete'. *Capitalism and Freedom* was dedicated to his two children 'and their contemporaries who must carry the torch of liberty on its next lap'. Johnson (1970, 43) accused the IMF of guarding the gates of the mythological hell of the 1930s and Friedman of guarding the gates of a 1930s mythological haven. Just like Patinkin (2003 [1969]), Johnson (2003 [1971]) accused his Chicago colleague of misrepresenting the Chicago tradition as embodying a collective Cassandra-style insight: a 'lonely light constantly burning in a secret shrine' which supposedly 'preserved understanding of the fundamental truth among a small band of the initiated through the dark years of the Keynesian despotism'.

Initially, Friedman (2003b [1974]) believed that this Chicago tradition provided immunity from the Keynesian virus: 'the small minority of economists who did not succumb to the Keynesian revolution consisted disproportionately of Chicago-trained economists...so far as policy was concerned, Keynes had nothing to offer those of us who sat at the feet of Simons, Mints, Knight and Viner'. Friedman (1953 [1942], 253, n. 2; 1972b, 13–14; 1975, 59) also reflected about what he believed to be the corrosive short-sightedness that the Washington atmosphere generates and acknowledged the 'corrupting' influence that 'the prevailing Keynesian temper' exerted over his own thinking. Prior to writing his autobiography he had 'completely forgotten how thoroughly Keynesian' he was during his time in Washington (Friedman and Friedman 1998, 113, Chapter 7, 124).

Stigler (1988, 52, 59–60) was employed in Galbraith's wartime Office of Price Administration, and Chicagoans such as Aaron Director,[7] Charles Hardy (1940),[8] Viner (1942)[9] and Wallis (1942)[10] were more sympathetic to the *Wartime Control of Prices* than perhaps they cared to remember. In a statement on 7 May 1942 before the House Ways and Means Committee, Friedman concluded that in addition to taxation, other anti-inflation devices included 'price control and rationing, control of consumers' credit, reduction in government spending, and war bond campaigns'. It is therefore possible that had Friedman stayed in Washington he might have been one of the architects of the regime of fixed exchange rates. The 'only regret' that he had in leaving his position in the wartime US Treasury was that he played no role in the construction of the Bretton Woods system (Friedman and Friedman 1998, 111–12, 124).[11] He might also have attended the first annual IMF meeting in Washington (along with Keynes) in March 1946. Instead, he returned to the University of Chicago.

The University of Chicago played a pivotal role both in Friedman's intellectual evolution and in the assault on the par value system. In the 1930s, Friedman, Stigler and Wallis, together with Rose and her brother Aaron Director, were 'key' members of the Knight 'cluster' who began to act 'in a loosely coordinated fashion to advance their common ideas' (Reder 1982, 9–10; 1987, 414). A special bond developed between Allen and Anne Wallis, George and Chick Stigler, Milton and Rose Friedman and Aaron Director.[12] Prior to Stigler's memorial service, Wallis (18 February 1992) wrote to Friedman about the deaths of their contemporaries including Knight's widow, Ethel:

> I guess at our ages we have to expect news like that every few days but I don't expect, and I'm still shocked by George's death. Anne [Wallis] is in a nursing home and doing as well as can be expected – which, of course, is not at all well. People ask whether she recognises me; she certainly does, so I visit nearly every day.

Friedman (26 February 1992) replied that:

> It is indeed depressing to hear about all the deaths but, as you say, we have to expect it. We have been exceedingly fortunate to have lasted as long as we have in such good shape. The probability calculation as of 1934 or 1935, let us say, would have shown a very low probability that of the six of us – you, Anne, Rose, me, George, and Chick – who were so close at that time, five would have survived to the age of 80.[13]

In 1934, Wallis sent Homer Jones a copy of Knight's essay 'Is Modern Thought Anti-intellectual? with the inscription 'Homer – you better read this and then frame it. W.A.W'.[14] A few months later as a result of a dinner party celebrating Knight's forty-ninth birthday (7 November 1934), four graduate students (Friedman, Stigler, Wallis and Jones) decided to publish a collection of Knight's (1935) essays (Friedman and Friedman 1998; Stigler 1988, 19).[15] In that collection of essays, Knight (1935, 355) reflected on the process by which an individual becomes

> as partial to his own ideas as he is to his own children.... When an idea gains acceptance, other data are easily harmonised with it and made to conform it...we must recognise that there is in our field no objective test for separating either truth from opinion or the urge to promote an opinion 'believed' to be true from the craving for personal aggrandisement.

This cohort of Chicago 'children' (or 'boys') were obviously highly regarded by their teachers. Meyer Burstein (22 February 1974) reported to Don Patinkin that Knight regarded Wallis as 'without question for sheer brainpower the brightest student I ever have had'. Knight also stated that 'capital theory is an impossible subject. Only Milton and I understand it.'[16]

In July 1956, Friedman was invited to join Eisenhower's CEA.[17] Theodore Schultz (20 July 1956), the Chairman of the Chicago Economics Department, wrote to Friedman warning him that

> the prestige would be bought at a price.... Let me also reveal a bias. It has been my belief that as an economist one is (always) more effective being on tap from his university post rather than being about in Washington on an appointment. I have known very few exceptions to this belief as I have read the signs in and about Washington since the early thirties.

Six days later, Schultz wrote to Friedman again: 'Three cheers on your decision! I hope it is the right one and that you will always look at it as such. Your being here next year is truly of extraordinary importance....'[18]

On several occasions, Theodore Schultz had tried unsuccessfully to bring Stigler back to Chicago from Columbia (Friedman and Friedman 1998, 275). In 1957, Wallis and Friedman conspired to engineer a successful 'coup'. Wallis (8 November 1957) reported to Friedman that he had made an unparalleled offer to Stigler: 'The salary is as high as any I know of... there are no prescribed duties.' After Stigler's acceptance, Friedman (2 December 1957) congratulated Wallis for

> pulling off this splendid coup. There is no doubt at all that the success was due to the techniques you adopted in pushing it including not only the financial aspects but also the excellent job that was done in showing George and Chick around Chicago. It gives me high hopes that perhaps this will prove the turning point in our efforts at Chicago.

Wallis (5 December 1957) replied that 'needless to say, we all feel pretty good about the Stigler affair – that it is coming off, and that we brought it off'.[19]

Burns (23 December 1957) wrote to Stigler about how depressed he was at losing him as a colleague: 'With your leaving and Leo [Wolman] retiring, I am in a very literal sense left with no one to talk to at the University. I cannot say that I like the prospect.'[20] But Stigler strengthened the Chicago cause, intellectually, ideologically and strategically. He and Friedman became 'Mr. Micro and Mr. Macro at Chicago' (Becker 1993, 762). In 1962, Wallis left to become President of the University of Rochester; but for five years these 'three musketeers' of the second-generation Chicago School enjoyed the same geographical and intellectual proximity that they experienced as graduate students (Leube 1986, xiii). In the same year, Wallis also brought Shultz and Friedman to Nixon's attention.

In 1956–57, Wallis and Theodore Schultz had been Fellows at Stanford University's Centre for Advanced Studies. Stigler and Friedman were Fellows in 1957–58 (Friedman and Friedman 1998, Chapter 19; Stigler 1988, 86). In summer 1964, Friedman was approached by Moses Abramovitz to accept a 'very attractive offer' from Stanford. Friedman had been close to Abramovitz since their days as graduate students at Columbia and they had spent summer 1934 co-authoring a business cycle treatise on 'Hoarding' (Friedman and Friedman 1998, 50, 370, 373–4; Rose Friedman 1998, 7–8).

Friedman asked his closest friends for advice. Aaron Director replied that 'I can only say, that if ten years ago, I had had an opportunity to go elsewhere, no conceivable advantages would have induced me to leave the place [Chicago] as long as George were here – assuming that you were neither here nor "there"'.[21] Friedman (21 July 1964) told Stigler that apart from 'sentimental loyalty' to the department 'only you are a strong [+ very strong] magnet in Chicago'.[22] Stigler (24 July 1964) replied that 'I am not sure that I would be capable of advising you to leave a place where I am, but I think so. *If* you were ten years older physically, and 30 years older mentally and psychologically, Stanford would be a nice place to retire to' [emphasis in original].[23] Wallis (5 January 1965) told Friedman that he was

> tremendously relieved by your decision. I had felt that there was a strong probability that in moving to Stanford you might be destroying some things that would turn out to be far more important, not only to you and to economics, but also to Rose, than the personal advantages of climate, housing and nearness to relatives.[24]

Friedman displayed an extraordinary loyalty to the economics department at Chicago and to the Chicago cause. Since 1931, his wife had waited for her 'dream' of living in San Francisco to 'come true'. But Rose Friedman had to wait 46 years for her dream to come true because her husband 'could not really face deserting the intellectual climate at Chicago...much to Rose's disappointment' (Friedman and Friedman 1998, 370, 373–4; Rose Friedman 1998, 7–8).[25] Friedman and Shultz confronted an establishment who had a similar degree of loyalty – 'loyalty to the institution they are serving' (Schweitzer 1976, 209). But loyalty to a cause or an institution becomes a source of intellectual weakness when unaccompanied by a lack of serious day-to-day exposure to alternative perspectives.

A healthy intellectual environment provides such an exposure. Friedman obviously thrived in a hothouse environment: as Stigler told Harry Johnson, for Friedman 'life without controversy would be a deadly prison'.[26] Friedman (20 May 1963) wrote to Stigler about a visit to the Bank of Japan: 'My biggest problem here is getting someone to say openly that he disagrees. The politeness in this respect is incredible.' Friedman found that when he expressed disagreement 'they would reply, maybe they were in error; I would say no, we just disagreed + there could be more than one point of view + what was theirs; + they would say they learned a great deal from my comments ...I shall keep on trying'.[27] One manifestation of this predilection was, in non-deferential circles, the emergence of 'the widespread sport of Friedman-sniping...full of snide and dirty digs' (Friedman to Stigler, 15 July 1965).[28]

Friedman attempted to understand his opponents' argument better than they did themselves – an attitude that was not always reciprocated. Thomas Mayer (1999, 111, n. 2) formed the impression that until the mid-1960s, thinking at the upper levels of the Fed was 'often rigid, defensive and out of touch with developments in economics'. As late as 10 December 1970, Eugene Leonard warned Burns that 'you do not have a good spokesman for the monetarist view among your many economists here at the Board'.[29]

This lack of serious day-to-day exposure generated confusion (mingled, perhaps, with a degree of contemptuousness). For example, senior Fed officials had regular meetings with 'Academic Consultants'. In 1969, Reed Irvine summarised for Governor Robertson the 'Advice' derived from this source over the previous five years. Irvine reported that at the 5 March 1965 meeting, Henry Wallich

> said he had never felt so uncomfortable about the dollar. We were moving towards foreign exchange controls or devaluation...Duesenberry, Friedman and Shaw thought one solution to our problems would be to devalue the dollar, Friedman favouring a freely floating rate. Duesenberry recognised this was not a practical possibility, however.

On 8 October 1965, 'Friedman said the choice was between devaluation, inflation and exchange controls. He preferred devaluation.' On 23 January 1969, Reed reported that Friedman complained that 'he saw similarities with the behaviour of the Board in 1929–33'. Irvine then summarised the 'Advice' for Robertson: 'Evaluation. Friedman is very predictable.'[30]

A similar attitude was expressed by Helmut Wendel in his report to the Federal Reserve Incomes Policy Group. Wendel reported that at the Treasury consultants meeting of 1 April 1971, 'Roosa pleaded for an immediate price–wage freeze followed by the setting up of national and local Price Wage Boards.' In opposition, Friedman supported cost of living clauses as an alternative to a wage–price freeze. But Wendel appeared to interpret Friedman's analysis of inflation as a cost-push story:

> Friedman seemed to think that inflationary expectations are now higher than actual inflationary forces and, as a result of negotiation, negotiations in terms of real wages would now tend to break the cost push spiral. There was not much discussion of these proposals by Friedman. They have a certain similarity to Friedman's proposals for flexible exchange rates....[31]

Friedman could not 'make any sense of the quote from Wendel'.[32] It appears that while an academic consensus was being forged about greater exchange rate flexibility, there was some incomprehension, if not confusion, within the bureaucracy about the nature of the arguments they were confronting.

15
Intellectuals

15.1 Lionel Robbins

Academic economists, like all scientists, exchange ideas and persuade each other in both formal and informal arenas. The informal process is inherently difficult to document. However, Friedman clearly devoted a significant amount of time and effort to persuading politicians, the general public and economists. For example, in the 1950s and 1960s few British economists exerted as much professional and political influence as Lionel Robbins. After the defeat of the 1945–51 Labour government, Robbins played an important role in formulating British macroeconomic and educational policy (Brittan 1964, 190–1).

In 1935, Robbins assisted Friedman, Stigler and Wallis in their efforts to publish a collection of Knight's essays (Stigler 1988, 19; Knight 1935). In 1934, Aaron Director (who also became Friedman's brother-in-law in 1938) had been denied tenure in the Chicago economics department, partly as a consequence of the split between the Knight and Paul Douglas factions (Director had initially been Douglas's co-author but had drifted into the Knight camp). In 1936, Director went to London (at Viner's suggestion) to undertake research at the Bank of England. Following its usual practice, Director was denied access to Bank of England data. Director thus gravitated towards the London School of Economics (LSE) where he came into contact with Robbins and Friedrich Hayek (Coase 1998; Friedman and Friedman 1998, 249).

But Robbins was 'prone to implacable reactions, often after only one incident'.[1] For example, in December 1951 Harry Johnson wrote a highly critical review of Meade's (1951) *Balance of Payments* which offended both Meade and Robbins. Graeme Dorrance saw Robbins shortly afterwards and found him to be 'almost incoherent'.[2] Robbins refused to talk to Johnson until Arnold Harberger's wedding in London in 1958 (Mundell 2001).[3]

According to Stigler (1988, 46, 140), the 'charged atmosphere' at the LSE in the 1930s displayed a similar intensity to the post-war Chicago atmosphere. In 1931, Robbins invited Hayek to the LSE, where he delivered some lectures which were subsequently published as *Prices and Production* (Hayek 1931). Robbins saw Hayek's work as an antidote to Keynes's *Treatise on Money* and so persuaded Hayek to join the LSE as the Tooke professor. The two become very close intellectually and personally: Robbins (1971, 128) recalled that his association with Hayek was 'an especially happy one'. Likewise, in 1943, Hayek described Robbins as his 'closest friend'. They were also intimately connected to the libertarian Mont Pelerin Society. Director regarded Robbins as the 'major figure' at the inaugural 1947 Mont Pelerin Society meeting, and as the senior libertarian, Robbins was entrusted with the task of drafting the Society's Statement of Aims. But in 1950, Hayek left both his wife and the LSE for Chicago. Robbins was disgusted by Hayek's treatment of his wife and in June 1950 declared that 'the man I knew is dead'. Robbins severed contacts with Hayek (and the Mont Pelerin Society) until they were apparently reconciled around the time of the wedding of Hayek's son in 1961 (Cockett 1995, 28, 116, 120; Hartwell 1995, 40–1).

Friedman had the sensitivity not to discuss Robbins with Hayek, and presumably learnt first-hand from Aaron Director about Robbins's temperament. But Robbins clearly needed to be handled carefully. Friedman's charm and kindness may have played at least a minor role in softening opposition to his policy proposals. In September 1949, Britain had been the second major Bretton Woods domino to fall. Friedman recalled that post-war Britain was an austere place: 'Food was rationed and poor. Price, wage, and exchange controls were extensive and rigid' (Friedman and Friedman 1998, 159). Both Knight and Viner experienced first-hand the pervasive shortages during visits to the LSE where they 'shared post-war austerities with [my] family' (Robbins 1971, 219). Robbins (12 January 1953) wrote:

> My dear Milton, This is to say thank you…for the lovely parcel of food which arrived the other day.… I am empowered to speak on behalf of the entire Robbins family in forwarding the warmest possible vote of thanks. How exceedingly kind of you to think of us. It has greatly enhanced the quality of our new year's entertainment.

Robbins even spoke flippantly of 'join[ing] the Friedman school at once'.[4]

Friedman could also be disarmingly modest. As a graduate student he had attended Knight's course on the history of economic thought, an area in which Robbins was an authority (Friedman and Friedman 1998, 36). Friedman (12 July 1951) wrote to Robbins describing himself as 'a tyro in the history of thought'. Friedman informed Robbins that his lectures on the classical economics had succeeded in 'punctur[ing]' some of his 'delusions.... You also whetted my appetite for Hume sufficiently to lead me to reread – or, I must confess, read – some of his essays and lo and behold, I find him, as has doubtless been noted again and again, recommending 100% reserves!' It appears that Robbins may have expressed to Friedman some apprehensions about publishing the lectures. Friedman was insistent:

> I hope you will not let the 'present state of the world' interfere with the prompt publication of these lectures. Their message is needed now so that it can help determine the policy position that will fill what seems to me a vacuum in current intellectual beliefs and that will be effective when (and if) the state of the world changes sufficiently to give more room for policy experimentation.[5]

The Left Keynesian Richard Kahn (1952, 250–1) found in Robbins's (1951) Stamp Lecture the objectionable 'Quantity Theory of Money, which has become, more than any other, subject to mysticism in its exposition.... Robbins might be regarded as an upholder of the old tradition.' Robbins (1951, 24, 28–9, 32) strongly opposed direct controls: 'My Utopia does not lie in that prison-house.' Robbins discussed sympathetically the 'powerful school of thought' which had recently 'arisen' which favoured flexible exchange rates as a concomitant of domestic monetary freedom. Citing Meade, Robbins noted that 'some of the most able, some of the most penetrating minds of our age have seen in such arrangements the monetary system of the future'. Robbins was concerned with the general impression that such an arrangement would 'render unnecessary internal financial vigilance.... If we do not...stop the inflation, stop it at all costs...then I fear that our days are numbered, certainly as a great power, perhaps even as a stable society.'

Friedman (21 January 1952) wrote to Robbins thanking him for sending him his 'magnificent' Stamp Lecture delivered only two months before: 'Your capacity to put these complex issues so elegantly and in such moving prose as always quite takes my breath away.' The purpose of Friedman's letter was to recruit Robbins in the project of burying Bretton Woods: 'I come not to honor but to quibble.... You will not be surprised to learn that I found your argument for a rigid exchange rate the least persuasive part of the lecture. And, reading between the lines, I rather infer that you do too.' Friedman continued: 'every argument for rigid exchange rates that I know and that has appeared in recent years rests on the invariably untested and usually unstated argument that private speculation in exchange rates would be destabilising'.[6]

In the 1930s, Robbins had been disgusted by Keynes's advocacy of a tariff (Moggridge 1992, 503–4). As Friedman (2003b [1974]) pointed out, Keynes (1936, 20, n. 2, 383) singled out Robbins as 'almost' the only consistent 'classical' economist who stood in the way of his 'fundamental diagnosis' of capitalism. Friedman reminded Robbins of his libertarian credentials: 'It is easy enough to understand why opponents of the price system should readily accept this view without evidence.... It is harder to understand how proponents of the price system can do so.' Friedman's economic analysis was interspersed with cutting political comments:

> there is of course the valid and strong argument for a rigid exchange rate for Britain under present circumstances, namely, that by reason of the exchange crises to which it is bound to give rise, it increases the expected amount of American aid. I wonder whether this has played any role, explicitly or implicitly?[7]

Friedman was spurred to take up the matter with Robbins in person. Robbins's (6 February 1952) five-page reply began: 'I cannot tell you how delighted we all are at this unexpected opportunity of having you with us for a few days.'[8] But Robbins also took exception to Friedman's casual empiricism regarding American aid: 'I showed this part of your letter to Frank Paish, upon whose sense of quantitative proportion in these matters I always place considerable reliance, and he has furnished me with the following figures.' Robbins then presented a table comparing the loss of foreign income to the gain from dollar aid. Robbins concluded that 'If these are right the minuses are still considerably predominate.'[9]

Robbins also had reservations about Friedman's libertarian agenda. In 1947, after the first Mont Pelerin meeting, Robbins returned to the LSE complaining that 'Friedman would even privatise telephones'.[10] Robbins (6 February 1952) took exception to having his libertarian credentials questioned by Friedman and sought to

> ventilate a purely ideological point. I have sometimes thought, when arguing with you and Aaron [Director] on this matter, that you tended to argue that a free exchange was an essentially liberal solution, whereas the fixed exchange was an interference with the general freedom of the price system. I confess this has never seemed to me at all persuasive.... My particular brand of liberalism is content to judge these things on their merits. I only want to claim that the argument for free exchanges should be judged on its own grounds and not buttressed by any special presumptions regarding the virtues of free markets.[11]

Having taken the scientific high ground, Robbins explained that any confidence he might otherwise have in Friedman's case was undermined by the state of prevailing opinion: 'Having regard to the present state of economic enlightenment in this particular community, I have more hope of positive monetary policy when there is a fixed exchange to fight for than when fluctuations are looked upon as everyday occurrences.'[12]

Friedman (22 February 1952) then sent Robbins a five-page letter which included two pages directly quoted from his '(unpublished) paper on free exchange rates I wrote a little over a year ago and which I have never gotten around to putting in final shape'. Friedman hurried to reassure him on a number of points: 'On the ideological point you raise, I am in complete agreement with you, and, on checking with Aaron, find he is as well. If we have given the impression that a free exchange rate is, and a fixed exchange rate is not, a liberal solution, it must have been in the heat of argument, and it is not a position that either of us would now want to defend. The question is, as you say, one to be decided on its merits. You may well be right that the end-result in a completely liberal world would be a single currency.'[13]

Friedman ended his letter: 'I look forward enormously to continuing this in London. We are so close together by now that we should be able to bridge the rest of the gap.' Robbins (4 March 1952) concurred: 'I found your observations intensely interesting and am inclined to think that you are right when you say that there is not so much between us as at first sight appeared.'[14]

Although he failed to persuade in this instance, Friedman obviously left an imprint on Robbins. Writing on 'The International Monetary Problem', Robbins (1968, 668–71) referred to 'the volume of heavyweight support' for floating exchange rates that emanated 'from my great friends Milton Friedman and James Meade outward and downward'. Robbins then considered the possibility that 'some world conference...were persuaded by Professor Friedman, or some other man of goodwill, to free all foreign exchanges'. Indeed, Robbins's essay was to a large extent a continuation of the conversation and correspondence with Friedman 16 years before.

Robbins (1971, 106) was a libertarian who believed that 'both personal liberty and economic efficiency were likely to be more prevalent under the dispersed initiatives of a system of markets and private property'. But referring to 'ideological considerations', Robbins (1968, 668–71) restated his position in a slightly defensive tone:

> I hope, though I am not so sure of this, that there would be some agreement that [the floating rate...as a general solution] is not a particularly liberal system. It is true that the idea of a freely fluctuating price for foreign exchange has a liberal flavor; it certainly sounds more liberal than the clutter of restrictions on capital movements and travel which advocates of Schachtian systems would impose on us. But the flavor is deceptive (see also Robbins 1976, 157–63).

Robbins (1968, 670, 676–7) was almost apocalyptic: 'I am afraid not only that the international economic problems will remain unsolved, but that what there is of a common civilisation of the West will go the way of other cultural entities of the past which had no ultimate will to survive.' Robbins emphasised that 'in the last analysis, the international monetary problem is essentially a political problem and...eventually it can only be solved on the political plane'. Robbins appeared to base his opposition to floating exchange rates on his British experiences: 'The economists who behind the scenes are arguing in and out of season for casting the pound loose are doing so, for the most part, just in order to be able to engineer a renewed expansion of money supply and spending.' Robbins's essay appeared in the *Journal of Political Economy* in July/August 1968, just as Friedman, behind the scenes, was bringing Shultz to Nixon's attention. On 15 October 1968 Friedman prepared a version of his case for Nixon (Friedman and Friedman 1998, 376).

15.2 Enoch Powell

Enoch Powell figured in Friedman's advocacy. In 1957, Powell, with two other Treasury ministers (Nigel Birch and Peter Thorneycroft), were engaged in an anti-inflationary 'crusade' which involved restraining the rate of growth of the money supply. When Friedman won the Nobel

Prize in 1976, Powell thought that Thorneycroft, Birch and himself should have been 'cut in on it. Because we invented monetarism too, there in the Treasury' (cited by Ranelagh 1991, 183).[15]

Samuel Brittan (1964, 190–6) interpreted their advocacy as a campaign to maintain the value of the pound: 'After the humiliation of Suez the sterling exchange rate...was one of the few status symbols we had left.' But Patrick Cosgrave (1989, 156, 164, 198) noted that in 1957 'Powell was alone in advocating the adoption of a floating currency'. Thorneycroft recalled Robbins back from holiday to support the 'crusade' which nevertheless ended in failure and the resignations of the three Treasury ministers (Brittan 1964, 191). After this incident, Robbins (1971, 234) recalled that 'standing in my club' a young economist 'said in a loud, slightly febrile voice, obviously intended to reach my ears, "This is the best news for years. *It is the death of the Quantity Theory of Money*".' Robbins reflected that the death notice was premature: 'Who would have thought the old man to have had so much blood in him?'

Powell (1970, 140) saw his failure in 1957 as a signpost for the redirection of world history: 'There has certainly, since about 1957, been a wave of prejudice in favour of the State, in favour of planning, in favour of state decision, in favour of state expenditure.' In 1967, Powell, by then back on the front bench as Shadow Defence spokesman, had an extensive exchange with Friedman and Paul Douglas in a Washington debate on 'How Big Should Government Be?' (Douglas and Powell 1968, 181–212). As the Bretton Woods system was weakened by the devaluation of sterling, Powell (1967, 7), during this speaking tour of the US, again broke ranks with respect to the 'sedulously eschewed' topic of flexible exchange rates. Consciously or otherwise, Powell was reiterating the position expressed in a letter to the *New York Times* which called for the United States to adopt 'exchange rate flexibility in free markets' and abandon 'controls' which 'suppress the forces of the market' (Fellner *et al.* 1967).

Two weeks after sterling was devalued, Powell (1969 [1967], 108) described the par value system as an attempt 'at mass self-deception'. Powell also broke ranks in other areas on his way to becoming *the* most controversial figure in British politics. Shortly after his exchange with Friedman (and nine months before Friedman's confidential memorandum), Heath sacked Powell from the Conservative Shadow Cabinet for making an inflammatory speech on immigration.[16] The editor of *The Times* denigrated his speech as 'Evil' and among leading British Conservatives he became a suspect figure.

From the left he was accused of hoisting 'the flag of racialism' similar to the one that fluttered 'over Dachau and Belsen' (Cosgrave 1989, 7, 251–2; Cockett 1995, 167).

Powell believed that within a few years 'there will be the whip-hand over the white man held by the immigrant' (cited by Smithies and Fiddick 1969, 36, 104). On 1 October 1968, the British Prime Minister Harold Wilson denigrated 'the virus of Powellism' (Powell 1970, 26, n.). Ten days later, Powell outlined an expenditure-reducing budget accompanied by a phrase that Friedman would later use as the title of a book and a television series: 'We are still free to choose.' Powell modestly added that 'I am the virus that kills Socialism.'

The financial press was incredulous. Writing in the *Observer*, Alan Day described Powell's budget as 'such utter rubbish'; in the *Sunday Telegraph*, Patrick Hutber described it as 'the work of an economic illiterate'. Powell (1970, 26–7, 44–5, 51) responded by ridiculing 'the sheer insolence of the reaction of "the top people". "The insolence of power"... If you want to know what arrogance can be, you need look no further than the economic columns and financial pages of some of the newspapers.' Powell unfavourably compared 'the economists whose words and writings have drenched us with the fashionable assumptions of state socialism from year to year' with the fawning pre-revolutionary French aristocracy.

A few days later, Friedman (1988b [15 October 1968], 438) described Powell in a memo to Nixon as 'the most intelligent and courageous of the Tory leaders' who would 'jump at the chance' of floating the pound. The other Tory leaders were described as 'less brilliant and more stodgy' who 'may well pass the opportunity by'.[17]

15.3 John Kenneth Galbraith

Galbraith, Samuelson and Friedman were the most well-known economists of their time. Left Keynesian, Right Keynesian and Anti-Keynesian, respectively, they symbolised the menu of post-war policy choice. Galbraith's (1977) television series, *The Age of Uncertainty*, competed for public approval against Friedman's television series, *Free to Choose* (Friedman and Friedman 1980). According to Galbraith (1949, 45), those who supported free markets did so because they perceived that this was 'the highest state of grace' attainable. In Galbraith's view, the market was perceived by Chicago economists as 'a mystique, a supernatural endowment which evokes, not technical, but religious, attitudes' (cited by Navasky 1967, 3).

Stigler (1966b) and Friedman (1962b) wrote *Price Theory* textbooks; Galbraith (1952) wrote *A Theory of Price Control.* In February 1951, Galbraith (1951, 12, 13, 15, 17) published an article in which he contended that the 'major unresolved question of mobilization policy in the United States is the role that should be assigned to direct price and wage controls...it seems probable that either inflation or controls are part of our future'. Galbraith opposed inflation, in part, because of the threat it posed to 'the conservation of democratic values.... It is clearly essential for this defense that the wage–price cycle be nailed down...this can be securely accomplished only by direct controls.' Underpinning Galbraith's analysis was a cost-push explanation: 'In the inflationary process the interaction of wages and prices is critical.'

The following month, Friedman visited Harvard: his economic analysis was clearly perceived to be in conflict with the prevailing attitudes in that institution. Nevertheless, Galbraith (27 March 1951) wrote to Friedman thanking him for his contribution: 'So far as I can tell...the students seem to have suffered no permanent damage. I hope your colleagues perceive no disconcerting changes in you. On second thought I hope they do.'[18]

Galbraith (1981, 124–6, 157) was the self-proclaimed *Price Czar Novitiate* 'in charge of the control of prices in the United States' at the wartime Office of Price Administration (OPA) where Nixon had been one of his employees. Nixon's economists, such as Herbert Stein, were demoralised by the economic situation: 'the fact and appearance of reluctantly sliding down hill with no end' (11 March 1971 memorandum). Stein (29 December 1970) also explained to Allan Meltzer that if the Nixon 'administration can't make it we are going into the long Galbraithian night'.[19]

Galbraith and Burns became involuntarily united as the focus of opposition from a variety of sources, including the labour movement. In 'The Nixon Administration and the Great Socialist Revival', Galbraith (1971 [1970], 94) suggested that the Fed-induced recession had hastened one of the 'dramatic tendencies of capitalism'. Burns was thus the Kerensky of this revolution. Meany complained that Burns from his 'ivory tower' was using organised labour as a 'whipping boy'. In September 1970, in reply to a question concerning the demise of the Democrat–Labour 'great coalition', Meany explained that 'left wing Democrats' including Galbraith, were increasingly 'asserting their influence' and alienating the labour movement (Robinson 1981, 300, 297).

Galbraith (1981, 31) complained that in 1970 Friedman used his position as AEA Past President to oppose his nomination as AEA

President. But Friedman was unsuccessful and, as expected, at the December 1972 AEA meeting, Galbraith (1973) used this platform to advocate policies that were highly uncongenial to the Chicago cause. AEA President-elect, Kenneth Arrow (31 December 1972), reported back to Friedman: 'Galbraith's [AEA] address was about as expected – high on wit and style (actually above his average) and a logical and empirical shambles'. Arrow was just as critical of Burns's (1978 [1973]) AEA address at the same meeting: 'Though couched in very different language and style, Burns's speech on inflation had essentially the same analysis as Galbraith's. It's all those powerful unions and firms.'[20]

Friedman replied to Arrow from Palm Springs where he was convalescing from open-heart surgery (Friedman and Friedman 1998, 420). The Friedmans were inundated with messages of goodwill including a phone call from Nixon and a telegram from Burns (14 December 1972): 'We need you and love you.'[21] Friedman (22 January 1973) recounted to Arrow how he had written to Galbraith shortly after 15 August 1971, saying that

> he must be as chagrined as I was to have Nixon as his pupil. He must be if not chagrined then certainly proud to have Arthur as his pupil. However, Arthur does give I believe more importance to monetary and fiscal effects than Galbraith does. He emphasises the unions and firms to get himself off the hook, or at least that is how I have interpreted it.[22]

15.4 Paul Samuelson

Samuelson was an undergraduate at Chicago (1932–35) and a postgraduate at Harvard before accepting a job offer from MIT in October 1940. In 1947, he was awarded the first AEA John Bates Clark award for the most distinguished work by an economist under the age of 40. The geographical configuration of modern economics could have been different had Samuelson accepted an offer to rejoin the Chicago department in that year.

Friedman (27 November 1947) wrote to Stigler that

> the Samuelson matter was again forced to a head – by [Paul] Douglas – + thanks mainly to his efforts we lost badly. The dep't has voted to make Samuelson an offer. We don't yet know the end of the story. But whatever it is, I am very much afraid that it means we're lost. The Keynesians have the votes + mean to use them.

Although he had been back at Chicago for only two months Friedman indicated that he was already contemplating other offers.[23] However, Samuelson rejected the offer in favour of a full professorship at MIT and Friedman remained at Chicago.

Samuelson later told Leonard Silk (1976, 17) that he rejected the Chicago offer because he had already located the position of 'balanced truth'. Interacting too much with an ideological eccentric such as Friedman would, he thought, 'radicalise me in a way I didn't want to be radicalised'.[24] This 'balanced truth' (circa 1947) presumably included a cost-push view of inflation and reservations about the merits of flexible exchange rates.

In his contribution to *Foreign Economic Policy for the United States*, Samuelson (1948, 404–6, 401, 411–12) argued that a case could be made 'if we still believe, as did Cassel, that Central Banks can, and do, easily control the quantity of money and, through the Quantity Theory, the level of prices'. But, Samuelson concluded, the activities of trade unions had more to do with the determination of inflation than did the Fed. The possibility of an endless inflation–devaluation spiral was 'entirely germane to the present scene'. Theoretically, 'a new free exchange rate' might be found to eliminate the post-war dollar shortage, but it would be an unstable equilibrium 'so that any momentary departure from equilibrium would be self-aggravating and cumulative'. Samuelson also argued that if a European socialist government imposed import restrictions on luxury goods the US could 'privately disapprove. But without risking the charge of supporting imperialism and being a propagandist, we cannot raise objections. Yet that is what insisting on free exchanges comes close to doing.' In his best-selling Keynesian textbook, Samuelson (1958, 697) also asserted that flexible exchange rates would reduce the volume of international trade by increasing risk.

Samuelson regarded Friedman as an 'eel' introduced into the barrel to keep economics 'lively and fresh' (cited by *Time* 19 December 1969, 65). He compared Friedman to 'a man with a foil attacking a battleship' (Samuelson cited by Davenport 1967, 154). But Friedman and Stigler did not have a high regard for Samuelson's ability to manipulate an audience. Friedman (6 February 1963) wrote to Stigler about a Samuelson–Stigler debate at Swarthmore College: 'Trust you took Paul to the cleaners.' Later (22 February 1963), he wrote: 'The kind of tactics you describe unquestionably lose an audience. One reason people like Sam are driven to them is that they are so unaccustomed to meeting serious intellectual opposition.'[25]

In a televised debate, a few months before Nixon's election victory, Friedman (1968d [28 February], 9) reminded Samuelson of the surprising events that had unfolded in Canada 20 years before. Samuelson (1968, 3, 5) replied:

> If that happens, and the chance that Professor Friedman even with his eloquence can make it happen, is not one in ten billion, if that happens, I will look upon the situation and rather approve, because ninety per cent of us academic economists, when we're academic say that that's a very interesting set up and maybe better than the present one. It isn't going to happen. I don't know whether we should waste the time of adults in discussing this.

Samuelson predicted that if the dollar exhibited greater disequilibrium 'then I think we'll have more direct controls of the sort which we have already have seen'.[26]

15.5 Charles Kindleberger

Three months later, at the May 1968 American Banking Association conference, Harry Johnson predicted that there was 'a fair probability that some crisis will lead the world to return to a system of floating currencies such as prevailed in the 1930s' (Rowen 1973). Samuelson's MIT colleague, Kindelberger (1970a, 99–100, 108) made a counter-prediction at the October 1969 Federal Reserve Bank of Boston conference. He was 'prepared to make a small wager' that Britain, France and Germany would continue to keep their currencies fixed in terms of dollars regardless of what the Americans chose to do. The major defect of flexible rates is that they would 'break up the world market.... In fact, such a system clearly would not last long.'

Kindleberger had been publishing prolifically on the international economy since 1937 and had played an important role in the post-war reconstruction of Europe. With Dillon, Roosa, Edward Bernstein and David Rockefeller he had served on President Johnson's Advisory Committee on International Monetary Policy (Kindleberger 1937; 1987; 1991, Chapter 19, 172–3). He had recently published *Foreign Trade and the National Economy* (1962), *Balance of Payments Deficits and the International Market for Liquidity* (1965), *International Monetary Arrangements* (1966a) and *Europe and the Dollar* (1966b). At the time, he was working on an extensive analysis of *The World in Depression 1929–1939* (1973) which attacked the Friedman–Schwartz explanation.

Kindleberger was as distinguished – and almost as practically experienced – an economist as Roosa (1967b) who, in debate with Friedman, had denied that a market for foreign exchange would emerge with flexible rates. Also in debate with Friedman, Kindleberger (1970a, 102–4) ridiculed the idea that forward markets would allow exchange risks to be hedged: 'In short, forward exchange is one of those complex topics which is reassuring to the lazy analyst, at least on my showing. For all its complexity, it changes nothing and can be ignored.' Thus the 'disintegration of the world market' would proceed apace with flexible exchange rates.

Friedman (1970, 15–16) congratulated the Federal Reserve Bank of Boston for focusing attention on the *International Adjustment Mechanism*. This revealed that the choice lay between either smooth exchange rate changes or 'variations in direct controls over trade and payments' with central bankers perpetuating 'this awful business of holding and holding and holding to the last gasp and then having to make a big change'. Kindleberger (1970a, 99–100) argued that flexible exchange rates 'would break up the world market.... This is akin to barter, the inefficiency of which is explained time and again by textbooks.' He had just published the fourth edition of *International Economics* (1968), the most successful post-war textbook of its kind (Blaug 1985, 112). In another textbook on *The Politics of International Money and World Language*, Kindleberger (1970b, 224) repeated his assertion that flexible exchange rates were 'a step toward barter'.

Friedman (1970, 109) dismissed Kindleberger's arguments for fixed exchange rates as an amusing 'collection of fallacies'. Subsequently, Kindleberger (1985, 254, 266, 291) accused Friedman of perpetrating an 'error' of historical understanding by favourably comparing Erhard's monetary reform of 1948 with the monetary policy of the occupation forces: 'a thoroughly misguided view, based on strong priors, although it is part of the legend'. The Friedman and Schwartz monetary explanation of the Great Depression was described as 'a fable'. Kindleberger even attributed to Friedman an 'oral tradition' about the feasibility of financing the Second World War 'with an equilibrium amount of money, a balanced budget and a constant price level.... For all its heuristic value, the suggestion, which Friedman may in fact not have made, embodies a touch of masochism.'[27]

Friedman (1970, 19, 117) suggested that Kindleberger's proposal for a world monetary authority would lead, at best, to 'a benevolent dictatorship of "experts" chosen in an arbitrary way' but still motivated in large part by self-interest: 'The desire on the part of the central banks to play an important part in the international monetary mechanism is too strong, I believe, to be frustrated by the mere fact that a floating rate works very well.'

Kindleberger and Friedman had known each other since graduate school at Columbia in the 1930s; Kindleberger had been AEA Vice President in 1966, the year that Friedman was AEA President-elect. Two decades later, Kindleberger (1986, 10) devoted part of his AEA Presidential address to an expression of nostalgia for the 1950s and 1960s when US officials took exchange rate policy seriously. Subsequently, this earnestness had been replaced by supposedly benevolent neglect for 'ideological' motives. Expressing an insight that had earlier been absent among the Bretton Woods veterans, Kindleberger noted that 'neglect can verge on sabotage'.

16
US Senators

16.1 Paul Douglas

Although he resisted formal Washington entanglements, Friedman was a highly political economist. Prior to the Nixon Presidency, his political influence was primarily exerted through informal channels. For example, in late January or early February 1951, he and six other Chicago economists issued a statement on 'The Failure of the Present Monetary Policy' (Friedman *et al.* 1951). The statement was sent to Senator Paul Douglas (1951, 1479, 1470) who read it to the Senate Congressional Record (22 February 1951). Douglas suggested that 'Next to the questions of foreign policy and defense, the threat of inflation is perhaps the most serious one which we face.' Douglas noted that the Fed was obliged to adopt an expansionary monetary policy to accommodate the Treasury's desire to keep interest rates low so as to keep at a minimum the cost of government borrowings. Douglas suggested that the Fed should restrain the rate of growth of the money supply. On 2 March 1951, the Fed and the Treasury reached an 'accord' (Tavlas 1977).

Friedman (16 March 1951) wrote a congratulatory letter to Douglas: 'It looks as if your good fight is paying big dividends. From here, however, it is hard to judge what is going on – whether the Reserve Board has become virtuous for good or only for the moment.... More power to you.' Friedman continued to keep open all sorts of channels of communication, offering a mixture of flattery and encouragement to those who might further the Chicago cause. Thus Friedman (6 November 1959) recorded for Douglas that he was

> very greatly impressed with the manner in which the [Joint Economic] Committee went about its task, with its objectivity in searching out

> material that could be relevant. I am sure that the material accumulated in the course of this study will serve an important academic as well as immediate political purpose in bringing together for the first time a vast amount of material. I hope that by now you have completely recovered from the cold that was bothering you on Friday. Best personal regards and wishes.[1]

On 14 November 1963, Friedman advocated floating exchange rates in a statement before the Joint Economic Committee Hearings on the Balance of Payments. When the 1964 Economic Report was published, Friedman (29 January 1964) wrote to Representative Thomas Curtis and Senator Jacob Javits complaining that the chapter on price and wage policy was 'balderdash…the standard defect of government pronouncements in this area'. The chapter on the balance of payments 'omits completely' any discussion of 'changes in exchange rates.… It is hard to believe that, as in discussing wage and price movements, the Council is not being deliberately disingenuous.'[2]

After 1964, the Joint Economic Committee of the US Congress continually bemoaned the lack of serious bureaucratic consideration given to floating exchange rates (Halm 1969, 3; de Vries 1976a, 528, n. 3, 536–7). Douglas also complained at this time that attempts to discuss flexible exchange rates with American IMF representatives or officials of the US Treasury elicited only a 'tropismatic response' (cited by Yeager 1976, 651, n. 16).[3] Friedman (5 December 1963) praised Douglas for the

> greater public service I believe you have performed by arranging for the hearings on flexible exchange rates. There has been something of a conspiracy of silence, or so it would seem, to keep any public discussions of this issue to a minimum. Needless to say, you added to your contribution by the extraordinarily effective way in which you conducted the sessions. More power to you and best personal regards.[4]

16.2 Barry Goldwater

With Douglas, Friedman was cultivating a relationship which had begun as a graduate student at Chicago in the 1930s and had also continued during their brief overlap at Chicago in the late 1940s. Friedman's influence on Senator Barry Goldwater illustrates the way in which he was capable (within six months) of converting a believer in the conventional exchange rate wisdom.

Friedman recalled that he 'entered the Washington political scene through association with the American Enterprise Institute' (AEI). William J. Baroody became AEI President in 1954, and he recruited W. Glenn Campbell as Research Director, a position he held until he left to become Director of the Hoover Institution. In 1956, Friedman declined to join Eisenhower's Council of Economic Advisers but did accept a position on the AEI Council of Academic Advisers. In the early 1960s, Baroody arranged for Friedman to act as adviser to a small group of Republican Congressmen, including Melvin Laird, Gerald Ford and also the Chicago Congressman, Donald Rumsfeld (Friedman and Friedman 1998, 344–5, 368).

Like Enoch Powell, Goldwater was a highly controversial politician with an extreme right-wing reputation and was often parodied as a hideous *Dr Strangelove* psychopath (Powers 1995, 314–15). Goldwater (1979, 11) almost managed to self-sabotage his own Presidential election campaign by exclaiming that 'It would be a good thing to saw off the eastern seaboard and let it float out into the Atlantic.' Republican economists such as Burns, McCracken and Wallich all distanced themselves from Goldwater (Silk 1976, 80). Friedman concluded that Goldwater needed some education about the merits of flexible exchange rates.

During May 1960, Goldwater (1979, 11) publicly attacked President Eisenhower's proposed budget as a 'dime-store New Deal'. In Goldwater's view, the campaign to resist the activities of Senator Joe McCarthy was a communist front operation (Latham 1966, 404). Goldwater (1960, 89, 93, 94, 112, 113, 122, 125) believed that America was being 'overwhelmed by alien forces…it cannot be long before a universal Communist Empire sits astride the globe'. The purpose of American foreign policy should not be 'to end the Cold War but to win it'. To achieve the aim 'we must develop and perfect a variety of small, clean nuclear weapons'. Regrettably, 'our government was originally pushed into suspending tests by communist induced hysteria on the subject of radioactive fallout'. Armed with these weapons the objective of American foreign policy should be 'to undertake military operations against vulnerable communist regimes…we would invite the communist leaders to choose between the total destruction of the Soviet Union, and accepting a local defeat'. The drive for 'military superiority' and 'decisive superiority in small, clean nuclear weapons' required that America must be 'economically strong'. Goldwater believed that for the nation to survive 'economic emancipation is equally imperative'. Almost immediately, Goldwater began his own personal odyssey of economic emancipation – heavily influenced by Friedman.

In March 1960, Goldwater published *The Conscience of a Conservative* which sold a total of 3.5 million copies, almost 700,000 copies in its first year. Goldwater (1970, 1; 1979, 100, 162) reflected that his intention had been to 'bridge the gap between theory and policy'. He also recalled that he began to receive 800 letters a day. One of these letters came from Friedman, written shortly after Nixon's defeat in the November 1960 presidential election. Friedman (12 December 1960) sought to bridge the gap between Goldwater's professed libertarianism and his acceptance of orthodoxy with respect to the foreign exchange market:

> As one of your admirers, as a fellow believer in a free society based on free enterprise, and as a professional economist, I write to urge you to rethink your position on the measures we should take to meet the gold drain – if indeed the *Wall Street Journal* report is correct that you favor imposing restrictions on the number of dollars tourists may take out of the country.... In promoting it, you are – unwittingly, I know – giving aid and comfort to the enemies of everything you and I hold most dear.

Citing his 1953 essay on flexible exchange rates, Friedman explained that Goldwater had without knowing joined 'a curious coalition of the most unreconstructed believers in the price system, in all its other roles [the central bankers of the world] and its most extreme opponents [the central planners]'.

Friedman enclosed a copy of a 1959 memorandum which he had written for 'some officials in Washington'. Friedman then asked:

> Are you planning to be in Chicago any time in the next few months? If so, would there be any possibility of your meeting with a group of us from the University to discuss both this issue and other economic issues? As you probably know, Chicago has for decades been the stronghold in the economics profession of believers in free enterprise – for a long time just about all by itself. This is why I believe such a meeting might further the aims we share.[5]

The Goldwaters, like the Friedmans and the Directors, were refugees from the 'oppressive' anti-Semitism of the Russian tsars (Goldwater 1979, 17; Friedman and Friedman 1998, 2). In his letter to Goldwater, Friedman traced the lineage of this fixed exchange rate coalition back to Schacht and the Nazis. In his reply, Goldwater (17 January 1961) revealed his thinking to be highly conventional: the

> protection of our currency is rapidly becoming a question of national survival. Consequently, I believe that all possible measures should be taken to reduce the outflow of gold and dollars.... This, I feel, is an area where restriction of a temporary nature becomes essential to the maintenance of our overall freedom.[6]

Goldwater (17 January 1961) declined the offer of a meeting with the Chicago economists but indicated to Friedman that his 'paper on floating exchange rates was read with interest and I plan to give it further study'. Six months later, Goldwater (16 July 1961) wrote a second letter to Friedman:

> I want you to know that I have enjoyed very much reading and rereading your paper on 'Floating Exchange Rates'. I find it to be in complete keeping with my thinking and if we could only present this in a reasonable way to all the members of Congress, I feel sure we could influence many of them.[7]

Goldwater's prospects for the 1964 Republican nomination had just received an enormous boost as a result of a five-page spread in *Time* magazine (June 1961) which provided 'very generous coverage to my political career.... It would be totally dishonest not to admit I was aware of and moved by this evidence of growing support of me for my party's presidential nomination' (Goldwater 1979, 155–6). Goldwater (16 July 1961) then proposed to meet with Friedman in Chicago in September 1961 (see also Friedman and Friedman 1998, 368).[8] The first 'Draft Goldwater' movement was launched at a Chicago meeting on 8 October 1961 by a small group including F. Clifton White, who was intent on 'desert[ing] the halls of academia to become a political activist' (Goldwater 1979, 149; White 1965, 116).

Goldwater (2 January 1962) sought Friedman's advice about potential American involvement in the expanding European common market. Friedman (12 January 1962) provided a 6-page 24-item reply:

> As libertarians, our strategic objective is free international trade.... Floating exchange rates (and a free market price for gold) are therefore the only market techniques now effectively available. (I enclose a recent article of mine expanding on this point.) As a practical matter, we shall not currently adopt floating rates except as the end product of a major exchange crisis that we have not been able to stem by other means.

Friedman added a note of urgency about the need to defeat policy proposals that Goldwater had held until very recently: 'Under present circumstances, and with the Administration's propensity to control, I fear exchange controls.'

Friedman (12 January 1962) offered his ongoing services to the chairman of the Republican Senatorial campaign committee:

> Needless to say, I appreciate very much your asking me for my opinion. If there is any way I or like-minded colleagues here can be of help to you, I hope you will call on us. You cannot know how heartening it is for all of us to have a Senator who is willing to take a stand on the principles of freedom and to fight on the public hustings for what we believe in. More power to you.[9]

Capitalism and Freedom sold over 500,000 copies and it transformed Friedman from an eccentric academic to a major public figure (Stigler 1988, 155). As Stigler (6 January 1963) explained to Robbins, 'the public is gradually discovering that [Friedman] is the leading conservative intellectual in the country and he takes to lecturing as he does to economics'.[10] Goldwater was apparently delighted by Friedman's contribution. Having received an advanced manuscript of *Capitalism and Freedom* Goldwater (13 July 1962) told Friedman that 'Professors sometimes have the habit of writing only for other professors, but your book is written in a way that the man on the street will understand and get your message. When this book comes out, I want to give it a plug in my column, I think so highly of it.'[11] Four months later the press were told that 'You won't have Nixon to kick around anymore' and a poll of Republican delegates to the 1960s convention revealed a strong majority for Goldwater as their next Presidential candidate (Goldwater 1979, 159; Summers 2001, 231).

On 29 August 1962, Friedman left for a year overseas. On his return, Baroody persuaded him to assist in the production of a Goldwater election platform and he soon became Goldwater's economic adviser (Friedman and Friedman 1998, 280, 367–8). During November 1963, Friedman scolded his pupil for making 'some comments on the dollar and devaluation that seem to me to be wrong in principle and extremely inexpedient politically, for the country as well as you personally'. Friedman then presented to Goldwater a draft of the speech that he believed Kennedy should have made early in 1961:

> We have decided…to make the dollar an honest dollar that can stand on its own feet without continuing government support by

> letting the free markets of the world determine its value in terms of other currencies. As to gold, we shall simply hold our present stock and refrain from buying or selling.

Friedman continued: 'If, as I hope, you were elected president, and if, as I fear, the balance of payments problem were still critical, would a measure along similar lines not be an effective way to give yourself desirable freedom?'[12]

Friedman was not mentioned in *The Making of the President 1964* (White 1965) nor in Goldwater's (1970) *The Conscience of a Majority* and only twice, in passing, in Goldwater's two autobiographies (1979, 304; 1988, 111). However, this remarkable personalised tutorial programme continued at great length on almost every conceivable political and economic issue up until Goldwater's death. It seemed as though Goldwater sought Friedman's advice every time he was confronted by an economic idea or a dilemma about which public positions he should adopt. Goldwater peppered Friedman with urgent requests by letter and telegram, sometimes adding that he would be most appreciative of his advice 'because, frankly, the Congress is made up of more economic morons than ever assembled in one place in history, and they need education' (28 March 1975). Friedman would reply immediately, often explaining that he would not delay Goldwater by checking the contents of his dictated letters: 'The issues involved are so important that I hesitate to delay your consideration of them' (Friedman to Goldwater 19 May 1975).[13]

In the second edition of *Capitalism and Freedom*, Friedman reflected on 'transition from the overwhelming defeat of Barry Goldwater in 1964 to the overwhelming victory of Ronald Reagan in 1980 – two men with essentially the same programme and the same message' (Friedman and Friedman 1982, viii). Goldwater (1970, 20) also documented his 'personal program of advocacy in the early days of this rebellion against liberalism...with all its Keynesian and Fabian trappings'. In '1964 in Retrospect', Goldwater reflected on the 'crackpot' label that been attached to his ideas. In 1964, it was not necessary to seriously engage these ideas; in 1980 it was.

Goldwater (1970, 30) was looking forward to a generation of Republican rule: 'Throughout the 50 states, cars are blossoming with Agnew bumper stickers such as "The Spiro of '76".' Shortly afterwards, the coalition of forces that had elected Nixon and Agnew began to crumble. In a December 1971 CEA document on 'The Economy in 1972', Stein explained to Nixon that 'we have created the conditions in which a Central Bank should feel safe with monetary expansion'. But Stein added: 'I don't think we should put all our eggs in the Federal Reserve basket.' The full employment balanced budget had 'genuine merit, but it was not handed down by Moses and may have to be subordinated to more pressing goals'.[14] Later (7 August 1974) Goldwater would deliver to Nixon in person the 'final kick' of his Presidency (Woodward and Bernstein 1976, 453).

But even before Watergate, Goldwater (4 February 1972) explained to Friedman that 'President Nixon's economics has me hanging on ropes and, frankly, his casual observance of deficit spending leads me very close to not being able to support him, but when I think of the alternatives it scares the living hell out of me.'[15] Friedman (21 February 1972) replied that he feared that Nixon's economic policy would lead to 'another twenty years of Democratic ascendancy'. Nixon was seeking to 'produce an appearance of a boom by November regardless of the longer run costs to the country or indeed to the party'. The consequences would be either 'a more extensive and rigorous imposition of direct controls on the one hand, or the creation of a really severe recession on the other hand'.[16] It is a measure of Friedman's influence that Goldwater should confide in him about this potential split in Republican ranks which could have cost Nixon the 1972 election (and could have put Goldwater on the White House hate list).

Much of Friedman's advice was organised about the theme of how best Goldwater could assist in the 'second American revolution', or 'Chicago tea-party': 'the only hope I can see for stopping the deterioration of a free society and the emergence of a collectivist society is via the combination of a tax revolt by the public plus their disillusionment with the federal government as the solver of all problems' (19 May 1975).[17] He obviously made a favourable impression on Goldwater. After he had been awarded the Nobel Prize, Goldwater (14 November 1977) expressed to Friedman how 'disappointing' it was that he declined to be the holder of the first Goldwater Chair at Arizona State University.[18]

17
The International Policemen

Jacobsson (1959, 30–1) declared to the IMF 1959 annual meeting that 'In all likelihood world inflation is over.' He left the 1959 meeting with 'no reason for pessimism about the outcome of our efforts'. After three years in office he had formed the 'general impression...that a much greater unanimity had been reached'. Two years later, he declared that 'We have saved the monetary system for the next generation' (cited by Jacobsson 1979, 314, 316, 327, 330).

The Per Jacobsson Foundation was incorporated in February 1964 to keep alive this shared vision. The Foundation's inaugural lectures were devoted to *economic growth and monetary stability*. Jacobsson's lifelong mission was described as using his anatomical skill so as to fine-tune the international economy. In this way, Jacobsson would succeed where Adam Smith, Thomas Malthus, John Stuart Mill, etc. had not (Wolf-Heidegger 1964, 1–2). Maurice Frere (1964, 25–6), honorary governor of the national bank of Belgium, described the Jacobsson legacy: 'It seems to be a lesson of history that without stable money neither justice nor progress can be assured, and that the human spirit cannot give of its best if it is harassed by all the uncertainties to which rapidly changing money values give rise.'

Frere (1964, 19, 23) also cited Jacobsson's anti-Simons preference for discretion rather than rules:

> In economic matters, one should always be prepared for the unexpected. Consequently one must not be rigid. The kind of measures which meet the needs of one situation may have to be reversed before many months have passed. There is a time for cheap money; and another for dear money; it all depends upon the circumstances, and especially on the dominant trend of business activity on each particular occasion.

Frere then explained why monetary policy 'must be entrusted as far as possible to specialists' who occupied a position above the political marketplace. Not only must these 'specialists' run monetary policy independently of elected representatives, but '*It is essential that this independence be supplemented by legal provisions giving those responsible for monetary policy a secure foundation which will enable them to resist effectively any pressure that the government may be tempted to exert on them*' [emphasis in text].

The President of the Per Jacobsson Foundation then thanked the Director-General of the Bank of Mexico for providing the 'very important parallel lesson' by which Third World countries could follow the correct path (Burgess 1964, 37). This lesson appeared to consist of accepting 'the decided support of the International Monetary Fund' and of implementing policies that 'coincide with those that Per Jacobsson himself spread with such vigour and enthusiasm' (Gomez 1964, 34–5, 37).

Roosa (1967a, 258) described the IMF system as an institutional apparatus through which senior officials from treasuries and central banks built up 'a growing intimacy of understanding'. When the Bretton Woods system was 'in full flower' there was a 'special sense of collegiality' among the international banking community (Volcker 1990, 6). These 'high priests, or perhaps stateless princes' met frequently, sometimes every six or eight weeks: 'It is hard today to reconstruct the atmosphere' (Volcker and Gyohten 1992, 29).

Observers compared the workings of the international monetary system with the 'Eleusinian mysteries' (Schlesinger 1965, 494). According to their critics, the bankers seemed to regard themselves as a 'Pythagorean priesthood possessing the vital mysteries whose power is diminished if they are exposed to vulgar eyes' (Gordon 1961, 22). Their preference was for an international monetary system run through 'large meetings' which were both 'effective and interesting' (Morse 1974, 189). The 'inner sanctum' of the bankers' system was often a regular dinner from which the lower ranks were excluded (Coombs 1976, 27). The frequency of the WP3 meeting to find solutions to the liquidity problems was made possible by the introduction of transatlantic jet transport which allowed 'incessant trans-Atlantic journeys' (Roosa 1967a, 27, 77, 79). Roosa and his fellow officials began to 'eat, sleep and dream the balance of payments'.[1]

When the Bundesbank revalued the Deutschmark despite opposition from Jacobsson, he was 'furious' with Otmar Emminger (Polak 1995, 740). Some of the advice offered to member countries was couched in the language of pre-revolutionary France ('Richesse oblige').

In 1962, Jacobsson explained to the Governor of the Bank of Canada that the IMF wished Canada to return to a parity system *pour encourager les autres*. The opposition to floating rates was 'for theological reasons'. Latin American countries with floating rates 'confess their sins and promise to mend their ways. But Canada rather defends its system. It persists in sin without any wish to mend its ways.' Jacobsson refused to recognise that the Canadian dollar was floating: it was 'merely a widening of the margin', thus minimising the extent of the heresy (Jacobsson 1979, 330, 335, 354, 383).

Newcomers were introduced to the 'custom' of the police force through what could be described as a vow of loyalty accompanied by threats. In public, the policemen made countless 'speeches and toasts...to the god of international cooperation'. But after his first WP3 meeting, Volcker found that he had been selected to join a secret 'core group' that regularly met for dinner at 'a rather mysterious hideaway'. Members of this nationally segregated group had taken an 'oath' of silence: 'It was not long before a European finger was being shaken in my face with this remark: "If all this talk about flexible exchange rates brings down the system, the blood will be on your American head"' (Volcker and Gyohten 1992, 144, 68).[2]

Roosa (1967a, 27–9, 77, 102, 114–15, 222, 258) was under the impression that the bankers' discussions exhibited an 'uninhibited freedom of inquiry...within a limited group and behind closed doors' these bankers had facilitated 'what is undoubtedly the most sustained, penetrating, frank and responsible exploration...that has ever occurred'. They had even considered 'the more extreme critics of the evolutionary approach we were following'. That elaborating upon some proposals was a 'fruitless exercise' was 'the inescapable conclusion dictated by the actual ways of the world – today and for any foreseeable future'. The case for flexible rates was dismissed as 'a long succession of neatly argued academic demonstrations' and as antithetical to the 'thinking and practice' of the IMF with 'little or no prospect' of success.

According to Roosa these meetings forced 'the critics' (whoever they were) to recognise the unwisdom of taking any of the 'supposed shortcuts to "balance of payments independence"'. Yet the conclusion that flowed from all of these uninhibited discussions was simply a repetition of the belief that 'there was no better alternative' than the par value system (Southard 1979, 24). The bureaucratic response emphasised the traditional mechanisms of adjustment: exchange rate flexibility was a 'taboo' subject (Brittan 1970, 88). Changes in exchange rates continued to be regarded as a last resort (Volcker and Gyohten 1992, 13).

From its inception, the IMF paid an unusual degree of attention to the theoretical underpinnings of the analysis it provided and consequently cultivated its connections with mainstream academic economists (Haberler 1978, 198, n. 1). Some IMF economists made substantial individual contributions to macroeconomic theory. For example, Marcus Fleming's (1962) analysis of targets and instruments under fixed and floating exchange rate regimes became part of the received fabric of the subject (the IS-LM-BP, or Mundell–Fleming model). Advice from heretics was perhaps less welcome. At least once in the early 1950s, one of the policemen (Jacobsson) was confronted, in debate, by a heretic (Friedman). Once was probably more than enough.

Jacobsson was fondly remembered for his didactic monologues and for being oblivious to the discomfort of his audience (McChesney Martin 1970, 5–6). He had an intimidating personality: 'One might start talking to him in the centre of the room, and find oneself after a time backed into a corner with his large frame and thick glasses still in attack' (Kindleberger 1991, 55). Harold James (1996, 106) referred to Jacobsson's 'ability to use his imposing physical presence and imposing personality in the service of institutional self-assertion. Some of the IMF staff later remembered him as a megalomaniac....'

But Friedman had a reputation for being 'the best debater in a profession that likes to debate' (Stigler 1987, 311; see also Galbraith 1987, 271).[3] Walter Heller (1969, 27), CEA Chairman under Kennedy and Johnson, noted that it was 'much easier to debate Milton in absentia than in person!' Friedman's Chicago training elevated 'the cogency of an argument' over 'the seniority' of the person espousing it (Friedman and Friedman 1998, 35). Perhaps the dynamics of discussion with the Bretton Woods establishment was more status-bound.[4] Either way, Jacobsson suggested that Friedman was 'too inflexible' in his opposition to monetary discretion, and the organisers of the debate were then obliged to curtail the evening with Friedman and Jacobsson 'standing, shouting, gesticulating and banging their chairs on the floor' (Jacobsson 1979, 260, 262).

Jacobsson came to the Fund with 'a strong reputation' as a professional economist and had been economic adviser to the Bank for International Settlements and IMF chief economist prior to becoming Managing Director (Polak 1995, 735; James 1996, 45, 82). But Jacobsson confided to his diary:

> Why do I quarrel so easily with economists.... Is it (according to Freud) that I have never been reconciled to the fact that I left University and have been just a marginal economist?...when I meet

> the 'real' economists – I have a deep 'envie' – more than the French 'envie', longing – I should have liked to have done what they have succeeded in doing.
>
> (Jacobsson 1979, 367, 398, 401, 402)

Jacobsson informed McChesney Martin that as Fed Chairman he was worth $1000 million to the US balance of payments (Jacobsson 1979, 314, 316, 327, 330). In turn, McChesney Martin (1970, 6) regarded Jacobsson as 'Mr World Central Bank'. Their shared vision was of 'a one world system, integrated by fixed exchange rates' (Wallich 1972, 19).

Jacobsson's successor asserted that the Fund possessed 'intellectually, the best possible staff you could find...they give their whole loyalty to the institution they are serving'. The Executive Directors had 'all evolved a kind of feeling of solidarity for the Fund' (Schweitzer 1976, 209).[5] There is no reason to doubt this assessment. The vital missing ingredient, however, was 'solidarity' from Nixon's Treasury.

The Treasury had previously been 'foursquare' behind the 'wonderful totem' of Bretton Woods (Coombs 1976, 20). President Kennedy appointed Douglas Dillon (an investment banker) as Treasury Secretary because he was 'a reassuring symbol of financial rectitude' (Volcker and Gyohten 1992, 20). Nixon's third Treasury Secretary had been both a Chicago academic and a skilled labour dispute negotiator. Shultz was cautious about how much to reveal to his fellow players; only after the demise of the Bretton Woods system did he declare that 'Santa Claus is dead' (cited by James 1996, 243).[6] Referring to Shultz, Friedman stated: 'Personalities do matter.'[7]

18
US Treasury Secretaries

18.1 David Kennedy

By the end of the 1960s, the case for floating exchange rates 'began to be taken more seriously' within the Bretton Woods bureaucracy (Volcker and Gyohten 1992, 46). Also, within the IMF there was thought to be a minority 'team' in favour of increased flexibility (Halm 1971, 14, 19).[1] But after Nixon's election victory, those who sought to patch up the Bretton Woods system were confronted by powerful adversaries in the US Treasury.

In December 1968, the 63-year-old Kennedy was nominated as Nixon's first Treasury Secretary 'primarily because he was not an Eastern banker'. He turned out to be a disappointment, even apparently in his own eyes (Safire 1975, 108, 498). Friedman (12 December 1970) attempted to cultivate an influence with Kennedy by writing to him directly:

> the great danger is, I believe, a lack of perspective and foresight. Because of all the drumfire of political and journalistic criticism, all based on a short-sighted view of events that disregards what has already been done, there are signs, that I hope I misread, of uncertainty, dismay, and frustration among Washington officials, with a tendency to react by pulling out all stops to reduce unemployment whatever the cost in inflation. There can be no greater mistake.[2]

When wage and price controls were raised at a Cabinet meeting (19 February 1970) Kennedy was part of the Shultz–McCracken alliance which opposed them (Reeves 2001, 165). With respect to international economic issues, Kennedy was sympathetic to the notion of greater exchange rate flexibility. Within the IMF he was regarded as being 'virtually alone' in wishing to consider a revision to the Articles of Agreement (de Vries 1976a, 504, 515). He confronted an international community almost completely committed to preserving the par value system.

After the November 1970 elections, Nixon gathered his aides to plan for 1972. He decided that 'Kennedy had to go'. In December 1970, Nixon announced to his Cabinet that he wanted a more forceful Treasury Secretary and had found one in John Connally, a Texan Johnson Democrat who was chosen partly because Nixon was determined not to lose Texas in 1972. He was also under consideration as a Vice Presidential running mate (Rather and Gates 1974, 276–7, 279; Safire 1975, 498; Reeves 2001, 171, 273, 280).

18.2 John Connally

On the same day as Burns's Pepperdine College speech, Nixon persuaded Connally to become Treasury Secretary, a position that was confirmed on 8 February 1971 (Reeves 2001, 285; De Marchi 1975, 338, n. 106). Haldeman (1994 [7 December 1970], 216) wrote in his diary: 'The Connally appointment and the repercussions of it will be one of the biggest things we've done and should be extremely effective in startling the media and the establishment.'

Friedman handed Connally a copy of the memorandum on floating exchange rates that he had written for President-elect Nixon on 15 October 1968 saying, 'Here is a memo I wrote for you two years ago' (Friedman and Friedman 1998, 377).[3] Simultaneously, the relationship between the IMF system and the US Treasury came under increasing strain. By the end of Connally's tenure as Treasury Secretary, the IMF had been snubbed, their system dismantled and replaced by an agreement which did not last.

By mid-1971, three major Bretton Woods currencies (the German Deutschmark, the Canadian dollar and the Netherlands guilder) were floating. There is evidence of Friedman's influence in Germany, where two decades before, he had first formulated his case for flexible exchange rates. Friedman's 1950 memorandum may have had more influence than he realised. In August 1952, the Germans joined the IMF; and on 19 July 1952, Erhard, the German Economics Minister, declared that European integration would fail if the rigid par value system were maintained. In September 1957, Emminger, the German central banker, noted that the Bretton Woods agreement could in principle allow exchange rates to float. From its inception in 1964, the

German Council of Economic Experts strongly advocated floating exchange rates (James 1996, 101–2, 196). In May 1968, at the American Banking Association conference, Karl Blessing, the head of the Bundesbank, created a 'sensation' by suggesting that the floating option had to be considered (Rowen 1973).

When sterling was devalued in November 1967, Schweitzer believed this would be 'good' for the international monetary system (de Vries 1976a, 447–8, 501, 513; Williamson 1987, 85). However, pressures continued to mount on the mark. Schweitzer (9 May 1969) telexed the Bundesbank about the 'alarming' volume of funds flowing into Germany: 'I feel I must warn that only prompt, courageous and effective action by German authorities can avoid very serious consequences for the international monetary system.... At the same time it would make a valuable contribution to solving Germany's own problems.'[4] The Germans were not inclined to take this advice about their own self-interest. In June 1969, Emminger publicly stated that it was necessary to investigate how exchange rates might be adjusted 'in an easier and more gradual way' (cited by James 1996, 201). Three months later, the mark was allowed to float, much to Friedman's (1970, 19) delight.

Friedman visited Germany the following year; a visit that was monitored by the US State Department. A State Department telegram (4 September 1970) was sent to the Treasury, the Fed, various US embassies and consulates plus the successor to the OEEC (the Organisation for Economic Cooperation and Development) explaining that in an interview with a German newspaper Friedman had

> emphasised that Germany's insistence on a fixed exchange rate ties its monetary expansion strongly to that of the US: 'you are chained to the dollar like a prisoner.' Friedman insisted that the only way for Germany to regain 'autonomous control' of its monetary expansion was to have freely floating exchange rates.[5]

A new revalued parity had been struck for the mark in October 1969. But in early May 1971, the mark was again floating. On 7 May 1971, Schweitzer and Southard met with the German Executive Director, Guenther Schleiminger, in a crisis meeting to discuss the German float. Schleiminger reported that 'Erhard had swung the opposition around ...the Bundesbank was no longer opposing it'. The IMF officials sought a German reassurance that the float would be limited by 'time and margins. Mr. Schleiminger replied in the negative, pointing out that no limits were set for Canada.'

Southard then tried a blunter approach by pointing out that if following Germany's example, 'four more important countries moved to floating rates, the undermining of the par value system could be very severe indeed'. This cut no ice with Schleiminger who 'contested this "bitter conclusion"'. Schleiminger advised the IMF to 'speed up our study of exchange flexibility.... He ended by saying that it was not the parity system which was being threatened, but the beginning of an orderly devaluation of the dollar.'[6]

In a press release on 9 May 1971, the IMF explained that despite the crisis affecting Germany, Belgium and the Netherlands the Fund would 'seek to maintain and strengthen the basic principles of the Bretton Woods system'.[7] In contrast, Friedman (1971, 4; 1972b, 112–13) welcomed the float by proclaiming that the Germans had established 'an effective automatic mechanism that will eliminate crises'. He also noted that the Bundesbank had lost well over $500 million to postpone the floating of the mark by two weeks.[8]

In discussing the May 1971 crisis, the South African Alternative Executive Director, G.P.C. de Kock, noted that 'an important school of thought in Germany' had embraced a more flexible exchange rate approach. L. Lajous, a Temporary Alternative Executive Director, noted that 'crises tended to reveal where the real power resided, and it was clear that the important political decisions would be taken elsewhere ...the Managing Director could and should play an important role in coordinating the important decisions which would have to be taken by the national authorities'.[9] But from the outset, Connally's relationship with the IMF and its Managing Director was tense.

Schweitzer's (1971) philosophy was expressed in an address on 'The Role of the Fund in the Quest for Financial Stability'. The Fund's role was 'central' and involved a continuing examination of 'the appropriate mix of countries' fiscal and monetary policies...problems of a political as well as purely economic nature'. Schweitzer believed that countries should 'increase their efforts' in this regard.[10] But he was mistaken in believing that he could appropriate Nixon's economic policy agenda to serve the interests of the par value system.

It appears that the IMF regarded Connally as someone who could be manipulated in a rather patronising way. Polak (5 April 1971) sent Schweitzer a memorandum to prepare him for a luncheon meeting with the newly installed Treasury Secretary. Polak was obviously an IMF veteran: he had been in the IMF Research Department since 1947, had been Director of Research since 1958 and Economic Counsellor since 1966 (de Vries 1976a, 643). He advised Schweitzer to briefly lecture

Connally on 'the need to bring inflation under control', the need to consider 'a more extensive use of incomes policies' and 'the need to take the balance of payments seriously'. Polak assumed that Connally would also require a lecture on the Special Drawing Rights 'background, with which the Secretary may not be familiar'. Polak continued:

> if the discussion develops well, I think it would be desirable for you to go one step further and mention: the exchange rate. Presumably this could be done in a negative way, in the sense that you would express the hope that balance could be achieved without a general readjustment of exchange rates.... These questions have been touched upon with Mr. Volcker; I think it would be desirable if the Secretary could be made aware that this subject was not out of your mind.[11]

But the 7 April meeting did not develop well and was, instead, 'very strained'. Connally 'rejected contemptuously' Schweitzer's attempt to interfere with US domestic economic policy (James 1996, 216–18, 244). Within the Nixon White House there was a tension between the 'Bretton Woods veterans' and those such as Shultz who believed passionately in the price mechanism. Volcker drafted a speech for Connally which included a 'vague paragraph' about the need for greater exchange rate flexibility (Safire 1975, 518; Volcker and Gyohten 1992, 74–5, 114). But Connally (28 May 1971) publicly announced that 'We are not going to devalue.'[12] Eleven days earlier, Schweitzer had earned Connally's lasting enmity by suggesting that the dollar should be devalued (James 1996, 216–18, 244).

Burns (19 May 1971) wrote to Connally stating that 'the international monetary crisis is not over. It is therefore highly important to plan ahead.' If the US were forced to suspend gold sales it was essential to 'make it appear that other governments have forced the action upon us.... In such a hostile environment, it might be significantly less likely that we could negotiate limited exchange-rate flexibility, a more equitable sharing of aid and defense burdens, and other important US objectives.'[13]

On 6 August 1971, the US Congress Joint Economic Committee on International Exchanges and Payments (chaired by Henry Reuss) issued a report which called for a realignment of exchange rates. This initiated a fresh wave of dollar selling and was interpreted as having 'precipitated the final crisis of the Bretton Woods system' (James 1996, 216–18, 244). On 9 August, the US Governor, William Dale, sent a memo to the members of the IMF Executive Board, summarising the Treasury response:

'No discussions are planned or anticipated with respect to exchange rate realignment at the International Monetary Fund or elsewhere.'[14]

Four days later, the President met with his advisers at Camp David to finalise the New Economic Policy (NEP). One of the Presidential orders issued on that weekend was for Shultz to brief Friedman on the move and to attempt to gain his support, or at least his empathy (Reeves 2001, 364–5). No such consideration was given to Schweitzer who at 7.30 p.m. on Sunday 15 August 1971, was summoned by Dale to the Treasury to watch Nixon's 9 p.m. television address announcing the NEP. Schweitzer was abruptly informed by letter that the US was dismissing itself from the IMF system.[15] Connally left Volcker to spell out to Schweitzer the details of the collapse of the IMF system. Worse still, Volcker interrupted the meeting with Schweitzer to take a confidential telephone call from Japan. Together with Shultz and McCracken, Connally had a more important engagement – with the press.[16]

A historian of the IMF noted that 'Choosing this method to inform the IMF of the end of America's commitment to a par value constituted a very clear breach of US obligations under the Bretton Woods Articles of Agreement' (James 1996, 219–20). Schweitzer (20 August) informed all the Governors of the Fund that he would rally against the forces of 'disorder and discrimination' to resurrect the IMF system. Schweitzer also explained that the IMF was not going to allow itself to be sidelined: 'I intend to press for rapid action to reach agreement on appropriate exchange rates....'[17] Schweitzer (22 August) reiterated this determination to the Italian C-20 deputy, Rinaldo Ossola: 'matters could not be allowed to drift'. Southard asked Ossola 'if in his talk with Mr. Volcker he had sensed that the United States viewed the need for negotiation with a sense of urgency or a lack of urgency. Mr Ossola replied that it was the latter.'[18]

Schweitzer made his determination public in two television interviews. Schweitzer (23 August) informed an NBC audience that the IMF was 'necessarily in the centre of...prompt collective action...because...we are in charge of carrying out law and order'.[19] The next day Schweitzer informed a BBC audience that he hoped that

> within weeks at most an international agreement could be negotiated to re-establish a satisfactory pattern of exchange rates.... In my opinion there is not the slightest chance that from the way markets are likely to operate there will emerge anything which will either achieve what is needed to put the US balance of payments in order, or what would constitute a satisfactory exchange rate pattern. I do

> not think you could rely on market forces to achieve that. In my opinion it needs, with the guidance and participation of the Fund, an international negotiation.[20]

A historian of the IMF interpreted this as a 'personal rebuke' to Connally (James 1996, 222).

The day after Nixon's NEP announcement, the IMF Executive Board instructed Polak, their Economic Counsellor, to provide a lodestar with the aid of MERM (the IMF multilateral exchange rate model). His advice was unambiguous. A floating regime was completely untenable: it could not 'even in theory be expected to lead to a viable system of rates'. What was required was the establishment of new parities derived 'on the basis of analysis'. The collapse of their system was considered likely to leave international monetary arrangements 'beyond repair'. All that was required was a once-and-for-all realignment based on the MERM computations (de Vries 1976a, 524, 537–8; 1985a, 126; 1987, 93; James 1996, 223).

Polak informed the IMF Executive Board that 'a satisfactory new pattern of exchange rates could not be found by letting all currencies float for a certain period'. But on 24 August the MERM table was leaked to two press sources causing both a 'sensation' and a 'debacle' (James 1996, 223). Schweitzer sent a confidential memo to all department heads about the leaks which 'threaten to do considerable harm to the trust and confidence in the Fund which is badly needed at all times but particularly now'.[21] The leaks further undermined the impression of competence and ever-diligent reliability that the IMF sought to project. The *Wall Street Journal* reported that, in contradiction to Polak's and Schweitzer's assertion, 'almost everyone agreed that there should be a relatively free market in currencies for a while' (James 1996, 223).

IMF officials appeared not to have realised how marginalised they had become. They appeared to be impatient with what they regarded as wasteful and presumptuous negotiations which did not involve the IMF. When Volcker visited the IMF on 7 September, Schweitzer 'began the discussion by remarking that he was concerned at the amount of time' that had been spent 'on bilateral meetings'. Southard asked Volcker 'what would happen next; when would the real negotiations start?'[22] Southard (12 November) wrote to Burns about 'the growing difficulties the Fund was having in carrying out operations under current conditions.... Up to now, we have not detected any willingness on the part of the United States to make its contribution to a solution of the problem.'[23]

Polak (15 November) warned Volcker in person that 'other countries might turn away from the dollar and move into a system that did not depend on the dollar'. Volcker replied that 'he would not be perturbed by Europe floating vis-à-vis the United States'. Polak's notes of the meeting continued: 'Referring to Mr Dale's complete silence at this morning's Board Meeting, the Managing Director raised the question of the US views on the future monetary system.' Volcker, however, declined to discuss the issue.[24]

It appears that the antagonism that Connally felt towards Schweitzer had increased. At the 7 September meeting, Schweitzer asked Volcker 'if there would be any useful purpose in a meeting with Secretary Connally' before what Volcker described as a G-10 'Ministerial confrontation in London'. The notes record that 'Mr Volcker said he would explore this matter.'[25] At the 15 November meeting, Schweitzer again 'inquired whether there would be any point in him seeing the Secretary'. Presumably reflecting the increased tensions, the notes record that 'Mr Volcker said with a smile that he would let the MD know if there was any point in this.'[26] On 30 November, the *New York Times* reported the details of the contemptuous manner in which the IMF officials had been treated on 15 August.[27]

In contrast, Friedman offered Connally more than strained lunches. In the atmosphere of impending crisis, Friedman (9 August 1971) wrote to Connally immediately after his appearance on *Face the Nation*, explaining that 'The country is fortunate to have so effective and vigorous a spokesman as you showed yourself to be on that program.'[28] In mid-September 1971, Shultz arranged a meeting between Friedman and Connally (and their wives) at a social gathering.

On 26 September 1971, Connally proposed to the G-10 (of which he was chairman) 'a general clean float' of major exchange rates as one of the conditions for the removal of the US import surcharge. It became clear that the US wished to postpone perhaps indefinitely the re-establishment of the convertibility of the dollar into gold (de Vries 1976a, 545–7, 551). Indeed, Connally stated that the US objective was to 'reduce, if not eliminate the role of gold in any new monetary system' and offered to reduce the US import surcharge for any country that allowed its currency to float. Connally was content to 'agree that we can't agree' and for the dollar to continue its float, but Burns and Kissinger persuaded Nixon that a return to a par value system was needed (Solomon 1982, 195–6, 199, 201, 205, 207, 217–18). Burns (1978 [1972], 440) argued that it was 'absolutely essential' for the Senate to pass the Par Value Modification Act which enshrined the Smithsonian currency realignment. However, within the

White House there was 'no evidence' of a commitment to preserve the Smithsonian realignment, and the defence of the arranged parities was largely left to the Europeans (Volcker and Gyohten 1992, 82, 104).

On 30 September 1971, Connally informed the IMF annual meeting that the US would remove the import surcharge if other governments dismantled trade barriers and were

> prepared to allow market realities freely to determine exchange rate for their currencies for a transitional period.... Freely floating rates will not necessarily, over any short time period, indicate a true longer-term equilibrium. But surely during this difficult period we should take care that we not reject the impersonal forces of the marketplace.

The Nixon White House was famous for its sense of paranoia and Connally had a reputation for being 'antiforeigner' (Haldeman 1994, 372). On the same day as his IMF speech, Friedman wrote to Connally inviting him to visit the Friedmans at their holiday home to 'enjoy fall New England colors.... From our hilltop in Vermont it is easier to take the long view and penetrate the mass of verbiage than it is in the hectic, crisis, short-sighted atmosphere in Washington.'[29] Friedman added: 'I trust that you will not be misled by the pressures from the foreign central bankers and IMF officials... [and] the Eastern Liberal press, which cannot get over the habit of serving as the voluntary representatives of European interests in this country.'[30]

Almost simultaneously, Schweitzer informed the 1971 IMF annual meeting that their first priority must be to re-establish the parity system (de Vries 1976a, 545–6). Schweitzer later interpreted the Smithsonian realignment of 17–18 December 1971 as a search for 'the appropriate monetary means and division of responsibilities for defending stable exchange rates' (cited by Solomon 1982, 209). He argued against 'dismantling the protection provided by the Articles of the Fund'. Stability of exchange rates offered protection against 'currency warfare'. Given the post-war commitment to macroeconomic management, it was 'unrealistic to suppose that governments would be prepared to accept alternative regimes that would put the rate of exchange at the mercy of market forces alone' (Schweitzer 1972a, 124–5).

Yet this was precisely one of the questions being seriously considered within the White House. Nixon appointed Peter Peterson as international trade representative in the White House. A recently declassified document stated that one of the post-NEP issues to be considered was 'do we or don't we want to return to fixed parities?'[31] Peterson consulted with Friedman prior to taking the job;[32] but when Nixon heard that Peterson had been to lunch with the IMF Managing Director, he told Haldeman (1994 [17 November 1971], 374–5) that 'Peterson is to quit talking to people such as Schweitzer.' It was Connally who was to be the exclusive economic voice of the administration.

In the period prior to the Smithsonian meeting, Friedman (3 December 1971) wrote to Connally about how 'extremely depressed' he was at the prospect of a new structure of fixed exchange rates. Friedman told Connally that hitherto 'you have done a yeoman's job in sticking to your guns', but now he was faced with an unholy alliance of

> European central bankers, their fellow travelers in the New York financial community, and the Eastern European-oriented journalists [who] are trying to conjure up the specter of crisis, world recession, trade war and all the rest unless there is prompt agreement on a new structure of fixed exchange rates. These are scare tactics directed at fooling us into entering once again into unwise commitments that will give foreign countries unjustified power over us.[33]

Friedman (1972b [20 December 1971], 115–17, 217) unsuccessfully campaigned to 'Keep the Dollar Free', warning Nixon and Connally that they would have 'snatched defeat from the jaws of victory' by agreeing to realign rates. Shultz pushed Nixon and Connally in the same direction: 'In reading over the years on this subject, I have never seen so many intelligent experts who disagree 180 degrees. George and others like the floating idea' (Nixon cited by Safire 1975, 514).

Before the Smithsonian realignment, Shultz 'made a very strong appeal' to Connally that floating rates should be at the centre of the new international order: the 'Shultz bombshell' (Volcker and Gyohten 1992, 47, 114). Connally's resistance to the re-establishment of fixed rates may have reflected Friedman's and Shultz's influence, or it may have been a bargaining posture (Solomon 1982, 213). But an IMF Executive Director remarked that Connally treated the Fund as 'a museum in which anything that wasn't already stuffed ought to be' (cited by Coombs 1976, 219).

The Smithsonian bargain, if not a Faustian bargain with the national forces of monetary independence, merely delayed the rendezvous with the political, economic and intellectual forces that were pushing hard against the system of fixed exchange rates. Nixon had hailed the realignment as 'the most significant monetary agreement in the history of the world. Now we have a new world, fortunately a much better world economically' (cited by Reeves 2001, 407–8). Burns (1978 [1972], 448) declared that it was in his 'judgment, solidly based'. According to Schweitzer, the Bretton Woods system had now survived the 'ordeal by fire…and has emerged with improved foundations' (cited by Emminger 1973, 5). In contrast, Volcker quipped, 'I hope it lasts three months' (Volcker and Gyohten 1992, 90). In retrospect, it became clear to the international policemen that it was a 'one sided agreement' (Coombs 1976, 225).

Friedman (17 March 1972) explained in a letter to Homer Jones that 'I don't really think our need is for good thinking [about the international economic situation], I do think it is for good policy. I think it's clear we know what to do, the problem is to be sure that we do it.'[34] Shultz recalled that 'we' were actually seeking a more fundamental reform and that the Smithsonian agreement was merely a prelude to such a reform. Defending the Smithsonian realignment was, he believed, 'a futile effort' (Shultz and Dam 1977a, 116–18, 127).

Nixon 'did not want to manage economic policy in detail himself. He wanted to have a manager of economic policy whom he could trust.… He found the person he wanted, first in John Connally…and then in George Shultz' (Stein 1995, 99; see also Ambrose 1994, 3). Connally had rejected Nixon's pre-inaugural request for him to become Secretary of the Treasury or of Defense (Reeves 2001, 171). Safire (1975, 497–508) described Nixon's initial feelings towards his newly appointed Treasury Secretary in a chapter called 'The President Falls in Love'.

But Connally had resisted the 'Shultz bombshell'. The following month, Shultz sought to establish a direct line of influence to Nixon and to undermine Connally's authority. Shultz brought up the 'whole Connally situation' with Haldeman:

> Shultz says he realized yesterday in the meeting with the P[resident] how disconnected he had become from the P[resident]…the P[resident] needs some people in the White House who are his own people, who know what's going on, for example, Shultz knows nothing about what's going on in international trade. Connally has the ball, he doesn't consult, he operates.… He says Nixon is a much deeper, more subtle man than Connally, has values, Connally doesn't. Connally has much less judgment. We are all Nixon men, not Connally men.… I had an opportunity a little later in the morning to get into all of this with the P[resident], which I did, reviewing basically all the

points that E[hrlichman] and Shultz had covered with me. P[resident] was very thoughtful about it and seemed to appreciate this (Haldeman 1994 [19 January 1972], 399).

On 9 March 1972, Shultz announced that 'he'd been analyzing Connally' who, he thought, had become a political liability to Nixon. Shultz 'feels that he has a totally different point of view about his basic approach to politics'. Shultz stated that Connally's attitude to opponents ('We should just brush the other guys off and not worry about them') did not fit with Nixon's. Haldeman (1994, 427) agreed: 'he's a Democrat and always has been in Democratic politics where they can do that because the press is with them. We can't afford that luxury.'

On 13 April 1972, Connally 'blew his stack...he feels there's clearly a conspiracy or at least a series of actions against him by White House staff' (Haldeman 1994, 439, 442). Connally then resigned to support the Democrats for Nixon campaign.[35] Shultz was sworn in as Treasury Secretary on 12 June 1972, three months before the IMF annual meeting. The fixed exchange rate system evaporated rapidly thereafter.

18.3 George Shultz

Shultz was Treasury Secretary during the crucial period when the fate of the par value system hung in the balance (Shultz 1993, 820; Shultz and Dam 1977a, 170). Friedman has 'always been proud' of the role he played in 'launching' Shultz's public career and apparently complained that Shultz had got his priorities wrong by turning down the opportunity to coordinate all the Nixon task forces in favour of finishing an academic book (Friedman and Friedman 1998, 376; Evans and Novak 1971, 25, n.; Reichley 1981, 75).

Friedman (1975 [1974], 55) was highly pleased with Shultz's contribution: 'He favoured the initial closing of the gold window, resisted repeated pressures from the Federal Reserve and from foreign central banks to intervene in exchange markets and pressed for the prompt end of exchange controls. He has played the major role in establishing a workable international economic order.'[36]

Unlike some other academics, Shultz made a successful transition to the political marketplace.[37] He was regarded as a vital if not indispensable figure by both the Presidents that he served: Reagan (1990, 361, 523) 'thank[ed] the Lord' having persuaded Shultz not to resign as Secretary of State. Visibly shocked as some of the tragedies of the era unfolded, Shultz nevertheless navigated his way through all sorts of difficult episodes.[38]

Shultz's integrity induced Nixon to contemplate criminal burglaries. Shultz refused to hand over the Internal Revenue Service (IRS) files of those on the White House hate list, leading Nixon to declare, 'There are ways' to obtain the files: 'Goddamit, sneak in in the middle of the night.'[39] Nixon threatened to fire Shultz.[40] When the White House tapes became public knowledge, this conversation became one of the most immediate threats to Nixon's Presidency: 'one problem remained: the conversation of September 15 [1972] in which the President threatened to fire the chief of the IRS and George Shultz' (Woodward and Bernstein 1976, 142, 153–5).[41]

Despite his reputation Shultz was in danger of being branded by his association with Nixon.[42] At a press conference, he was accused of making an 'inoperative' statement (a code word for 'lie' during the Watergate years).[43] However, William Safire (1975, 10) remarked that Shultz was one of the few not to be tarnished by association with the Nixon administration: 'proof that the system does not corrupt an incorruptible man'. Friedman observed that Shultz emerged from his involvement with Nixon 'without any mark on his character' (Friedman and Friedman 1998, 376).

To Shultz (1995, 8), Friedman was 'a source of wise and practical counsel over many years'. One of the issues on which Friedman advised was on the optimal moment to resign. Two months after the generalised float, Nixon announced another 60-day price and wage freeze (mark IV).[44] Shultz (1993, 820) had been unhappy with the August 1971 freeze and by his own account decided to 'drop out' from public life in protest over this further interference with the price mechanism.[45] Friedman (24 May 1973) advised Shultz that he should resign: 'You now have enormous credit for your principled stance. You would erode that credit by again accepting controls. More important, the chance of fending off permanent controls is enormously reduced if there is no protest on grounds of principle by anyone involved.'[46]

The IMF historian noted that Shultz was 'ideologically in favor' of floating rates (de Vries 1985a, 238). Shultz bemoaned that economic policy had 'too often been the enemy of the market economy'. Abandoning 'fashionable ideology' and relying instead on 'the market system' offered a 'brightly optimistic' future (Shultz and Dam 1977a, 205). Shultz (1993, 23, 29) noted that 'the price of money is the most important price in an economy'; he also recalled that he had helped to 'achieve a major transformation in the international monetary system', the emergence of 'a flexible rate system'.

There was certainly no doubt in the minds of insiders such as Volcker, the principal US participant in the negotiations that failed to rescue Bretton Woods, that Shultz had been 'captivated' by Friedman: 'in terms of ideology there was no question as to who was the teacher and who was the student'. Shultz exercised an enormous influence in pushing the case for floating exchange rates: 'His tactics and approach were very different, but we ended up with floating rates' (Volcker and Gyohten 1992, xiv, 82, 107, 118, 120; see also Stigler 1988, 161; Brandon 1973, 221; Evans and Novak 1971, 194).

Friedman's influence on Shultz is difficult to document in full because much of the contact was through unrecorded conversations. For example, Friedman (5 November 1971) wrote to Shultz: 'Your phone call stimulated me to set down on paper my views about current monetary policy and the traps ahead.' Friedman repeated that the Fed should ensure that M1 grew at 4–5 per cent per year and 'should forget about interest rates.... I feel like an unimaginative dullard to say the same thing over and over again.' Friedman added that the Fed should 'change its operating procedure (preferably by firing some people both in New York and Washington...)'. He concluded by stating that he was 'taking the liberty of sending a copy of this letter to Arthur'. On the same day Friedman wrote a second letter to Shultz which began: 'I am writing this as a separate letter because I did not want to send a copy to Arthur. It concerns possible nominees for the Federal Reserve Board.'[47]

Likewise, Friedman (23 October 1970) wrote to Shultz explaining that he was coming to Washington for a Federal Reserve consultants' meeting which was 'usually over by 4 p.m. at the latest, so I could be available from then until the last plane to Chicago that evening'. In addition to providing advice, Friedman kept Shultz posted about what he should be reading: 'Let me urge you to read Alan Greenspan's presidential address to the association of business economists. It is unusually thoughtful and perceptive and has important implications for your task.'[48]

Shultz (16 April 1971) wrote to Friedman explaining that he was due to meet Lord Cromer, the Governor of the Bank of England, for dinner on 29 April and would like the opportunity of talking with Friedman beforehand: 'Could you come to my office in the late afternoon for a talk? I will see that you get a ride to the airport.'[49] A talk Shultz (22 April 1971) gave to the Economic Club of Chicago on 'Prescription for Economic Policy: 'Steady As You Go'' illustrates the relationship between the two.

Shultz (1971, 1, 3, 4, 10, 14) noted that 'the pressures mount to alter the course and to steer, not by the compass but by the wind, tossing caution to the wind in the process. I can assure you that these counsels meet strong resistance from the President.' The 'school of thought' that was being resisted advocated 'that more Government management is needed not only temporarily to cure our current inflation, but indefinitely'. Shultz argued that inflation had recorded its lowest quarterly increase since 1967.2. Increasing industrial disputation was 'evidence that the system is working – reacting, as it must, to the end of the spiraling rate of inflation'. The Nixon administration was determined to begin phase two of the battle against inflation: 'time and the guts to take the time, not additional medicine, are required for the sickness to disappear...we will not be drawn into a series of steps that will lead to wage and price controls, rationing, and black markets, and a loss of the effectiveness of the free enterprise system'. Shultz ended his talk by invoking Friedman's authority: 'A colleague of mine at the University of Chicago, in a recent *Newsweek* column, said the major threat to prudent management of the economy is the "For God's sake, let's do something" philosophy. I think there is a great deal of merit in what he says.'

The following month, the *New York Times* reported that Shultz's 'Steady As You Go' speech had been criticised by various employer groups and that members of the Business Council voted to condemn the administration's failure to secure smaller wage increases (De Marchi 1975, 340). In June 1971, Shultz's 'Steady As You Go' approach to inflation control had prevailed at a Camp David economic summit (Safire 1975, 512). But on 23 July 1971, Burns criticised the Nixon administration's 'stand-pat' economic game plan: 'I wish I could report that we are making substantial progress in dampening the inflationary spiral. I cannot do so' (cited by Silberman 1971, 14).

Friedman (1972b [26 July 1971], 13–14) devoted his last *Newsweek* column before the NEP to Shultz's 'little-noticed talk' to the Economic Club of Chicago.[50] Friedman pleaded against some of the proposals that would form the basis of the NEP. Nixon had served in the Navy and liked naval analogies: 'The captain will still be on the bridge. I will not retreat' (Nixon cited by Reeves 2001, 132). Friedman cited Shultz's Chicago talk and Nixon's rhetoric: what is required is 'time and guts to take the time, not additional medicine.... The voice from the bridge [the President] says "Steady as you go".' But hitherto, Nixon had

> not received the credit he deserves. Washington generates an atmosphere in which it takes great will power and moral courage to look very far ahead.... Just when [his] policy is producing demonstrable results, there is increasing pressure on the President to alter course...to establish a wage–price review board, or to freeze wages

> and prices.... Mr. Nixon has not given into the pressure. Instead, he has announced that he is sticking with his policies. Once again, he has shown the vision and courage to pursue long-run stability rather than short-term gains.[51]

Shultz appeared anxious to keep in touch with Friedman even during his sabbatical in Hawaii. Friedman (15 January 1972) wrote to Shultz: 'I appreciate very much receiving a copy of your excellent talk to the Press Club. But I appreciated even more the remarks about me that you made in answer to questions, as reported in the *Wall Street Journal*.' Friedman added that Hawaii was 'wonderful...I never expect to get closer to paradise, in this world or the next'. His beachfront apartment had 'an extra bedroom that is yours needless to say for the asking if you can find some excuse to get out this way'.[52] Judging by their correspondence, Shultz clearly appreciated the advice and encouragement offered by his fellow Chicagoan.

Friedman advised Shultz on all aspects of the fight. For example, after a meeting (25 September 1971) with a variety of IMF and foreign central bank officials, he fired off an epistle to Shultz: 'I believe that the key element in our long-run position should be that "a dollar is a dollar" and nothing else, that we should under no circumstances assume any obligation to convert the dollar into something else.' Friedman always considered political feasibility: 'I remain opposed to a change in the price of gold. However, my confidence in that position is somewhat weakened. There appear to be greater short-run political advantages to a book-keeping change than I had recognised.'

Friedman also weighed up the quality of the opposition. In 1957, Emminger, of the German central bank, had 'defended passionately' the floating exchange rate alternative. Jacobsson concluded that Emminger was 'very ambitious but not yet wise' (cited by James 1996, 112–13). In contrast, Friedman regarded Emminger as an 'extremely intelligent, knowledgeable, and thoughtful person'. With regard to the other 'experts' at the September 1971 meeting: 'I was strongly impressed with the air of unreality in their comments and attitude. They had not faced up to the fact that this is a new ball game.'[53]

18.4 William Simon

In February 1973, Shultz had prevailed on Nixon to appoint Simon (1978, 8) as his Deputy; in April 1974 Simon was nominated to succeed Shultz as Treasury Secretary. Simon (1978, 87) recalls that he was pilloried in the press for being a 'Neanderthal' and a 'prisoner of a theology which sees market forces as totally benign and government as evil'. Simon had been heavily influenced by Friedman through correspondence and the popular dissemination of libertarian ideas.

Friedman (18 April 1974) wrote to him:

> The country is to be congratulated at having such a splendid replacement for George.... You will have a hard time living up to the standard set by George...so best wishes and good luck are more called for than congratulations. But I have every confidence that you will succeed. Here's hoping and praying.

Simon (29 May) replied:

> I know that it will be a difficult and challenging task, but I will do my best to continue the fine example set by George. You know that I have always respected your advice and I hope that I can count on you now for help. I haven't forgotten our plans to get together and will call you soon to set up a time.[54]

Simon (18 October 1974) wrote to Friedman 'please let me know the next time you are in Washington so we can have lunch or dinner'. Following on a debate with Hubert Humphrey, Friedman (4 February 1976) wrote reassuringly to Simon that the defeated 1968 Democratic Party Presidential candidate was 'as usual being liberal with someone else's belongings. More power to you. It warms the cockles of the heart to have someone as stalwart and effective as you.' After watching Simon on television, Friedman (20 June 1976) wrote that 'you were your usual candid effective persuasive self. Glad to see you are still uncorrupted.'[55]

When Friedman won the Nobel Prize, Simon (15 October 1976) wrote to Friedman that he was 'proud to know and count you as a friend'. Friedman (21 October 1976) replied that such comments were 'one of the nicest things about the award. I am encouraged that there are more of us than we sometimes think. Few are as outspoken and effective and courageous as you have proved to be, but they are there to back us up and to share in our all too occasional triumphs.'[56]

Friedman (1978, xiv) thought that Simon was a 'splendid' Treasury Secretary. In return, Simon (1978, 14, 87, 224) reflected that Friedman and his fellow libertarians had 'kept the torch of economic liberty burning and are passing it on to younger generations'. Simon was 'resolved to fight for the free enterprise system...the reason for discussing economic issues is not to inspire a national pastime for bookkeeping, but to inspire a national awareness of the connection between economic and political freedom.... That was my constant thesis as Secretary of the Treasury.'

19
Chairmen of the Federal Reserve System

19.1 William McChesney Martin

Friedman tended not to ingratiate himself with central bankers. When invited by Lionel Robbins to deliver two lectures at the LSE in May 1952, Friedman (22 February 1952) explained to Robbins that he would like to use the opportunity to discuss 'the question of automatic vs. discretionary monetary policy, in which connection I should display the Federal Reserve Board as the horrible example'.[1] In his published work he was hardly more flattering: it would be 'politically intolerable' to have independent central banks because 'Money is too important to be left to central bankers.' Friedman (1968a [1962], 173, 178, 182) approvingly noted that central bankers 'tended to oppose many of the proposals for extending the scope of government' which he regarded as a 'requisite for a free society'. Yet when he read the memoirs of prominent central bankers he realised how 'thoroughly dictatorial and totalitarian' some of them tended to be.

After Greenspan became Fed Chairman, Friedman (8 August 1989) wrote him 'a fan letter' for apparently resisting the temptation to deflect criticisms: 'I do not recall a single case in which any Federal Reserve Chairman ever admitted the possibility that the Federal Reserve might make a mistake.' Friedman (4 May 1989) also told Greenspan that there had always existed 'an informal boycott on referring to our book [Friedman and Schwartz 1963] in Federal Reserve Board publications'. He was therefore 'delighted to see that under your more tolerant leadership that boycott has been ended'. Friedman explained that when they had finished the book

> we sent a draft to the Fed (Bill Martin was then chairman) asking for criticisms and corrections, and indicating that because many of the

> documents we would have liked to see were not available to us, we were not sure we had interpreted all the events correctly and would appreciate the Fed's corrections. We never got a formal answer from the Federal Reserve although we discovered informally that a long internal review had been written of our book. In addition, the Fed proceeded then to change its rules about making minutes of Open Market Committee meetings available and hired an outside economist to write a history to show ours up.[2]

Throughout McChesney Martin's last year in office, Friedman grew increasingly apprehensive about a Fed-induced recession. In August 1969, Friedman warned in his *Newsweek* column and in conversations with McChesney Martin and others that restrictive monetary policy was in danger of creating a recession. He compared the situation in 1969 to the Fed-induced recession of 1960–61 which had undermined Nixon's Presidential campaign and facilitated Kennedy's victory (De Marchi 1975).[3] McChesney Martin was reported to have wanted 'no more economists' on the Fed Board – he preferred bankers, lawyers and those with 'worldly judgment' (Malkin 1971, 149).

19.2 Arthur Burns

According to Friedman (1975, 162, 166, 178), between 6 March 1933 (when Roosevelt fixed the price of gold at $35 per ounce and ended the internal convertibility of dollars into gold) and 15 August 1971 (when Nixon suspended the external convertibility of dollars into gold) events 'unfolded with the inevitability of a Greek tragedy'. It was a 'beautiful example' of how the hubris and 'prejudices of central bankers and government officials' were destined to meet their nemesis in the form of 'basic economic forces'. In Stigler's (1988, between 116 and 117) autobiography, there is a photographic montage of the 'brooding eminence' of Burns juxtaposed with the mock-Grecian temple that housed the Federal Reserve Board. Between January and May 1970, the Burns–Friedman relationship evolved with all the angst of a Greek tragedy.

Friedman (whose 'natural father' died when he was 15) went to Rutgers University at age 16 where Assistant Professor Burns became his 'mentor, guide and surrogate father'. It was Burns and Homer Jones who were responsible for Friedman becoming an economist rather than an actuary.[4] In 1948, on Wesley Clare Mitchell's death, it was Burns who invited Friedman to become Director of a three-year National Bureau of Economic Research (NBER) project on monetary factors in business cycles (Hammond 1996, 48; Friedman and Friedman 1998, xi, 228; Burns 1969 [1950], 90). Friedman (to Homer Jones 22 July 1969) was very keen for Burns to become Fed Chairman: 'he would be absolutely first-rate and far away the best of anybody I can think of'.[5] In celebration of Burns's appointment, Friedman, Wallis and Greenspan signed a five-dollar 'Arthur Burns Money' note which on the reverse side stated: 'In Arthur We Trust' (*Coin World* 1 April 1970, 3). Shultz composed a celebratory ballad.[6] But within months, a major cleavage emerged.

There was an institutional component of the conflict between the Fed Chairman and the Treasury Secretary. Under the Johnson administration, Douglas Dillon organised a continuing seminar on international monetary policy through which the New York Fed and the Treasury could coordinate thinking. Dillon had donated $30,000 to Nixon's 1960 campaign against Kennedy, and was a strong candidate to become Nixon's Secretary of State (Reeves 1993, 27; Reichley 1981, 65). The first Nixon administration, however, dispensed with the Dillon Committee, thus opening up a potential fissure between the Treasury and the Fed (Coombs 1976, 204; Mayer 1981, 149–50). Superimposed on this institutional fissure was an intense disagreement about economic policy and the future of the par value system.

The early rhetoric of the Nixon campaign and administration had been highly congenial to the Chicago cause. Indeed, the price of Shultz's acceptance of Nixon's offer of the post of Secretary of Labor was an apparent agreement to end the Kennedy–Johnson practice of 'jawboning' and intervening in industrial disputes. In an election broadcast, Nixon (21 October 1968) complained that Hubert Humphrey was 'not thinking of treating the *causes* of the high cost of living today. The old leadership is thinking of treating the *symptoms* of inflation by bringing to bear the most harmful tool in the economist's kit: Wage and Price Controls'.[7]

Burns was a Mont Pelerin libertarian (Hartwell 1995, 158, 213). During 1965, he wrote to President Johnson supporting the build-up of American forces in Vietnam but opposing the price and wage guidelines.[8] In 1964, Burns (1969 [1964], 241, 248–9, 251–3) explained that he opposed wage and price guidelines because they tended to 'throttle the forces of competition'. He also regarded them as a Trojan horse for more insidious forces: 'from whatever angle we examine the guidelines, direct controls pop up dangerously around the corner'. He associated the guideposts with the worst of outcomes: there was the 'serious' risk in 'a time of trouble or emergency' that they would 'move our nation's economy in an authoritarian direction'. Moreover, the social responsibility of business and trade unions argument was a smokescreen behind which the government could abandon their own responsibility for controlling inflation: 'Once the government looks to trade unions and business firms to stave off inflation, there is the danger that it will not discharge adequately its own traditional responsibility' of controlling the money supply and 'maintaining an environment of competition'.

In *Dollars and Deficits*, Friedman (1968a [1954], 88) republished his essay on 'Why the American Economy is Depression Proof' in which he stated that President Eisenhower and his CEA, of which Burns was chairman, 'deserve unreserved tribute for their political courage and economic wisdom' for the policies that they had followed. Burns's view of unemployment policy was similar to Friedman's: aggregate demand could not, and should not, be used to target 'the volume or rate of unemployment', since unemployment–vacancies was the crucial underlying relationship. Just as Friedman (1968b) in his December 1967 AEA Presidential address argued that the natural rate was not targetable because it was unobservable, so Burns (1969 [1967], 280–1) in April 1967 still further distanced aggregate demand policies from unemployment targeting on the grounds that there were no adequate statistics on vacancies.

In 'The Perils of Inflation' Burns (1969 [1968], 291, 295) provided specific measures of the rate of growth of the money supply, before concluding that 'the new inflation is mainly the result of excessively rapid creation of the money supply and of our unbalanced budgets'. Burns favoured the 'prudent control of the money supply'. Nixon's CEA Chairman declared himself to be 'Friedmanesque' (McCracken, cited by Blumenthal 1986, 109, 111) and it was a reasonable inference to place his Fed Chairman also in the monetarist camp.

Friedman (1972b [2 February 1970], xii, 27, 54, 57) echoed Nixon's phrase about Burns being 'the right man in the right place at the right time'.[9] Friedman predicted that under the influence of his 'close friend and former teacher' the nation could 'for the first time in its history, have a monetary framework for stable economic growth'. This was because Burns 'understands the monetary system and its relation to the economy at a depth and subtlety there has not been equaled by any past chairman of the board'. Friedman implied that Burns was also a monetarist: he would not make the mistake of allowing erratic movements in the quantity of money. Friedman also contrasted the position of 'the critics' with 'those of us who have stressed the importance of money ...inflation is always and everywhere a monetary phenomenon. And inflation is today our major economic problem.'[10]

Friedman had left the US Treasury and so had missed the opportunity of attending the Bretton Woods conference in New Hampshire in summer 1944. However, from 1949 to 1967 he spent his summers in New Hampshire working on the NBER project on monetary factors in business cycles: the genesis of the monetarist framework. In 1948, Arthur and Helen Burns assisted Milton and Rose Friedman (1998, Chapter 11) in renting their first summer cottage in Vermont. In late 1967, they took possession of 'Capitaf' (paid for by the royalties from *Capitalism and Freedom*) their 'dream home' in Vermont, close to the Burnses.

This proximity of vacation entered popular perceptions about the prospects for monetarism. In an essay on 'How Burns will Change the Fed: New Chairman Likely to Put More Stress on Managing Money Supply', *Business Week* (25 October 1969) suggested that Burns and Friedman were part of 'a tightly knit band of mostly conservative economists who usually summer together at Eli, Vt.' Underneath a picture of Friedman ran the commentary, 'Money supply ideas of Milton Friedman may get test at the Fed under Burns.' Yet within three months of Burns becoming Fed Chairman, Friedman felt 'betrayed' by his surrogate father. Ironically his correspondence with Homer Jones reveals much about the depth of his professional annoyance with Burns.

Burns also received counsel from sources other than his vacation associates, such as Edwin Nourse who, like Burns, been both an early CEA Chairman and the director of an economic research institute (the Brookings Institution). Nourse (27 January 1970) wrote to Burns commiserating that

> alleged friends should try so flagrantly to put [you] in a box... when Friedman himself in effect writes an inaugural message for you in his Newsweek column, that's too much.... I credit you with being enough of a scholarly Houdini to be able to extricate yourself from any box that friend or enemy thinks he has locked you in.[11]

Burns (30 January 1970) sent a reply to Nourse: 'Thanks for your letter. I appreciate it ever so much. I need hardly tell you that I see "Friedmanism" just as you do. I wish the world were as simple as the Friedmanites and Keynesians wish to make it; but it never has been, and I dare say, it never will be.'[12] The following day at his swearing-in ceremony as Fed Chairman, Burns described his duties in a sentence the first part of which could not have heartened Friedman: 'To do what I can to help protect the integrity of the dollar and to help foster a stable prosperity for our Nation.'[13]

One Washington adage is that 'where you stand depends on where you sit', and after a year in the job Burns declared that he was 'less of a monetarist now than when I came here'. But Burns also added that he 'never was a monetarist in the accepted sense' (Malkin 1971, 151). Burns (1978, preface, 19, 256, 367–9, 382, 417, 418) retired as Fed Chairman denying that inflation was always and everywhere a monetary phenomenon. Instead, a responsible collective bargaining was required plus 'a growth of understanding' and the 'will' to fight inflation, which, he hoped, might 'be forged someday'. Such sentiments were repeated through his Chairmanship. Burns expressed his deep opposition to monetarism and to bill H.R 212 which sought to impose monetary targeting on the Fed: 'There is a school of thought which holds that the Federal Reserve need pay no attention to interest rates, that the only thing that matters is how this or that monetary aggregate is behaving. We at the Federal Reserve cannot afford the luxury of such a mechanical rule.'[14] The consequences of adopting such a proposal 'could prove very damaging to our nation's economy'.

It was, he asserted, far preferable to leave monetary policy to the discretion of the 'highly qualified individuals' at the Fed who 'live and work under a Spartan code'. Burns reflected that 'men without morality corrupt power' and described the Federal Reserve as 'a collegial body of great moral and intellectual distinction'. While there was a relationship between money growth and inflation, 'the catch is that nowadays there are tremendous nonmonetary pressures in our economy that are tending to drive costs and prices higher'. Therefore, monetary rules were inadequate. Fortunately, the Fed did possess 'considerable discretion' to accommodate 'the pressures of the marketplace less than fully'. Indeed, the Fed was consistently 'engaged in probing and testing our capacity' to exert that discretion.

Burns repeated such sentiments at a meeting with business writers in May 1975. It was 'difficult to clarify monetary policy for the public, or for economists, few of whom understand this mysterious art.... You are the victims of what a number of professors learnt 20 years ago.' According to Burns, monetarism and the emphasis on monetary targets at the expense of interest rates was 'simplistic nonsense' (Rowen 1975).

Nevertheless, the Burns–Friedman correspondence reveals a continuing depth of affection on both sides. For example, there may have been a few internal tensions within the NBER regarding Burns's 'elevation' to the position of Honorary Chairman. When in early 1970 the NBER organised a dinner to honour Burns, Friedman (to Burns 11 February 1970) declined to attend because of his 'great reluctance to take part in a mass act of hypocrisy. You have my sympathy for your part in it.'[15] Burns (15 February 1970) replied to Friedman that he too wished he could avoid attending: 'You are right about the NBER dinner. It is exactly the way I feel. How I envy you!'[16]

Shultz, who had worked for Burns as a staff economist at the CEA in the 1950s and whom Burns had recommended as Secretary of Labor, was invited to give a speech at the 1970 fiftieth anniversary NBER dinner, at which Burns was guest of honour. However, rather than an innocuous ceremonial speech, Shultz made some controversial and stirring remarks about current policy alternatives.

Given the importance of the later dispute between Burns on one side and Friedman and Shultz on the other, it is worth exploring the background of these remarks. The Burns and Mitchell (1946) NBER method of *Measuring Business Cycles* had been derided by the structural econometricians as 'measurement without theory'; they studied business cycles 'as if they were the eruptions of a mysterious volcano' (Koopmans 1947; 1949). The NBER and the econometrically inclined Cowles Commission were indulging in 'product differentiation campaigns [and competing] for funds from the same foundations' (Hammond 1996, 23). Rutledge Vining (1949, 77, 85) responded that the 'Koopmans group' were pursuing 'an exceedingly narrow class of methods, and an insistent appeal to use them, and them alone, [is] an invitation to put a straight jacket on economic research'. Vining noted that 'Tycho and Kepler are becoming fairly regular attenders of economic discussions these days' and warned that the econometricians resembled the Inquisition hounding Galileo: 'I should feel much safer in bringing my little work before the Commissar of Research if that chair were occupied by Burns or Mitchell than if [Tjalling] Koopmans were the occupant.' With the installation of 'Commissar Koopmans', Vining felt that his 'liquidation as an inquirer' would be rapid.

Burns and the NBER had also been involved in a long-standing dispute over Keynesian economics with Hansen. In his NBER Annual Report on *Economic Research and Keynesian Thinking of Our Times*, Burns (1946, 12, 27) criticised the 'simple determinism of Keynesian doctrine' as 'an illusion'. NBER-style 'painstaking studies of experience' furnished 'a better basis than now exists for dealing with grave issues of business-cycle theory and policy'. In 'How Keynes Came to America', Galbraith (1971, 45–8) referred to Burns's essay and the 'attempt at counter-revolution', adding that 'Hansen replied rather sharply'. In the *Review of Economic Statistics*, Hansen (1946) accused Burns of expressing 'a number of elementary misconceptions'.

In the Friedman archives there exists some correspondence – presumably forwarded to Friedman by Burns – which casts some light on the background of this dispute. Burns (21 January 1947) wrote to Hansen explaining that he was 'interested and eager to know what these misconceptions are. Would you be good enough to jot them down some time for my benefit?' In a brief and dismissive reply, Hansen (29 January 1947) explained that one of his graduate students had analysed Burns's essay: 'I understand he plans to send you a copy.' This understandably failed to satisfy Burns (7 February 1947): 'I am still eager to know what misconceptions you yourself have found in my essay on Keynes, and I earnestly hope that you will inform me.' Hansen (13 February 1947) was then obliged to send a three-page analysis, concluding that he found 'what seems to me misconceptions, or at least doubtful statements, in almost every paragraph'. But Burns (26 February 1947) was not impressed:

> while I failed to see any good flowing from controversy along these lines, many people have been puzzled by a statement in the *Review* [*of Economic Statistics*] and have asked me to do what I can to clear up the puzzle. You understand, of course, that there is not much that I can do about this, unless you are willing to assume a certain responsibility in the matter.[17]

Hansen (1947), forced to defend his position in public, suggested that Burns had implicitly claimed that 'once the massive studies of the Bureau are completed' economics would be capable of reaching '*definitive* conclusions' [emphasis in original]. Hansen added: 'Perhaps; but one is entitled to be skeptical.' Hansen (1939) devoted his AEA Presidential address to his exposition of the principles of secular stagnation; Burns (1969 [1960], 126) used his AEA Presidential address to remind economists of the defects of the Hansen-style analysis of secular stagnation: 'Parts of their analysis were faulty and their predictions have proved wrong.'

Burns (9 May 1947) complained to Stigler that 'A good part of my time, I am sorry to say, has been wasted in quarrels with people like Hansen, Harris, and Koopmans.' Stigler's (1963, 58) response was to accuse Hansen (and also Harris) of making wild empirical assertions: 'almost studied carelessness in the use of facts'. But Hansen was 'the American Keynes...the man behind the men who are reshaping U.S. economic policy' (*U.S. News and World Report* 27 February 1961, 59). Hansen (1962, 28–9) complained that those who 'opposed any expansion in the role of government have found the balanced budget dogma to be a powerful propaganda device'. The 'credit taboo' was simply 'irrational behaviour': it was 'the budget balancers that are fiscally irresponsible'. Bond-financed fiscal expansion could close the $40 billion Okun gap between actual and potential output. In his celebratory essay on the 'full bloom' of Keynesian ideas, Hansen (1966, 226) again referred to this 1961 dispute between Burns and Kennedy's CEA over the Okun gap.

Arthur Okun's work was highly influential in the 1960s; he was CEA Chairman immediately prior to Burns's appointment as Counselor to the President in 1969. In 1961 Heller, CEA Chairman under Kennedy and Johnson, calculated the Okun or 'performance gap' to be $50 billion and 5 million jobs. In May 1962, President Kennedy publicly attacked the 'myth…that Federal deficits create inflation'. It was interpreted that Kennedy, 'student of Heller and Samuelson, had become a disciple of Keynes'. But Kennedy refused Heller's request to be photographed with all previous CEA Chairmen on the grounds that Burns had been 'kicking me in the balls every day' (Reeves 1993, 318, 320, 328).

To celebrate his retirement from active NBER work, Burns (1969 [1968], 292–4, [1967], 282, 303, 308) published a collection of essays in which – on several recent occasions – he had referred to the influential policy of closing the Okun gap and the associated corollary 'that wage and price guidelines would serve to keep the price level stable while these stimuli were being applied'. Burns described this as one of the 'articles of faith' of the Keynesian 'new economics'. In reality, 'as experienced observers had predicted, the price–wage guidelines proved a fragile barrier to inflation once labor and commodity markets tightened'. Burns reflected on the potency of this approach: 'theories have a power that administrators, no matter how able, cannot fully control'.

Burns (1947) noted that Keynesian doctrines had 'stirred the world'. Perhaps to stir Burns in a direction congenial to Chicago perceptions, Shultz took the opportunity of the NBER dinner to launch what was regarded as a 'personal attack' on Okun for his advocacy of an incomes policy. Shultz had previously criticised the Fed's policies and he was reportedly prevented by Treasury Secretary Kennedy from delivering a 'vitriolic' speech attacking the Board (Malkin 1971, 260). At the NBER dinner, Shultz's strategy backfired: Burns was 'deeply embarrassed' and 'felt impelled to rise to Okun's defense' (Malkin 1971, 148, 260; De Marchi 1975, 317).

Indeed, Burns was now aligning himself more closely with Okun than with Friedman and Shultz. Burns (29 April 1970) made a speech in which he argued that 'we have moved from demand-pull inflation to a transitional phase in which cost-push adjustments are prevalent' (cited by De Marchi 1975, 316). According to a letter from Friedman (18 May 1970) to Burns, it appears that sometime shortly after this speech Burns phoned Friedman and explained that 'it might be necessary to think the unthinkable'. Friedman (29 May 1970) wrote to Burns that he had been 'repressing dismay ever since. I thought I would at least have the chance to argue it out with you before you committed yourself in public.' Friedman had had a lot of success in outlining the merits of floating to recalcitrant libertarians such as Robbins and Goldwater, but his failure to influence Burns left him, within 11 days, feeling 'foolishly impulsive' to have tried.[18]

Burns (1978 [18 May 1970], 99) informed the annual monetary conference of the American Bankers' Association that

> we should not close our minds to the possibility that an incomes policy, provided that it stopped well short of direct price and wage controls and was used merely as a supplement to overall fiscal and monetary measures, might speed us through this transitional period of cost-push inflation.

That night, Friedman (18 May 1970) wrote to Burns explaining that his talk of an incomes policy had left him unable to sleep:

> It is hard for me to recall any newspaper story that so saddened, dismayed + depressed me...the word that keeps coming to mind is 'betrayed'.... Never in my wildest dreams did I believe that the Central Bank virus was so potent that it could corrupt even you in so short a time. For you, of all persons, to pull the rug out from under those of us – including yourself – who have been holding out against the barbarians! Who have been trying to defend reason and economic analysis against the unions + subconscious socialists. To lend your immense prestige and standing to evasion and fallacy![19]

The following day, Friedman spoke at a fund-raiser for the Jewish United Fund where he attacked Burns's speech. The following day he wrote to Burns explaining that 'one of the reasons I feel so badly – and so deeply – about your incomes policy speech is that I shall have to attack it publicly – as I was forced to last night – which I hate to do'. Friedman then asked: 'Is there any way we can have a moratorium on speeches?' Shortly afterwards, Friedman sent Burns a draft of his *Newsweek* column (dated 24 May 1970) in which he portrayed Burns as an all-too-early captive of central bank 'gimmicks'.[20] For Friedman (1975 [1970], 121–3), it was 'disheartening' to see Burns advocate the 'dangerous expedient' of an incomes policy as an antidote to inflation.

Further telephone calls caused Friedman more sleepless nights. He wrote to Burns (29 May 1970) that he was

> dismayed by our phone conversation last night. When you said that you did not want to talk to *anyone* this weekend you were clearly politely saying that you did not want to talk to *me*. I was so taken aback + so slow in comprehending what you were really saying that I feel I lapsed into incoherence. Your reaction means that my earlier letter was a major blunder. I had no intention of wrecking a friendship of near 40 years standing or a personal relation that has meant and now means so much to me. I owe a sincere apology to you and even more to myself, since the harm to me is clearly greater than to you.[21]

Friedman (13 December 1971) wrote to Burns (with a copy to Shultz) asking,

> What in God's name is happening?...In early 1960, you correctly warned Mr. Nixon of the danger of recession, arising at least partly from the sharp monetary slowdown, and you urged the Fed, as I did also from my much more junior position, to reverse course. The Fed did not do so until June 1960, by which time it was too late to prevent a recession. In 1971, you were at the head of the Fed, and *a far sharper slowdown has occurred in monetary growth than in 1959* [Friedman's emphasis]...continuation of the slowdown for many more months would almost certainly abort the revival that is now under way.

The Fed had been following a policy which was the antithesis of monetarism: 'Monetary growth has been more erratic in 1971 than in any year in the past several decades. Try as I may, I find it hard to see any excuse for such an irresponsible policy. The Fed can avoid such wild swings. It must accept full responsibility for them and their consequences.'[22]

Later, Friedman described the Nixon administration as 'an enormous disappointment'. He blamed Burns for his lack of influence in the early years of Nixon's Presidency (Friedman and Friedman 1998, 376). He explained to Homer Jones (17 March 1972):

> I had great hopes when Arthur took over, but unfortunately, the statements which Arthur makes are almost all unobjectionable and indeed extremely good, the actual policies and actions followed by the Fed are very far from it. I have the impression that the people in Washington are simply in a state of panic and are willing to pour on any amount of steam in order to get a short run increase in employment regardless of the consequences for more distant future.[23]

Friedman's disillusionment with Burns was widespread. Burns attended his first meeting of the Fed's Open Market Committee on 10 February 1970 (Malkin 1971, 150). The following day, Friedman wrote to Burns urging him to appoint someone from 'outside' the Fed to investigate the money supply figures. Burns set up a Committee on Financial Statistics, with Friedman as a member. Friedman (17 March 1970) wrote to Burns: 'all reports that I hear concur about the excellent changes that you have been producing at the Fed'.[24]

Walter Heller (1969 [1968], 20) referred to the Federal Reserve Bank of St Louis as 'the unofficial statistical arm of the Chicago School'; to which Friedman (1969b [1968], 60) replied 'well, we ought to have one out of twelve anyway'. Friedman (7 July 1970) informed Homer Jones that he was

> impressed by the fact [that with] all the Federal Reserve people I talked to (this morning it was Frank Morris of Boston who was calling about something) there is a wholly different attitude of concern about what has been happening to the monetary aggregates [than] would have been manifested even a year ago, and certainly [than] would have been manifested two years ago.[25]

Fifteen months later, Friedman (31 October 1973) complained to Homer Jones that it was 'disgraceful that the Federal Reserve's measurement of the money supply should be so defective'.

Friedman (1975, [1 March 1971] 70; [27 August 1973], 84; 1972b, xiv; 1972c, 13) berated the 'inexcusable' inability of the Fed to measure the monetary aggregates it was targeting. Friedman also complained that the Fed had become 'an engine of inflation', and 'terrible' monetary policy had been driven by 'erroneous economic theories'. The Fed, not the President, was the 'culprit'. In the private sector 'Heads would roll. So should they at the Fed.'

20
Within the White House

20.1 Pierre Rinfret

Friedman attempted to both cultivate contacts and to neutralise the influence of opponents. This latter project is illustrated by his antagonistic exchanges with one of Nixon's friends, Pierre Rinfret, an influential New York investment adviser, who had been under consideration both as a CEA member and as Treasury Secretary (Ehrlichman 1982, 258). Rinfret was sufficiently close to Nixon to be used by Burns as a messenger. According to Rinfret, in spring 1971 he was invited to have lunch with Burns so as to relay the message to Nixon that the Fed would 'not be party to inflation'. But Nixon told Rinfret he was 'about the hundredth person Dr Burns has asked to deliver the message'.[1]

At Burns's swearing-in ceremony as Fed Chairman in January 1970, Nixon apparently informed Rinfret that 'Friedman did not agree with your concerns' and indicated that he would welcome a confrontation between the two. Moreover, according to Rinfret's testimony, Burns acknowledged that he agreed with 'most' of his criticisms: 'The interesting thing about that remark is that the money supply began to expand the very next week.'[2] According to Rinfret, Friedman could not be found at Burns's swearing-in ceremony – but the confrontation was merely delayed.

Nixon had repeatedly denounced controls – 'rationing, black markets, regimentation' – as 'the wrong road for America'. In January 1970, Nixon indicated that he would 'continue to avoid the use of presidential persuasion to convince business and labor to hold prices and wages down'. He stated that the 'primary responsibility for controlling inflation rests with the national administration and its handling of fiscal and monetary affairs'. The business community had to be guided by 'the interests of the organisation that they represent' and should not be controlled by guidelines and exhortation (*The Washington Post* 31 January 1970; Evans and Novak 1971, 185; De Marchi 1975, 299; Reeves 2001, 263). One consequence of this disavowal of Presidential responsibility for wage outcomes was the adoption of sole Presidential responsibility for inflation without having the alibi of 'irresponsible' labour and management.

Nixon's apparent support for Friedman's repudiation of the 'social responsibility of business' had not gone down well with some in the business community, and had led instead to the development of an 'inflationary psychology'.[3] This was threatening to derail the administration into a more interventionist position. Rinfret (3 July 1969) circulated a two-page memorandum to his clients accusing the new administration of entering office with 'slogans and little else' and in believing that 'inflation could easily be turned off' through monetary policy alone. In reality the administration was 'fostering, abetting and creating inflation' through the 'abandonment of the wage and price guidelines, which created "open sesame" on prices and wages'. Rinfret advised his clients to raise their prices, since controlling inflation was now the responsibility of the monetary authorities (Evans and Novak 1971, 186, 189).

Friedman (1986, 86) believed he had 'escaped [Washington] before I caught Potomac Fever'.[4] Friedman (1972b [22 December 1969], 6) wrote about the 'near-hysterical tones [of] the current flood of talk about inflation'. On 27 April 1970, Friedman met with Nixon and Rinfret in the Oval Office. According to Rinfret, Friedman tried to persuade Nixon that the unemployment rate would not be a factor in the forthcoming election. According to Nixon's press officer, Friedman 'nearly came to blows' with Rinfret over the issue, 'but the President asked me not to take notes of those fireworks' (Safire 1975, 183).[5]

The following day, Nixon advised Americans to invest in the stock market (Safire 1975, 349). Galbraith (1971 [7 June 1970], 74) wrote in the *New York Times Magazine* that Rinfret's advice to raise prices was a direct consequence of the decision to rule out price and wage restraint which would inevitably 'promote inflation'. The next year, Friedman (1975 [5 July 1971], 72) ridiculed the forecasts of the 'Ebullient Pierre Rinfret...New Economists, 0; monetarists, 3'. Presumably to in part neutralise Rinfret's influence, Friedman sent Shultz a copy of this *Newsweek* column. Shultz (15 July 1971) replied: 'Thanks for sending me a copy of your column – and for writing it. The president will see it and appreciate your generous comments, especially since everyone knows you only write what you believe.'[6]

20.2 Richard Nixon

Nixon's deep-seated animosities might have prevented him from being associated with economists from the University of Chicago. Other universities later appeared on his hate list, and he believed that it was in Chicago where he had been robbed of victory in 1960. The Eisenhower–Nixon opponent in 1952 was Adlai Stevenson the ex-governor of Illinois, whom Nixon described as 'Adlai the appeaser' and a 'Ph.D. graduate of Dean Acheson's cowardly college of Communist containment'. Nixon, a virulent anti-communist, was echoing the rhetoric of Senator Joe McCarthy who described Secretary of State Acheson as the 'Red Dean of Fashion'. McCarthy also denigrated William Benton, a former vice president of the University of Chicago, as 'a clever propagandist' who for years had been 'paralleling the Communist Party line down to the last period, the last comma' (cited by Wittner 1978, 108, 99, 100).

For Nixon, accepting the Republican nomination at their Chicago convention in July 1960 was 'the greatest moment in my life' (cited by White 1965, 207). He appeared to lose the election in the famous television debate with Kennedy in Chicago in September during which he looked as if he had been 'embalmed' (Mayor Daley cited by Summers 2001, 208). Shortly after he left Chicago airport at midnight on election night to return to Los Angeles, he was obliged to concede defeat.

In 1960, there was evidence of electoral fraud in Chicago where the voting took place under Daley's 'watchful eye' (Manchester 1975, 884–5). Chicago mobsters may also have played a role (Summers 2001, 217). After the polls closed, Joseph P. Kennedy told his son that if he had changed his mind about being President it was not too late: 'They're still counting votes up in Cook County.' It was these votes (some apparently cast from beyond the grave) which Nixon believed had decisively and illegitimately carried Chicago, and thus the nation, for Kennedy. Had 32,500 additional votes in Illinois and Texas been cast for Nixon he would have become the thirty-fifth President (Reeves 1993, 25, 110; Safire 1975, 311; White 1965, 317, 350).

But according to Stigler and Friedman, the University of Chicago required no electoral fraud to register its Democratic affiliations. Stigler (27 October 1964) reported to Frank Knight that 97 per cent of the University of Chicago supported Johnson in preference to Goldwater.[7] Friedman (1978, xiii) noted that 'There was, I suspect, no precinct in Mayor Daley's Chicago whose vote was consistently more predictable and one-sided than the University of Chicago's Hyde Park.'

Nixon was paranoid about machinations in Chicago. In 1968 he mounted Operation Eagle Eye, designed to thwart Mayor Daley's attempt to rig the election in Humphrey's favour (Summers 2001, 309). But with Nixon and his aides it was always 'Us' against 'Them' and Chicago economists assisted the victory push of both 1968 and 1972. Nixon's speechwriter – one of the certified members of the 'Long March Back' – had lifted the key phrase 'Silent Majority' from a speech from ex-Chicago economist Senator Douglas. During his first term, this 'new majority' solidified and changed the mood of the administration in an ugly direction: from 'an analytical how-do-we-run-against-them to a satisfied run-'em-out-of-town' (Safire 1975, 14, 50, 309). Shultz played a pivotal role in creating this 'new majority' by neutralising the labour movement (see Chapter 21).

Nixon's personal association with Chicago economists went back at least as far as the last year of the Eisenhower administration when he had enjoyed a working relationship with W. Allen Wallis, who was special assistant to the President working with the Cabinet Committee on Price Stability for Economic Growth chaired by Nixon.[8] Wallis was highly regarded by Eisenhower (Safire 1975, 25). In a seven-page invited response to Nixon on Kennedy's proposal to cut taxes, Wallis (15 January 1962) brought Friedman and Shultz to Nixon's attention. Wallis arranged for Friedman to 'have a long visit with Nixon'.[9]

In 1968 Burns recruited Friedman to serve on Nixon's Advisory Group on the Economy (in company with Rinfret, Greenspan, McCracken, Maurice Stans and Don Paarlberg). He rapidly became an inside player able to exploit numerous contacts within the bureaucracy.[10] Friedman reflected that 'perhaps the most important positive effect of the Task Force process was to bring George Shultz to Nixon's notice' (Friedman and Friedman 1998, 375).

Friedman's advocacy did not, of course, always prevail. For example, Friedman (26 February 1974) wrote to CEA Chairman, Alan Greenspan, in an apparently unsuccessful attempt to recruit him to the Mont Pelerin Society.[11] In the same year, Greenspan (1974) described monetary policy in a non-monetarist fashion as 'a very sensitive and flexible counter-cyclical tool'. But he also concluded that Friedman's views 'have had as much, if not more, impact on the way we think about monetary policy and many other important economic issues as those of any other person in the last half of the twentieth century' (cited by Taylor 2000, 101). Friedman (to Greenspan 13 July 1983) also indicated that he had failed to persuade Reagan to appoint Greenspan as Fed Chairman instead of reappointing Volcker.[12]

But even when he lost the immediate argument, Friedman left an impression on those he was seeking to influence. According to Evans and Novak (1971, 371), Nixon's initial resistance to wage and price controls was 'reinforced by George Shultz's doctrinaire opposition'. Shultz recalled that 'In the end, the only people opposed to controls were Richard Nixon, Milton Friedman and myself' (cited by Reichley 1981, 222).

Nixon (1980, 238–9, 245) reflected that the controls went against his 'every instinct about what is good for the American economy.... The economy is not just the realm of accountants. It is also the realm of the spirit.' Citing Friedman, he concluded that 'Most important, there is a direct relationship between human liberties and a free economy.... The best economic advice I can give to my successors in office is to resist firmly political pressures to impose wage and price controls.'

Part V

End Game

21
Secretary Shultz

Shultz was a powerful figure inside the White House prior to becoming Treasury Secretary. One of the Governors of the Federal Reserve System observed that he was 'the strongest economic voice in the Administration' (Maisel 1973, 268). Safire (1975, 467) dated the beginning of Shultz's domestic ascendancy (vis-à-vis Burns) from late 1969 (see also Ehrlichman 1982, 89, 92; Anderson 1990, 267; Solomon 1982, 220, 272; Rather and Gates 1974, 47; Evans and Novak 1971, 369).

In May 1971, *Fortune* reported on the conflict between the Shultz-led 'ideologists' and Burns 'the practical politician' (Malkin 1971, 148, 260). But Shultz was also a highly skilled practical politician. From his time at Chicago, Shultz (1993, 28; 1995, 2) 'learned early on that I must be able to persuade if I was going to be effective'. His 'training as an economist has taught me also to be a strategist who tries to understand the constellation of forces present in a situation and arrange them to point towards a desirable result'.

While Burns and others exacerbated Nixon's problems associated with the traditional hostility of the labour unions, Shultz reduced them. Tass (the Soviet news agency) reported Burns's 7 December speech as being part of an 'anti-labor' programme. Tass also reported Meany's complaint that Burns was seeking 'to roll America back to the nineteenth century'.[1] The *Journal of Commerce* (24 March 1971) portrayed labour leaders as seeking an expansion of the money supply, not a restriction on wages. Burns, they thought, was making 'Tory' statements and 'should go back to school and learn his economic lessons again'.[2] Meany (12 March 1971) ridiculed Burns as 'the good doctor' who wanted to 'starve them out' and as someone who 'never worked with his hands for wages in his life' (Robinson 1981, 301). Burns was 'one of those semi-skilled intellectuals who play with other people's lives'

(Meany cited by Goulden 1972, 422). On 14 April 1971, Burns received a telegram detailing Meany's hostility: 'If [Burns] were in the Soviet area he would have been sent to Siberia', he said in a speech. In the memo attached to the telegram Chas Molony noted: 'Seems to me he's either (1) developing a fixation or (2) figuring you as the prime influence in swinging the President into income policy action – and hence trying to back you off.'[3]

In 1964, Meany perceived similarities between Goldwater and Hitler. Goldwater attributed his defeat to the campaigning activities of the AFL-CIO Committee on Political Education. In 1968, Meany and the union movement launched unprecedented efforts to defeat Nixon (Robinson 1981, 240–1). Shultz sought to capitalise on blue-collar discontent with the Democratic Party and to neutralise Meany's opposition to the Nixon administration (Goulden 1972, 416).

Nixon was prepared to raise public suspicions about his own integrity so as to achieve his objectives. For example, Frank Fitsimmons, the Teamsters President, sat on one of the bodies supervising Phase Two of Nixon's wage and price control apparatus along with Meany and Leonard Woodcock of the United Automobile Workers. At the AFL-CIO convention, 18–28 November 1971, Meany attacked both the administration and Burns for his Pepperdine College speech.[4] In Christmas week 1971, Nixon pardoned Jimmy Hoffa, the Teamsters leader, in an attempt to guarantee their future support (Manchester 1975, 1254–5).

As a staunch anti-communist, Meany was not impressed with Nixon's policy of détente towards China and the USSR. As Labor Secretary, Shultz recognised the 'considerable political power' wielded by trade union leaders such as Meany, and presumably to minimise further difficulties, Shultz played golf with the 78-year-old Meany and guaranteed him 'quiet access to the President' (Shultz and Dam 1977a, 5; Shultz 1993). Shultz also flattered him about his golfing prowess. In turn, Meany reflected that Shultz 'made a good Labor Secretary' (Robinson 1981, 280; Goulden 1972, 406, 428).

Shultz's approach to the labour movement prevailed over powerful forces within the Nixon administration. On 30 November 1970, Acting Treasury Secretary Charles Walker advised Nixon to 'take off the gloves' and 'enter open battle' with the labour unions.[5] Burns had raised with Nixon the possibility of suspending the Davis–Bacon Act and Nixon had initially included the suggestion in a 4 December 1970 speech. However, Shultz had intervened and persuaded Nixon that he would antagonise important sections of the labour movement. When Nixon wanted to invoke the Taft–Hartley Act to intervene in the September 1971 dock dispute, Shultz advised against it (De Marchi 1975, 327; Goulden 1972, 406; Safire 1975, 586; Haldeman 1994, 350, 357).

In December 1971, Meany was hospitalised with a heart attack and denied access to media reports by his doctors. However, Shultz was able to keep the White House informed: 'Shultz reported that a good friend of his had seen Meany in the hospital and gave him a pretty good report on the true situation' (Haldeman 1994, 380). In March 1972, as Shultz predicted, Meany and Woodcock withdrew their support for the wage and price control apparatus. Walker recommended that 'Big Labor' and Meany be identified as the major enemy in the 1972 election. Connally also sought a 'get tough approach on wages that would offend labor'. But in contrast, 'Shultz's contacts with Meany became more frequent' – although these conversations were deliberately kept 'private' (Safire 1975, 586, 588–92; Manchester 1975, 1254–5; Robinson 1981, 319–20).

On 18 June 1972, Shultz relayed to Nixon the message that Meany had (over a game of golf) assured him that he would not support George McGovern in the forthcoming Presidential election. This secured the 'benevolent neutrality' of a large part of organised labour by detaching Meany from the traditional Democratic coalition (Haldeman 1994, 471; Ambrose 1989, 585; Safire 1975, 584; Ehrlichman 1982, 94). Nixon (1978, 626, 672) recalled that Shultz's news provided 'a tremendous boost' to his re-election chances.

Safire (1975, 589–91) noted that Shultz had an important ulterior motive for the tactics he pursued with organised labour:

> he was worried about controls becoming too popular, which could result in the end of collective bargaining and the free market system. Government management, he feared, would sap initiative the way it had done in the railroad industry. The ultimate protection against this, Shultz knew, was not philosophical purity but the refusal of the unions to go along.

At the NEP planning meeting at Camp David, he assured Nixon that price and wage controls 'will stop when labor blows it up with a big strike' (cited by Reeves 2001, 358).

Shultz displayed powerful skills of rhetoric in his dealings with Nixon: the phrase 'a bridge from welfare to work' had gone down especially well (Reeves 2001, 98). Kissinger (1982, 81) observed that using these skills Shultz became 'the dominant member of every committee he joined'. When persuasion was insufficient, Shultz (1993, 13, n. 2) used other tactics to achieve his desired results.[6] In particular, Shultz was determined that the Treasury should maintain control of the negotiations about the future of the international monetary system (Shultz and Dam 1977a, 61, 122). One of his first acts as Treasury Secretary was to exert 'concerted pressure to make progress' with monetary reform (Volcker and Gyohten 1992, 118–19).

Meanwhile, the IMF undertook a 'marathon' series of meetings so that their report on the *Reform of the International Monetary System* could be agreed upon prior to the September 1972 annual meeting (de Vries 1985a, 136). It expressed a 'touching faith' in prompt parity adjustments as the salvation of the system. But observers noticed evidence within the report of 'strong differences of opinion' on the question of automatic adjustments of parity. The US was the only country that did not welcome the *Reform* report (Williamson 1977, 61–2, 66). Shultz became Treasury Secretary as the report was being written.

The September 1972 IMF meeting provided an opportunity to reflect about the disturbing events of the previous year. Henry Wallich (1972, 19, 45, 49–50) noted that ten years ago 'we were bitterly divided' with no common ground between the fixed and flexible diehards. Now there was a growing consensus on limited flexibility, at least in the short run. The 1971 experience of floating was described as 'an unmitigated disaster', but a parity based on effective exchange rates might usher in his desired outcome of 'one world of fixed exchange rates'. I. G. Patel (1972, 64, 67) noted with alarm that the idea that flexible exchange rates allowed countries to pursue their national objectives in a more unfettered way was a 'misguided psychology' that was 'gaining ground'.

Jeremy Morse (1972, 51, 54–8) reflected that the temporary period of disorder had not produced a 'general mind-defeating disintegration' but had been 'closed by the Smithsonian bargain'. On this the international bankers could 'stand with recovered confidence'. A 'massive exchange of views' had led to the creation of a 'new slogan of "a one-world system"'. International cooperation, 'the utopian vision of earlier times has become the accepted thing in the age of jet and telex'. The Bretton Woods experience had reinforced the attachment to fixed rates: 'Behind this satisfaction with the post war experience lie darker memories of the thirties.' Some calculations made by WP3 revealed that the system contained a 'depreciation bias'. But the Smithsonian bureaucrats were determined to prevent a recurrence of the crisis by controlling the recurrent trend towards maintaining an undervalued exchange rate. The crisis of 1971 had been helpful in this respect: 'Once the crisis exposed this trend, one could see that it had been running like an underground river through the twenty five years of the Bretton Woods system, generally suppressed by the acceptance of fixed rates.' But – at least in Morse's lecture – there was no understanding of the intellectual currents which after 25 years were about to sweep away the foundations of the par value system.

At the September meeting, the US delegation was unsuccessful in their attempts to prevent the Committee of Twenty (C-20) electing Morse as Chairman of the Deputies. The US preferred Rinaldo Ossolo 'partly because he was not hostile to floating exchange rates' (de Vries 1985a, 158). Morse (1974, 186) set himself the task of reconstructing Bretton Woods by providing 'a complete design for an international monetary system that would last for 25 years'. The reform deliberations of the C-20 were expected to last two years. Yet within six months the par value system collapsed. Henceforth the edicts of the international policemen lost their potency. On 27 March 1973, as floating became generalised, the C-20 at their second meeting insisted that the 'reformed system' must be based on 'stable but adjustable par values…within the framework of a strengthened International Monetary Fund'.[7] But they were just 'too out of touch with reality' (Williamson 1977, 67, 70–1).

Nixon (1972, 6) opened the 1972 IMF annual meeting by commending the various proposals that Secretary Shultz was about to make as 'the best thinking of my top economic advisers'. Shultz sought to reassure his audience: he was aware that most countries were committed to fixing the value of their currency. However, he added that provision needed 'to be made for countries which decide to float their currencies'. This 'surprised the world' and appeared to the Europeans to be evidence that the 'religious war' was over and that the Americans would adopt a more cooperative international stance (Solomon 1982, 226, 228; Williamson 1977, 61–2, 66, 82). In reality, Shultz had spent his first summer as Treasury Secretary formulating an elaborate plan based on a 'simple core idea…a system in which exchange rates could move freely' (Shultz and Dam 1977a, 126).

In the Friedman archives there is a 'Confidential' document entitled 'A Sketch of a World Monetary System' presumably written by Shultz. The document states explicitly that 'In specific monetary terms, we or others will not "buy" a heavily IMF-directed, rigid fixed exchange rate system combined with free movement of trade and capital – even if such a system should demonstrably maximise international trade, investment, and total real world income.' The objective of US policy was clearly stated: 'we want the apparent "freedom" of the looser exchange rate regime, while keeping the advantages of a strong international consensus as to certain basic rules of good behavior'. Shultz (1972a, 2, 12) acknowledged that 'reasonable international standards against competitive undervaluation' had to be incorporated into the new system but that 'in the end, we could adopt the floating option for the US'.

Kenneth Dam (1982, 224) recalled that the US proposal was formulated by Friedman and articulated to Shultz, Dam and Arthur Laffer over dinner on 22 May 1972. The US proposal was designed as a part of the transition to a floating system: 'But it was not so presented', because of the opposition of Burns and others. A historian of the IMF noted that Shultz believed in the floating solution but 'was at least at the outset unwilling to articulate this position in an international context'. On 14 June 1972, in a meeting with IMF officials, Laffer 'merely argued not "that a floating rate system would be a preferred alternative but rather that it might not be such a bad alternative"' (James 1996, 234–5).

Just ten days before the Friedman–Shultz–Dam–Laffer dinner, Burns (1978 [12 May 1972], 447–8) delivered an address in Montreal on 'Some Essentials of International Monetary Reform' in which he described the 1971 experience of floating as inconsistent 'with the model usually sketched in academic writings'. Contrary to what Friedman and others had promised, the world, Burns asserted, had witnessed an alarming retreat back towards the 1930s: 'signs of political friction among friendly nations proliferated'. But Burns was upbeat about the return to the par value system: 'Fortunately, this dangerous trend towards competitive and even antagonistic national policies was halted by the Smithsonian Agreement' which had been 'worked out with care by practical and well-informed men, and I am confident that the central banks and governments of all the major countries will continue to give it strong support'. The Smithsonian realignment was 'solidly based'; the alternative was 'not pleasant to contemplate'.

Business Week (20 May 1972, 28) reported that Burns's speech might have been an indication that the US was changing its attitude to international monetary reform. With Connally's departure there were rumours that 'Burns and Connally had battled and that Burns had triumphed'. Connally's replacement – Shultz – was a novice because the international arena was 'alien ground' to him. Foreign central bankers hoped that 'Shultz is more in line with the Burns approach'.

But the supporters of exchange rate flexibility had other hopes. Nine months later, when the Smithsonian realignment broke down, Haberler (and Friedman) exerted intense backstairs pressure so as to impair the chances of a revival of the par value system (de Vries 1985a, 113). In response to the Montreal speech, Haberler (15 May 1972) wrote to

Burns, attempting to enlist him in allowing the dollar to float according to the principle of benign neglect:

> aversion to flexibility is unfortunately a fact of life, at least at present ...I was glad that you did not say what you had been reported to have said on an earlier occasion, that last year's events have shown that flexible exchange rates cannot work...I am glad you stressed 'autonomy of domestic policies'. This is, of course, the main pillar of the policy of benign neglect.[8]

Since the early 1960s, the Fed and the Treasury had intervened in the foreign exchange markets; buying and selling currency to support exchange rate parities (Wallich and Axilrod 1964, 140). As early as March 1972, Volcker had made it clear that the Smithsonian agreement would have to be defended by the other leading countries (Coombs 1976, 226–7; Southard 1979, 42; James 1996, 241). It was becoming increasingly obvious that there was a 'clear split' between the Treasury and the Fed on the issue (Volcker and Gyohten 1992, 130). In July 1972, following 'interminable arguments', the Treasury agreed to provide a 'shoestring' to support the dollar against the Deutschmark (for the first time since August 1971). Two days later, Shultz's Treasury removed even this 'grudging' support. Henceforth the Fed would have to attempt its defence of the Smithsonian system without Treasury support.

Burns (30 August 1972) obtained legal advice about this intervention. In a confidential document entitled 'Respective Powers of the Federal Reserve and the Treasury in the Foreign Currency Area', Burns was informed that 'the System's authority to engage in foreign currency operations is not legally subject to direction or control by the Treasury'.[9] On 14 November 1972, Burns forwarded to Shultz an excerpt from a letter from Dr Klasen, head of the Bundesbank, which stated that 'I shall always continue to be an indefatigable opponent against a European floating of exchange rates, as long as this would be planned without the explicit consent of the United States. Such floating – and here I concur emphatically in your views – would split the liberal world.'[10]

The split between Burns and the Treasury appeared to be widening. *Time* (22 May 1972, 85) reported that Burns regarded his 'ten point' Montreal programme as 'a pretty fair summary of the US position'. But Burns's address did not attract support from the Treasury. At a press conference, Treasury Under-Secretary Volcker stressed that Burns had not provided 'any kind of model for reform'. Using diplomatic language, Volcker explained that 'the emphasis may vary' between the

Fed and the Treasury. Specifically, while Burns stressed that the convertibility of the dollar was an essential element, Volcker merely stated that it was 'one of the subjects under discussion'. When asked whether he thought that Burns's lecture was 'purely personal' he replied that 'We have no ten point program.' One journalist stated that 'Rightly or wrongly, a number of Europeans have, in fact mentioned, that they have no idea what the United States wants.' When asked to comment on Burns's expressed faith in 'basically fixed parities...with perhaps more flexibility than we have had in the past', Volcker replied, 'I really don't know quite how to answer that.' But Volcker did find 'wisdom' in the words 'said by someone' that although we knew how fixed and floating rates worked we weren't sure 'how any of these things in between worked'.[11]

In his September 1972 Annual Report to the Board of IMF Governors, Schweitzer (1972b, 3, 5, 7) reflected on the 'marked contrast' with the previous year's situation where 'most exchange rates were floating without guidelines for their regulation or for the reconciliation of conflicting national objectives'. He expressed his 'belief' in powers that transcended market forces: incomes policies and the rather ponderous 'high purpose' which had informed his predecessors.[12] In his statement the following day, Shultz (1972b, 3, 5) expressed another belief: 'The belief is widespread – and we share it – that the exchange rate system must be more flexible.... Provision needs also to be made for countries which decide to float their currencies.'

Some have suggested that Friedman actually drafted Shultz's speech (de Vries 1985b, 964; Volcker and Gyohten 1992, xiv, 82, 107, 118, 120). Shultz (1972b, 2) certainly referred to 'stimulating contributions to our thinking from a wide variety of other sources – public and private'. Friedman, however, denies playing any drafting role but is prepared to accept that he may have discussed the speech with Shultz prior to the 1972 meeting.[13] Certainly, the proposal to allow the US to float while leaving other countries with the option to follow suit or peg against the dollar was similar to that outlined by Friedman (1969c) shortly after Nixon's first election victory. In his concluding remarks at the end of the IMF meeting, however, Schweitzer explained that he was 'impressed by the tone' of the meeting and 'even more convinced' by the validity of the IMF framework: 'I have been heartened by the confidence that so many Governors have expressed in the Fund.'[14]

Six months later, the 'final collapse' of the IMF system was 'unexpected' within the Fund (de Vries 1985a, 119). However, White House rhetoric suggested a different perspective than that of the Fund officials.

With respect to the NEP, Friedman (1974b [1971], 426) welcomed 'the President's bold actions...[which] gave a formal signal that the Bretton Woods system is dead, that it will no longer be revived'. The 1973 Economic Report of the President echoed these words: Nixon's 'bold initiatives ... gave public recognition to the fact that ... the Bretton Woods system had become untenable' (cited by de Vries 1985a, 111). The IMF Executive Board expected to exercise a 'leadership position' in reforming the international monetary system. But the USA wished to exclude the IMF from discussions about the international economy because Fund officials 'would be excessively influenced by the history and past operation of the Fund and excessively biased in favor of a system of par values' (Coombs 1976, 220; de Vries 1985a, 118, 130, 150; Solomon 1982, 225, 228; James 1996, 244).

But Nixon was also preoccupied with Watergate and disinclined to support attempts to rescue the par value system.[15] On 23 June 1972, Nixon and Haldeman formulated a plan to call in the CIA to restrain the FBI investigation into the Watergate break-in (Kutler 1997, 69).[16] On the very same day, Haldeman informed him that the pound was floating, but Nixon replied 'I don't care about it'. Haldeman pressed him to take an interest in the international monetary crisis, telling him that Burns, the Fed Chairman, was 'concerned about speculation against the lira'. Nixon retorted to Haldeman: 'Well, I don't give a [expletive deleted] about the lira' (cited by Williamson 1977, 175; Ambrose 1991, 414).

Besides, the heroic self-sacrifice of the par value rhetoric was being revealed as hollow. At the September 1970 annual meeting of the IMF the British Chancellor, Anthony Barber, made an attack on floating exchange rates that was regarded as 'a sermon against atheism before a convocation of bishops' (Volcker and Gyohten 1992, 105). On 15 February 1972, Barber gave a speech on 'new currency solutions' in which he stated that he was 'impressed by the very wide area of basic agreement on objectives. All want a system with fixed rates.'[17] But the British government had fought for three years to avoid devaluation in the 1960s; in 1972 they resisted for about a week. On 23 June 1972, the pound started to float for what was announced to be 'a temporary period' (Solomon 1982, 175, 220–1). The Italian lira was also under pressure. However, on 17 July 1972 Barber announced that the EEC Finance Ministers remained committed to a system 'based on fixed but adjustable par values'.[18] Friedman (1975 [1972], 175–8) welcomed the float of the pound: the 'sooner the Smithsonian agreement is undermined the better'.

Part of the reason for the lack of US commitment to the Smithsonian realignment was the perception that the negotiated devaluation was still insufficient (Volcker 1978–79, 7). But had Nixon been exclusively advised by advocates such as Burns, the par value system may have survived much longer. Nixon regarded himself as a Presidential peacemaker and could, presumably, have been susceptible to pressure to see himself as the defender of international economic morality and peace. Inter-war analogies were plentiful at this time. To manipulate Nixon, Connally drew analogies with the one-term Republican Presidency of Herbert Hoover (Rather and Gates 1974, 279). Nixon was so obsessed with Neville Chamberlain returning from Munich in 1938 with 'Peace in Our Time' and an umbrella that as Vice President he reportedly prohibited staff members from carrying umbrellas when meeting him from airports (Reeves 2001, 468). In par value mythology, flexible exchange rates were a species of nationalistic territorial demands and their toleration was a species of appeasement. Thus Burns (1 February 1973) wrote to Nixon in London about the dollar coming 'under attack in recent days' and the fear of 'individual nations becoming more nationalistic…lead[ing] to international trouble.… I feel it is important that you alert Prime Minister Heath to this danger.'[19]

Burns (1978 [1972], 154) devoted his December 1972 AEA address to the need to build on the new economic policy and thus 'facilitate the rebuilding of the international monetary system'. But Burns had rejected Nixon's pressure to expand the money supply and had even failed to respond to a Presidential letter on the matter: 'No answer is to be made to this letter. It's outrageous' (Burns cited by Reeves 2001, 423). More importantly, after January 1973, Shultz combined the job as Treasury Secretary with new roles as Assistant to the President for Economic Policy, Chairman of the newly formed Council on Economic Policy and Chairman of the Council on International Economic Policy (CIEP). This was the vehicle through which Shultz imposed his authority on US economic policy and through which the Treasury dominated international economic policy.

As the par value system was disintegrating even Nixon came to think that Shultz wielded too much power. Nixon told Haldeman (1994 [16 March 1973], 588) that he felt that 'Shultz is spread way too thin, he's the senior man on labor, Russian trade, economic policy, Treasury items, monetary policy, energy, and so forth.' Shultz used his position to achieve all sorts of long-held objectives. As OMB Director, Shultz (2 March 1971) attempted to persuade the CIEP that the capital control programmes should be 'abandoned' because 'the balance of payments argument is irrelevant'.[20] In February 1973, Shultz again pressed for the removal of all remaining controls on capital outflow (Volcker and Gyohten 1992, 107). By 1974, he was in a position to remove them (Shultz and Dam 1977a, 19).

Shultz's stated philosophy was to 'do nothing' in response to both Presidential instructions to harass perceived enemies and to the expectation that the administration should intervene to resolve industrial disputes (Shultz and Dam 1977a, 2, 7, 176–7). He now brought this market-based philosophy to bear on the par value system.

Shultz was regarded as 'the creative synthesiser...the man who could conjure up a surprisingly different way to an agreed upon objective' (Safire 1975, 215). His post-Bretton Woods 'synthesis' proved more conducive to floating rates than the fixed rate advocates would have wished. On 11 January 1973, Shultz announced that Phase Three of the economic stabilisation programme would entail 'volunteerism.... From this point on, we have a self-administered system' with the number of Internal Revenue workers monitoring price performance cut in half.[21] The perception that wage and price controls had been abandoned put pressure on the dollar (James 1996, 241). Between 1 and 9 February 1973, the Bundesbank spent almost US$6 billion defending the Smithsonian realignment. It was the 'last gasp' of the Bretton Woods system (Haberler 1988, 135; Scammell 1983, 184; de Vries 1985a, 66).[22]

Burns (1978 [1970], 17) reflected, 'If you can keep your head while all about you are losing theirs, perhaps you don't understand the gravity of the situation.' The Federal Reserve kept their head and sold $320 million worth of marks to defend the fixed parity system. But the day after the defence began, newspapers reported that Shultz was sympathetic to the float of the mark, thus rendering the defence an expensive but pointless exercise (Friedman 1975, 181). Coombs (1976, 228) realised that 'the ball game is over'. On 12 February 1973, Shultz announced a 10 per cent devaluation of the dollar, noting that the US had 'undertaken no obligation' to intervene in foreign exchange markets.[23]

Of further symbolic importance was the fact that Shultz sent Volcker to Europe and Japan to discuss the impending changes, rather than negotiate via the IMF who, he believed, had a vested institutional interest in maintaining a par value system (Shultz and Dam 1977a, 121). When the agreement had been reached, the IMF were given a copy of Shultz's press statement: 'Perhaps for the first time in the Fund's history, the Executive Board did not have a paper prepared by the staff. In these circumstances there was little that the Executive Board could do.... Such a situation was far from welcome.' The IMF had been deliberately excluded from decision-making about the very issue that they believed defined their existence (de Vries 1985a, 66–9, 117). At an internal crisis meeting on 9 February 1973, IMF officials expressed the fear that the death of the parity system might be a prelude to the death of the IMF. Henceforth it was safest to keep 'a low profile' so as to avoid aggravating the Americans still further (James 1996, 242).

On 5 March 1973, a group met in Shultz's office to plan for the forthcoming C-20 meeting. The agenda noted that 'the world seems to be accepting de facto more floating than C-20 discussions have assumed.... Is floating to be considered a transitional arrangement or a more or less permanent or indefinite situation?'[24] On 27 March 1973, the C-20 (1974, 215) recognised that 'floating rates could provide a useful technique in particular situations'. But Shultz successfully resisted the effort to insert the word 'temporary' before 'floating rates' (Solomon 1982, 228, 230, 248). This wording remained in the final report, although the IMF (1974, 8, 12) sought to make floating 'subject to Fund authorisation, surveillance and review'.

By March 1973, the yen, the Swiss franc and the Italian lira were floating, in addition to sterling and the Canadian dollar. On 1 March 1973, the Bundesbank issued DM 8 billion (equivalent to 16 per cent of the currency in circulation) to buy US $2.7 billion, the largest amount ever purchased by a central bank in a single day (Emminger 1977, 36; James 1996, 242). Throughout the 1973 crisis, Friedman and Haberler exerted relentless pressure on Emminger and the Bundesbank to again float the Deutschmark (de Vries 1985a, 113). Schweitzer sent a telex to the German Finance Minister urging massive currency intervention. But Emminger concluded that the market had sounded 'the death knell for the Bretton Woods system' (cited by James 1996, 242).

On 2 March 1973, the Bank of France was forced to close the Paris exchange market after 90 minutes' trading. On that day, Volcker was presented with an IMF staff paper outlining the tools by which the US could use the Fund's resources for a concerted defence of the existing structure of rates. Volcker replied that the US had accepted the system of floating rates (de Vries 1985a, 76–7). The system of fixed exchange rates thus effectively collapsed into a generalised float.

On 9 March 1973, Shultz 'politely refused' a request from the EEC Finance Ministers to intervene in the exchange markets (Solomon 1982, 232). A historian of the IMF noted that Shultz now 'sounded only half convincing.... Behind the scenes he was as unhelpful in maintaining the new parities or rescuing the system as could be imagined. He did not return the anxious telephone calls of the German Finance Minister

Helmut Schmidt, and he showed no sign of being concerned about the situation' (James 1996, 242).

The six European countries of the 'snake' plus Sweden began to float jointly while attempting to fix exchange rates among themselves. Outside the IMF it was 'universally' recognised that a new regime of floating rates had been initiated. But the IMF thought it best to pretend that the Europeans were not really floating and so decided to treat them not as separate countries but as a group: 'The joint float might then be construed as a step towards the restoration of a system of adjustable parities' (de Vries 1985a, 80). But even this was short-lived: by the end of 1974 only Germany, the Benelux countries, Denmark, Norway and Sweden remained committed to the system (Greenspan 1988, 301). In 1973, there was also an effort to pretend that countries were committed to 'central rates' even when a country's intervention currency was floating. It became necessary to dilute still further this rather meaningless concept, although the IMF Executive Board, apparently paralysed by indecision, took two months to agree on this 'seemingly minor question' (de Vries 1985a, 281).

A press release (13 June 1974) began with a familiar tone: 'There is widespread agreement that the behavior of governments with respect to exchange rates is a matter of international concern and a matter for consultation and surveillance in the Fund.' However, the IMF was now obliged to offer 'guidelines rather than rules to indicate their tentative and experimental character'. Indeed, the 'Staff Comment on Guidelines for Floating' emphasised that the 'steps the Fund would take to "encourage" a hesitant member to follow Fund recommendations are not specified'.[25] More importantly, the Americans were prepared to accept the IMF guidelines on the understanding that they would be activated only 'in exceptional circumstances and very cautiously. The Fund should be under no illusion that the guideline is intended to provide the Fund with a handle to determine exchange rates or to promote an early return to fixed exchange rates.'[26]

The *Washington Post* (8 March 1973) reported that an intellectual revolution had occurred: 'some of the unshakeable concepts have been shattered, never to be restored'. Floating exchange rates had previously been 'dismissed as fuzzy headed' because 'the monetary authorities of the world simply won't go along'. But now the monetary authorities were confronted by a new situation and a different kind of Treasury Secretary who was 'strongly inclined towards the flexible exchange rate posture, and the free market philosophy best espoused by Milton Friedman' (Rowen 1973).

Various further attempts were made to salvage something, but the futility and exhaustion were plain to see. As one official put it, 'the most urgent aspect of international monetary reform is to return to a system of fixed weekends and free evenings with very wide bands around them' (cited by Solomon 1982, 336; see also Fleming 1974, 9). After the oil price rises, attempts to return to exchange rate fixity were simply overtaken by events (Greenspan 1988, 311). Henceforth, Shultz concluded, 'markets, rather than governments were explicitly in charge' of exchange rates (Shultz and Dam 1977a, 128).[27]

22
Secretary Simon

Shultz's influence lived on in the system of sometimes managed floats. The summit meetings between the leading industrial nations at which efforts were occasionally made to influence currency outcomes had their origins in the Group of Five or 'Shultz's Library Group' which first met in the White House in April 1973, immediately after the abandonment of the fixed exchange rate system. Shultz also acted as the American 'sherpa' at the November 1975 Rambouillet summit meeting which was part of the process that provided a legal basis for floating exchange rates (Volcker and Gyohten 1992, 126–7, 141; Shultz and Dam 1977a, 12; James 1996, 266–7). The 1976 Jamaica revision of the IMF Articles which legitimised floating was driven by free market sentiments (de Vries 1985b, 761).

The debate over exchange rate regimes had become somewhat 'doctrinal'. The French wished to return to fixed rates, but at the 1974 IMF annual meeting, Simon insisted that 'flexible exchange rates...have served us well' (cited by de Vries 1985b, 701). The official US position as expressed by Secretary Simon was that 'We believe strongly that countries must be free to choose their own exchange rate system.' At the 1975 IMF annual meeting, Simon declared that 'The right to float must be clear and unencumbered' (IMF 1975, 269).

His two deputies (Jack Bennett and later Edwin Yeo) were 'convinced currency floaters' who were determined to resolve international negotiations in a manner that would 'not prejudice the monetary system against floating rates' (Volcker and Gyohten 1992, 141). Simon and Bennett were regarded as 'even stronger advocates of free markets' than their predecessors, Shultz and Volcker (de Vries 1985b, 814).

The *Wall Street Journal* (22 May 1975) reported that Bennett had complained that the 'French are off on the extreme'. A French source was reported as saying that an agreement was unlikely 'as long as the

US is represented by Mr Bennett' (Gannon 1975). The French representative described a floating regime as 'a dangerous phenomenon that disturbs the world economic order...the very raison d'être [of the IMF] is at stake' (IMF 1975, 268–9). Giscard d'Estaing described floating rates as 'a sort of monetary LSD' (de Vries 1976a, 503). The French insisted that the US were in violation of the Fund's Articles by not adhering to a par value system. Simon's response was that the Fund's Articles should be amended accordingly (de Vries 1985b, 736, 738–9).

In a October 1975 Treasury document on 'International Monetary Problems', the French were described as being motivated by '(a) traditional French attraction to fixed prices and organized markets; (b) fear of US competition (heightened by the loss of the Belgian aircraft contract); (c) nostalgia for the world of the 1950s and 60s'. The Treasury position was that 'Any attempt to restore the rigid, speculative, and crisis-ridden Bretton Woods system would fail.... The US should not accept an amendment to the Articles which contains a legal or moral commitment to establish a par value for the dollar.' A Fed commentary on the paper perhaps reflected a long-standing difference with the Treasury: 'It is curious that there is no explicit mention in the paper of the role of the IMF guidelines for floating and no mention of possibly expanding their role. Of course the concept of exchange-rate zones is mentioned in the paper; the IMF role in this connection is not mentioned.'[1]

A French–US deal broke down when the French saw in English the phrase 'a stable system of exchange rates' rather than the 'system of stable exchange rates' that had been agreed upon verbally. The international policemen felt like Sisyphus 'eternally damned to see their efforts undone' (de Vries 1985b, 740–1).

Simon then sent Yeo across the Atlantic with 'dizzying frequency' to negotiate in secret with the French, whose resistance weakened as a result of a deal struck on gold. As part of this deal, Simon persuaded officials from the five largest IMF countries that there should be no attempts to peg the price of gold. Other compromises were made to appease the French. In the mid-1960s there had been a French–US monetary 'cold war' (Triffin 1968, 113). In 1967 de Gaulle insisted that the US remove their military bases from France, and the US demanded $400 million in compensation. In the middle of the negotiations over exchange rates, the French offered $100 million which President Ford (1979, 223) and Simon accepted without quibble. In response, the French President appeared to redefine the word 'parity' to mean an exchange rate not necessarily attached to a par value. The French were now prepared to accept 'limited flexibility of the system'.

President Giscard d'Estaing's after-dinner announcement of the 'stunning' news of the French–US agreement was met with 'total silence' by the Rambouillet delegates. Such was the 'elation' that three of the five Finance Ministers initialled an agreement that they had not even seen. The resulting November 1975 'Declaration of Rambouillet' legitimised floating rates, and proposed frequent consultations to prevent erratic fluctuations. When in December 1975, Polak, the representative of the IMF Managing Director, was allowed to see the agreement about a revision to the IMF Articles, he made himself 'highly unpopular' by unfavourably comparing the French–US agreement with the draft prepared by the Fund's staff. The deputies of the G-10 were prepared to tolerate only minor legalistic redrafting of the Rambouillet agreement – without any input from Polak (de Vries 1985b, 746–9).

The agreement was embodied as Article IV section 2(b) of the revised IMF Articles of Agreement which legitimised and legalised floating exchange rates by declaring that 'members may choose the exchange arrangements they wish to apply' (de Vries 1985a, 326; 1985b, 751; Solomon 1982, 268, 271–4, 278). James Callaghan (1987, 437, 480) left the Rambouillet meeting with no doubt about the 'United States' determination to adhere to floating exchange rates'. He also observed that Simon's influence on US economic policy was 'paramount' and appeared to exceed that of President Ford. Simon compared the agreement over the revised Article IV to the original Bretton Woods agreement: 'one of the most significant and beneficial international developments of the present decade' (cited by Emminger 1976, 21).

John Williamson (1977, 67, 70–1, 75) reflected that 'One country, at least, seemed happy enough with a non-system.' Shultz recalled that the agreement was deliberately designed so that the US could 'defeat' any attempt to return to a regime of fixed exchange rates by requiring an 85 per cent vote in the IMF, thus giving the US an effective veto (Shultz and Dam 1977a, 131; Scammell 1983, 208). The French were offered 'vague allusions to a return to a general par value system' and so were able to represent the agreement as a step in that direction (Volcker and Gyohten 1992, 141; Solomon 1982, 273). To one observer at least, the linguistic compromises embodied in the final agreement were 'worthy of a slapstick comedy' (Triffin 1976, 47). As Friedman's Chicago colleague, Arnold Harberger, pointed out, the terminology 'non-system' was conceived by those whose systems had been rejected (cited by Williamson 1987, 32).

23 Conclusion

With the benefit of hindsight it is clear that neither adversarial position with respect to exchange rate regimes was fully vindicated by subsequent events. Behind the public analysis offered by the Bretton Woods administrators lay the fear that floating exchange rates would open a Pandora's box which therefore had to be left closed. For example, in 1964, Roosa 'emphatically' and privately informed the recently appointed British Chancellor that it would be impossible to maintain the post-war system if a currency realignment was even attempted. Therefore, if the idea was merely 'floated the subsequent failure would be disastrous for the stability of the international monetary system' (Callaghan 1987, 171). Not surprisingly, after this Pandora's box was opened, the policemen looked at the world 'with an unusual mixture of hope and uneasiness' (de Vries 1985a, 85).

But contrary to Roosa's public assertion, a market for foreign exchange did emerge. Friedman, Shultz and Simon played pivotal parts in this process also. After the NEP, the Chicago Mercantile Exchange commissioned Friedman to prepare a report on 'The Need for Futures Markets in Currencies'. Friedman's (1971, 2–4) report proclaimed that Bretton Woods is now 'dead', and the moment of death was dated to the initiation of the two-tier gold market in March 1968. Friedman's report which predicted a 'great expansion in the demand for foreign cover' was sent to Shultz who 'offered immediate and warm support…and embraced Friedman's philosophical rationale'. Burns and Stein were also courted: in both cases, Friedman's paper thus paved the way for a 'receptive encounter'. The International Monetary Market (IMM) opened on 16 May 1972. But consent to institute Treasury futures did not occur until Friedman intervened with Secretary Simon who 'readily agreed'. In all of this, Friedman 'provided us with the intellectual courage to proceed undaunted' (Melamed 1988b, 421–2).

After March 1973, there were numerous attempts to re-establish some sort of parity regime through international cooperation. Friedman's initial 1950 memorandum advocating flexible exchange rates was written with German and European considerations in mind. Half a century later, the European Union proceeded down the alternative path of the most fixed of all exchange rate choices: a monetary union. With the benefit of hindsight, the literature on optimal currency areas probably had as profound an impact on world history as the much 'louder' dispute between fixers and floaters (see for example, Mundell 1963, 1973a, 1973b; McKinnon 1963, 2002; Kenen 1969).

The par value system may or may not have withstood the strains associated with the oil price rises of the mid-1970s. Either way, the world learned to live with floating and the IMF rapidly adjusted to the loss of its defining role and focused instead on policing other areas of the international economy. As Shultz (1995, 5) noted, 'In the tradition of skilled bureaucracies, the IMF has turned to new areas and has managed to expand substantially its financial resources and in the process its influence.' The IMF had 'more money than mission'.

It also became clear that floating did not deliver the hoped for 'escape'. During the last 13 years of fixed exchange rates (1960–72), the seven leading industrial countries experienced real growth rates at double the rate of the 1973–90 period, and as growth rates were cut in half, inflation and unemployment more than doubled (Bordo and Jonung 1996, 177–88; Salvatore 1993, 614; Volcker and Gyohten 1992, 293, 304). The post-1973 period also exhibited larger and more persistent inflation differentials than under the Bretton Woods system (Alogoskoufis 1992; Aldcroft and Oliver 1998, 174). Country-by-country changes in real behaviour are not easily traced to individual post-1973 decisions to float or fix (although fixing in a generally floating world is different from fixing in a fixed world); and some evidence suggests that the exchange rate regime has little significance in explaining pre- and post-1973 economic performance. But the volatility of exports, imports and the real exchange rate increased in the post-1973 period (Baxter and Stockman 1989).

But after the collapse of fixed exchange rates there was no return to unemployment-exporting efforts of the competitive devaluations of the 1930s. Instead, the adoption of domestic monetarism led to soaring interest rates and, in effect, to competitive *appreciations* (Solomon 1982, 360).[1] It had been argued that flexible exchange rates would assist the free movement of capital which Friedman (1967) sought to 'welcome and encourage' and facilitate the associated domestic adjustment: 'the exchange rate will then move and this will tend to create the balance-of-trade difference required to accommodate the capital movement'. But anti-inflationary monetary targeting in the UK forced the real exchange rate to rise from 106.3 in March 1978 to over 140 in 1980 (March 1973 = 100): 'by far the most excessive overvaluation which any major currency has experienced in recent monetary history' (Emminger cited by Keegan 1984, 171). Between 1977 and the first half of 1982, the volume of world trade rose by 18 per cent while UK exports of manufactured goods were unchanged. Domestically over the same period, import volumes rose by 40 per cent and output of the UK manufacturing sector fell by 14 per cent. Between 1979 and January 1983, UK unemployment increased from 5.5 to 13.3 per cent (Keegan 1984, 131, 179–80).

For Friedman (2000) a pegged exchange rate is 'a ticking bomb'. The 'Shultz bombshell' was the regime of floating exchange rates that was rejected prior to the Smithsonian meeting (Volcker and Gyohten 1992, 47, 114). Emminger (1977, 29) concluded that the Smithsonian realignment 'collapsed like a house of cards' because, after December 1971, 'the various difficulties which could threaten and break down any system of fixed parities succeeded one another in textbook fashion'. The IMF were all too conscious of the economic difficulties, but perhaps insufficiently informed about the intellectual 'bomb' carried by Friedman and Shultz. When the final currency crisis came it was, for the IMF, 'as if a trapdoor had opened' (de Vries 1996, 133–4).

Connally, with his 'screw or be screwed' attitude, had advocated 'a floating of the dollar' to 'get us away from being the victim of foreign governments that are arbitrarily floating their currencies and leaving us hanging' (Haldeman 1994 [2 August 1971], 335–6). Influential agents within (or with access to) the Nixon administration were determined from the outset to allow the par value system to twist in the breeze. The policy of 'benign neglect' was indistinguishable from the policy of waiting for the final collapse, which, in the absence of US intervention, was the likely consequence of the *next* currency crisis. Later, Kissinger (1979, 953) recognised that the policy of 'benign neglect' meant, in effect, allowing the dollar to eventually float. Coombs (1976, 207–8) also belatedly realised that the policy also involved maintaining an indignant public position to the contrary.

The US negotiating position may have appeared to contain a commitment to a return to the par value. But throughout this period the lack of US Treasury commitment was clearly visible, as was the lack of US–German policy coordination (Emminger 1977, 31–2). Those whose system had been vanquished had misread the straws in the wind. Their faith in some modified version of the status quo had persuaded them that the alternative to their own writ was quite literally unthinkable.

In the process, two sacred symbols of the post-war order, the macroeconomic pursuit of full employment and the regime of fixed exchange rates, were jettisoned and replaced by monetary targeting. Friedman's (1953, Chapter 1) methodology of positive economics nominated predictive success as the criterion of reliable science. Using that methodology, Friedman (1968b) successfully predicted that microeconomic forces would increase unemployment as inflation rose. Since the success of this prediction had taken his opponents by surprise, this increased the attractiveness of Friedman's framework of analysis and enhanced the status of the natural rate of unemployment model. With respect to the subject matter of this essay, Friedman (1965, 179) also predicted that 'the Emperor is naked'. In reply, Edward Bernstein (1965, 182), a member of President Johnson's Advisory Committee on International Monetary Policy, and the Director of the IMF Research and Statistics Department, 'predict[ed] that Mr Friedman is going to be pleasantly surprised by the survival power of the present international monetary system'. Again, it was Friedman who, in this instance, appeared entitled to don the mantle of predictive accuracy.

Shultz and Dam (1977a, 127–8; 1977b, 143) later reflected on the 'gamesmanship' inherent in price-fixing arrangements: 'It is a continual process of interplay and interrelation through which those who control develop ways of doing whatever it is they really want to do.' With respect to the international monetary system, they recalled that 'from the outset we envisaged the road to reform as consisting of two lanes: the one of negotiations and the other of reality'. The defenders of the par value system relished travelling along the lane of negotiation largely oblivious to the realities of the lane that was being travelled by their flexible rate opponents. When those travelling along the negotiation lane realised that their destination all along had been a 'flexible market system' that was 'a bitter pill for some to swallow'.

Friedman (1965, 181) concluded that the 'political aspect of the monetary arrangements is the ghost that haunts the discussion. It needs to be brought out into the open.' Friedman (1968a, 3) described himself as 'an amateur political scientist' and his interest in flexible exchange rates was 'a minor avocation rather than a vocation'.[2] This study has described the process by which this self-proclaimed amateur constructed and disseminated an argument which over the course of a quarter of a century, became the effective organising principle for the international monetary system and provided the necessary precondition for the domestic monetary revolution that followed.

Notes

2 The Combatants

1 In a letter to Abraham Hirsch (5 December 1983). George Stigler Papers, Box 8, Friedman file.

2 Friedman (correspondence to the author, 1 September 2002) suspects that I have overemphasised his role:

> So far as my role is concerned, you make it appear much more deliberate and planned than I regard it as having been. The invisible hand not the master planner was at work.... I would like to believe that I played as important a role as you assign to me, but I cannot persuade myself that I did. If I were that good, I would have finished the job by getting rid of the IMF.

3 In a speech on the occasion of Friedman's retirement from Chicago. George Stigler Papers, Box 8, Friedman file. This unofficial 'position' may account, in part, for Friedman's remarkable generosity in patiently responding to his numerous correspondents (some of whom were reacting to his newspaper articles). Academics sometimes write books for 'the educated layperson'; but how many Nobel Prize winners are prepared to provide individual correspondence courses to newspaper readers (some of whom were clearly not well informed about basic economics)? Friedman's explanation (conversation, 9 November 2000) is that 'If someone has taken the time to write to me, then I feel that I should take the time to write back to them.'

4 Like Irving Fisher, Friedman (1987, 651) had a high regard for Simon Newcomb: 'a truly renaissance man'. Fisher (1922) dedicated *The Purchasing Power of Money* to 'the memory' of Newcomb.

5 Friedman's private office, Correspondence, George Shultz file, not yet processed into the Archives.

6 Arnold Weber, a Chicago professor, was an assistant OMB director (Safire 1975, 521). By 1973, Weber was at Carnegie Mellon.

7 During his time in the Nixon administration, Laffer became embroiled in controversy at Chicago by claiming to have fully completed his Stanford thesis. An 'Ad Hoc Committee on Arthur Laffer' concluded (2 June 1971) that

> Laffer became an assistant and then an associate professor without fulfilling the known requirements for these appointments and at a very minimum permitted misunderstandings favourable to himself to persist. We consider this conduct deplorable.... This cloud of suspicion, whether of judgement or character, introduces a serious impairment of Laffer's value to the University of Chicago.

This conclusion was stronger than that reported on the front page of the *Los Angeles Times* (22 March 1985) in which the Committee was supposed to have found Laffer guilty of nothing more than 'carelessness'. George Stigler Papers, Box 10, Laffer file.

8 Burns Papers, Box N41, Presidential, Outgoing, R.M. Nixon.

9 George Stigler Papers, Supplementary Box, Milton Friedman file.

10 James's book is, in other respects, very useful. Chapter 5 contains sections on 'The Clash of Ideas', 'The Sociology of Politics' and 'The Politics of the International System' but in the context of development issues not exchange rate issues.

3 Full Employment, Free Trade and Fixed Exchange Rates

1 Brofoss, Minutes of Executive Board Meeting, 71/38, 5 May 1971, Box S123 Monetary Crisis Not Resulting in General Revaluation, 1968–July 1971, IMF Archives. See also de Vries (1976a, 628).

2 When asked by Seymour Harris (22 March 1948) to contribute a paper to the 1948 AEA meeting, Friedman (1 April 1948) replied that he would only agree if he could elaborate on his 'Framework' by posing (among others) the following question: 'What are the international implications of alternative anticyclical policies? I.e. don't all proposals to use of fiscal and monetary policy to produce internal stability logically imply free exchange rates?' Friedman Archives, Correspondence, Seymour Harris file.

3 Haberler (1961, 67) concluded that 'Needless to say, this [deflation] solution to the balance-of-payments problem is totally unacceptable nowadays.'

4 A similar logic underpins the use of tight monetary policy to target the current account deficit: in effect, destroying large sections of the domestic economy to prevent it from falling into enemy (i.e. foreign) hands. The Reserve Bank of Australia embraced and then discarded this approach in large part because of a campaign led by John Pitchford (1990).

5 The Bretton Woods Establishment

1 Bury, Executive Board Meeting, 53/91, 16 December 1953, IMF Archives.

2 Southard, Executive Board Meeting, 53/82, C/Czech/761, IMF Archives.

3 Paranagua, Executive Board Meeting, 54/47, 11 August 1954, IMF Archives. It seems likely that Czechoslovakia was deliberately being uncooperative, probably for Cold War political reasons, probably at the behest of the Soviet Union. However, the purpose of this study is not to offer a legalistic evaluation of IMF decisions but to analyse the attitudes that were revealed.

4 Box S123, Monetary Crisis Not Resulting in General Revaluation, 1968–July 1971, IMF Archives.

5 Southard, Memorandum for Files, Subject: Meeting with Under Secretary Volcker, September 24, 1969, Box S123, Monetary Crisis Not Resulting in General Revaluation, 1968–July 1971, September 25, 1969, IMF Archives. An alternative interpretation is that the IMF officials did not wish the G-10 to hijack the issue, but wanted a more inclusive examination of the issue.

6 Minutes of Executive Board Meeting, 71/38, 5 May 1971, Box S123 Monetary Crisis Not Resulting in General Revaluation, 1968–July 1971, IMF Archives.
7 Minutes of Executive Board Meeting, 71/38, 5 May 1971, Box S123 Monetary Crisis Not Resulting in General Revaluation, 1968–July 1971, IMF Archives.

6 The Early History of the Case for Floating Exchange Rates

1 In *The Case for Freedom*, Anthony Fisher (1949, 12, 27) described the law of supply and demand 'no more easily defied than the principles of Mathematics or the Law of Gravity'. Fisher preferred gold over paper money, and described the British fixed exchange rate as 'disastrous...if a currency is "freed" so too must be its value'. In 1955, Fisher (1974, 104) founded the Institute of Economic Affairs whose first publication was entitled *The Free Convertibility of Sterling*. According to Alfred Sherman, without the IEA 'there would have been no Thatcher revolution. They prepared the ground. They were the John the Baptist of the 1950s and 1960s – *pace* Enoch Powell – the voice crying in the wilderness' (cited by Ranelagh 1991, 198).
2 Likewise, Christopher McMahon (1964, 60) explained that 'in principle' there was 'much to be said' for floating rates; but 'to float would be to act in defiance of all that has been developed in the way of international monetary co-operation since the war'.
3 Hansen's (1948, 379) doubts 'related to serious questioning that, in many if not most cases, a deficit in the balance of payments can be cured by a change in the exchange rate. I do not deny, however, that along with other measures a change in the exchange rate may, in certain specific cases, help.' Earlier, in his analysis of 'The International Monetary Situation', Hansen (1936, 26–7, 36) warned of an impending devaluation of the French franc caused by the widening disparity between French and foreign costs that would inevitably follow from the concessions made to labour by the newly elected Popular Front government. Hansen cautioned that if the franc were 'permitted to fluctuate according to uncontrolled market forces' this would have 'deadly consequences upon the current world situation. England and the United States would be particularly vulnerable.' Fortunately, he concluded, it was 'the opinion of leading responsible authorities in France and elsewhere that the...method of freely fluctuating exchanges will...very definitely not be adopted'. Hansen concluded on an apocalyptic note: 'Will the continued pressure for huge governmental expenditures finally bankrupt the capitalist system?' Shortly afterwards, Hansen underwent an intellectual transformation and became 'the American Keynes' (Barber 1987; Leeson forthcoming). By 1939, the 'Hansen ideology' was associated with a permanent role for large-scale government expenditures (Crawford 1939). But there was much greater continuity with respect to Hansen's aversion to floating exchange rates.
4 George Stigler Papers, Supplementary Box, Friedman file.
5 Friedman Archives, Correspondence, John Davenport file.
6 Friedman (27 March 1964) wrote to John Davenport at *Fortune* explaining that 'I see no possibility whatsoever of moving towards the world of freer

trade and less restrictions except under the protective umbrella of floating exchange rates'. Friedman Archives, Correspondence, John Davenport file.

7 Unlike Hayek, the inspiration behind the Mont Pelerin Society, who followed the breakdown of the Bretton Woods system so loosely that when asked to write a Foreword for William Simon's *A Time for Truth* he was apparently unaware that the author had been US Treasury Secretary for three years. Hayek (1978, xv) appeared to think that holding such a position was inconceivable for someone with Chicagoan or libertarian credentials and that the writings of such an office holder were of little or no interest to him: 'How a man with his views could ever have become U.S. Secretary of the Treasury is still something of a puzzle to me.' Simon's predecessor as US Treasury Secretary was Shultz, Hayek's Chicago colleague.

8 Both Machlup and Haberler were 'close disciples' of Ludwig von Mises (Hayek 1967 [1951], 198). Machlup met Friedman and Stigler during a visit to Chicago in 1933 (Stigler 1988, 25).

7 An Emerging Academic Consensus

1 G. Gordon Liddy (1980, 170–1, 239, 371) hated the 'Beautiful People' and planned to launch 'an undeclared war…for the President' (he also acquired forged Treasury authorisation to carry a gun). This war escalated after June 1971, when the Supreme Court allowed the *Washington Post* to publish the leaked Pentagon Papers. Nixon did not take this judicial defeat well and demanded that a 'Plumber's' unit be established to plug any future leaks. Nixon (1978, 512–13) 'wanted someone to light a fire under the FBI in its investigations of [Daniel] Ellsberg' whom Nixon believed had stolen the papers. Nixon also wanted to get hold of sensitive information that he thought was being held at the Brookings Institution: an academic research organisation that he wanted to 'smash' (Ambrose 1989, 448; Summers 2001, 385–9). Nixon (1978, 512) made it clear that he wanted the material returned 'right now – even if it meant having to get it surreptitiously'. Liddy therefore targeted the Brookings for fire bombing (Dean 1976, 45, 316; Woodward and Bernstein 1976, 324–5; Kutler 1997, 6, 8). Liddy (1980, 225–6, 276, 438) planned to acquire an authentic-looking fire engine so that a group of Cubans (later of Watergate infamy) could imitate fire fighters while 'calmly loading the "rescued" material into a van'. Who knows what might have happened had Liddy been disturbed in this operation by Dillon, who was Chairman of the Board of Trustees of the Brookings Institution, or anyone else for that matter. Liddy appeared to have been obsessed with killing his 'enemies'. His first thought on being left alone with John Dean was to interpret the pencil lying on the desk as a coded instruction from someone in authority to kill: 'In a second I could drive it up through the underside of his jaw, through the soft palate and deep into his brain.' Had the fire bombing taken place Nixon could have been driven from office for covering up the Brookings scandal. As it happened it was Liddy's bungled operation GEMSTONE which lit that particular fuse.

2 Friedman initially accepted membership of the Study Group but regretted 'exceedingly' that he was unable to eventually attend (Friedman 1965, 178; Machlup *et al.* 1964, 11).

8 1966: Four Conferences

1 Friedman (13 December 1965) explained in a letter to Fellner that signing the statement represented 'very much an exception to my general policy which is to sign nothing in the nature of joint statements. However, this seems to me a clearly exceptional case both because in terms of the importance of the issue and the public misunderstanding of the position of economists about it.' Friedman Archives, Correspondence, William Fellner file.

2 The CEA report was 'not a scientific discussion. It was...a political discussion' (Friedman 1967, 135).

9 1967: the AEA President versus the AFA President

1 Loose leaf attached to Friedman and Roosa (1967).

2 Roosa also recalled that the 'frustrated' Kennedy economists were 'continually being reminded that the balance-of-payments position prevented all-out efforts for their own programs'. The external constraint was regarded not as 'warts on the economic body, quite unrelated to its own functioning' but as 'a kind of mirror, reflecting whether or not the home economy itself was functioning in a sustainable way within the limits of its own resources'.

3 When asked in 1962 by a Russian about the price of gold, Per Jacobsson explained that he was a Marxian on the issue. After offering some witticism about the current price being the proper price because it reflected the cost of production he confided to his diary: 'There was laughter!! When they left the Russians asked me to visit Moscow. I would be well received' (Jacobsson 1979, 393).

4 The threat of competitive depreciation was 'a false issue...a herring'. In the 1930s, the floating countries 'got out of the depression first'. But the analogy with the Depression was misplaced: 'There is no mileage to be gained from competitive depreciation by anyone in a world of reasonably full employment' (Friedman 1967, 90–1).

5 Friedman (1967, 185): 'Do you deny that the market will set a price?' Roosa: 'I deny that an actual market will exist.' Friedman: 'You deny that a market will exist in exchange?' Roosa: 'I do, yes.'

10 From Academia to Washington

1 He thought that most economists would still not favour completely floating rates.

2 Friedman Archives, Correspondence, Fritz Machlup file.

3 Friedman Archives, Correspondence, Fritz Machlup file.

4 The editor of *The Times* William Rees-Mogg (1977) published an IEA paper on *Democracy and the Value of Money: the Theory of Money from Locke to Keynes* which was highly sympathetic to monetarist conclusions.

5 In January 1969, a 'confrontation between academic economists and practitioners' resulted in Friedman and Roosa drawing up two alternative agendas for a further conference. Roosa (1970, 53, 56) acknowledged that the choice now lay between 'one or more of the new approaches'. In the first decade of

convertibility there had been a 'bias' towards fixity; the second decade required 'a presumption' in favour of greater flexibility 'with the objective of dissolving political stalemates' associated with the resistance to adjust rates.

6 At the March 1970 Madrid conference, fixed rate advocates were so much on the intellectual defensive that they were obliged to produce a positive 'case' as Friedman had done when in a minority in 1953 (Johnson and Swoboda 1973, 18).

11 Flexible Exchange Rates as a Vehicle for Nixon's Re-election

1 The non-dissenting members were Fellner, Haberler, Hendrik Houthakker, Herbert Prochnow, William Schmidt, Henry Wallich and Thomas Willett. The dissenting statement was not included in the final report.

2 Friedman Archives, Correspondence, Peter Flanigan file.

3 Friedman Archives, Correspondence, Bryce Harlow file.

4 Just six years earlier, Houthakker (1962, 304) informed the Joint Economic Committee that it was 'not up to academic economists to strike a balance between the pros and cons of exchange rate adjustment'.

5 Burns Papers, Box A29, Treasury (15).

12 The Cross of Gold

1 Nixon's staff pondered about the rhetorical impact of the NEP. The idea that the 90-day freeze should be extended by 10 days simply to mimic FDR's 100 days was rejected on historical analogy grounds: the phrase 'hundred days' originally measured the time between Napoleon's escape from exile in Elba to his ultimate defeat at Waterloo. But with respect to the associations attached to the NEP, Safire (1975, 523, 525) recalled that he 'had a nagging feeling it was not original, but I could not pinpoint my objection. It turned out to be Lenin's slogan.'

2 At a September 1971 bilateral meeting in Chicago it appeared that the Japanese would accept a maximum of 8–10 per cent revaluation of the yen (CIEP memo 25 September 1971, Burns Papers Box B24 CIEP 1). Three months later at the Smithsonian meeting, the Japanese persuaded Connally (who had been hit by one of the bullets aimed at President Kennedy in 1963) to accept a 16.88 per cent revaluation of the yen rather than the 17 per cent proposed because the Finance Minister who agreed to a 17 per cent devaluation in 1930 had been assassinated (Volcker and Gyohten 1992, 97). Connally told other Finance Ministers that he feared that Mikio Mizuta, the Japanese Finance Minister, might commit hara-kiri if pressed to revalue further (James 1996, 237).

3 Burns Papers, Box B52, Gold 1971–2 (1).

4 Friedman's private office, Correspondence, George Shultz file, not yet processed into the Archives.

5 Burns instructed Ralph Wood to investigate whether there was any truth in Friedman's assertion in *Newsweek* (16 August 1971) that in 1933 private US holders of gold 'were required to turn their gold over to the U.S. Treasury at

$20.67 an ounce when the market price was well above this sum'. Wood (2 March 1972) reported to Burns that Friedman's charge 'seems to be a gross distortion of the facts'. Burns Papers, Box B52, Gold 1971–2 (1).

13 Price and Wage Regulation, Exchange Rate Deregulation

1 Burns was referring to President Kennedy's budgetary practices.
2 James Callaghan was in the audience for Friedman's lecture. Callaghan's 1976 denouncement of Keynesian economics may have been influenced by Friedman via his son-in-law Peter Jay (Cockett 1995, 100, 187).
3 George Stigler Papers, Supplementary Box, Friedman file.
4 Burns Papers, Box A1, AFL-CIO.
5 Memo to Burns from Alexander Christie, legislative consultant. Burns Papers, Box A1, AFL-CIO.
6 'Nixon and Burns Spar Amiably at Swearing-In Rites'. Freedom and Union, March 1970: 7.
7 The economists were described as 'technicians' and (presumably reflecting the new administration's cost-cutting emphasis) were informed that they would have to purchase their own lunch. Burns Papers, Box A29, Treasury (12) and (14).
8 ABC Issues and Answers. Burns Papers, Box A12, Interviews.
9 Burns Papers, Box A12, Interviews (2).
10 Burns Papers, Box A28, Treasury (5).
11 Burns Papers, Box B100, Treasury, November–December 1970.
12 Burns Papers, Box B59, Incomes Policy 1970.
13 Robert Solomon (21 October 1970) sent Burns a State Department summary of a speech by Sir Leslie O'Brien, Governor of the Bank of England, calling for 'a long run incomes policy based on general consent'. Burns Papers, Box B59, Incomes Policy 1970.
14 13 January 1973, Burns Papers, Box B90, Prices and Wages.
15 Burns Papers, Box B23, CEA 1970.
16 Burns Papers, Box B90, Price and Wage Control.
17 Burns to Nixon (1 May 1974) Burns Papers, Box B89, Nixon meetings.
18 Burns Papers, Box A12, Interviews.
19 Burns Papers, Box A12, Interviews.
20 'Strictly Confidential' memo, Grimwold to Burns, Burns Papers, Box B90, Price and Wage Control.
21 Burns Papers, Box B90, Prices and Wages (1).
22 Burns (28 December 1972) sent Shultz a copy of an earlier letter about the decision to increase the salary of departmental head while keeping Fed salaries fixed: 'monetary policy had become completely immobilised and was regarded by the Keynesians as having little or no significance'. Burns Papers, Box B101, Treasury November–December 1972.
23 Burns Papers, Box B9, Press Clippings June–December 1971, dated 'received July 30 1971'. The same report also noted that Agnew had previously tried to set up the press as a scapegoat.
24 Burns Papers, Box B9, Press Clippings June–December 1971.
25 Burns Papers, Box B100, Treasury April–July 1971.

26 In a March 1958 speech at the University of Chicago, Burns supported a permanent $5 billion tax cut (Stein 1969, 335).
27 At a press conference (21 March 1972) the President's press officer Ron Ziegler expressed great sensitivity about the prospect of increased interest rates: 'we are not pursuing a policy – we are not pursuing a policy – that would lead to increased interest rates'. Asked if Burns was 'in the same boat with you' Ziegler responded: 'that is what the Wage–Price Board is about; that is what the Committee on Interest Rates and Dividends headed by Dr. Burns is about, and that is to see that the interest rates don't rise in this country'. Burns Papers, Box B90, Prices and Wages.
28 Friedman Archives, Correspondence, Homer Jones file.

14 The Nature and Origins of Friedman's Influence

1 This was how Mundell (to Friedman 29 May 1967) interpreted Friedman's advocacy: 'you are writing to three audiences – the public, economists and Roosa'. Friedman Archives, Correspondence, Robert Mundell file.
2 *Newshour* 19 November 2001, Pentagon press conference. In retrospect, it appears that this strategy did not achieve its stated objectives.
3 Patinkin Papers, Box 27.
4 Friedman continued: 'If you or I were in charge of one of those economies and had to operate with rigid exchange rates under present conditions I very much fear we would use direct controls over trade too. There was some sentiment for flexible exchange rates but not enough in high places.' (Friedman dated the letter 1950, but 1951 is a more plausible date.) Friedman (16 September 1961) told Stigler that 'Berlin I fear is gone, the Congo is on the way and Algeria is next. Can we be far behind?' George Stigler Papers, Supplementary Box, Friedman file.
5 Friedman (5 December 1983) informed Abraham Hirsch that one of the most important influences that Wesley Mitchell exerted upon him was 'his emphasis on the distinction that John Neville Keynes made between positive and normative'. Friedman also recalled 'I have not done any serious work in the field of methodology – frankly, either before or since writing the essay on the methodology of positive economics'. He concluded that 'What Mitchell was interested in was not theory as such but rather the sociology of knowledge.' George Stigler Papers, Box 8, Friedman file.
6 While at Columbia in 1964–65, Friedman as economic adviser to Presidential candidate Goldwater, found himself to be in great demand to speak to academics, the media and the financial community because there were, apparently, very few New York intellectuals who would speak on Goldwater's behalf. The six weeks prior to the election were a 'blur of one meeting or interview or talk after another'. But Friedman was 'appalled' at what he found:

> There was an unbelievable degree of intellectual homogeneity, of acceptance of a standard set of views complete with cliché answers to every objection, of smug self-satisfaction at belonging to an in-group.... To exaggerate only slightly, they had never talked to anyone who really believed, and had thought deeply about, views drastically different from their own (Friedman and Friedman 1998, 370–1).

7 Aaron Director assisted in the preparation of the *Wartime Control of Prices* 'until the research had been substantially complete' and 'greatly aided' the project by discussing 'almost every portion of the work' (Nourse 1940, vii).

8 The Brookings report concluded that 'it is obvious that price controls must be imposed at the spots where the price advances begin'. What was required was 'the development of co-ordinated administrative machinery'. The project began with a discussion of the price mechanism: 'even under normal peacetime conditions we no longer place exclusive reliance upon an unregulated price and profit mechanism'. Wartime price controls had to be integrated with other anti-inflation policies: 'The proper standard of both credit and fiscal policy, if a war is to be fought without inflation, is...the movement of the price level.' This was inappropriate under peacetime conditions because other factors such as 'the volume of employment' had also to guide policy. But under wartime conditions 'we see no better criterion of the need for an increase or a decrease in the supply of bank credit than the movement of the price level'. But they explained, 'we are not arguing for the classical quantity of money which would explain the causal relationship as running entirely from the monetary situation to the price situation'. Instead, a cost-push mechanism was postulated. A 'labor agency should have full control' to ensure 'coordination of policy.... Control of wages presents, in a democratic country, the most difficult problem in the whole field of selective price control', in part because 'the monopoly power of labor organisations enters into the determination of public policy'. Wage rises reflected this trade union power and collective bargaining had become a 'quasi-legislative process'. Such wage increases were a

> matter of grave concern to the public, because of the irresistible pressure they create for price increases to cover them. A substantial drive on the part of labor organisations towards a general increase in wages in advance of a corresponding rise in other parts of national income, such as occurred in 1937, would wreck any plans for waging a war without inflation (Hardy 1940, 14, 17, 42–3, 74, 78–9, 93).

9 Viner (1942, 687, 689, 692, 701, 702) advocated discretion rather than rules and inflation control was not discussed in terms of monetary policy: 'effective prevention of inflation requires tax and direct control measures...this excess of civilian spending power must in one way or another be tapped by the Treasury or frozen into immobility by direct controls; otherwise the possibility of inflation will be unlimited'. Increased taxation was 'the most obvious method'. Forced savings were also required. But if they did not 'quite suffice to keep the over-all price ceiling intact, a little more *ad hoc* application of taxation, a little more *ad hoc* application of direct control, should remedy the deficiency. A genuine freezing of the wage structure, however, must be included in the direct controls.' Freezing wages had significantly contributed to the 'apparently very complete success of the Canadian ceiling'.

10 In 'How to Ration Consumers' Goods and Control Their Prices', Wallis (1942, 502, 512) explained how to 'prevent inflation and facilitate economic mobilization'. With respect to the 'inflationary gap', Wallis concluded that

'To rely on the normal operation of the price system during the war' would encourage

> further injustices in the distribution of goods, aggravating the inflationary movement.... A system of total-expenditure rationing, coupled with a steeply progressive tax on all expenditures in excess of the basic ration, would be enormously superior to the devices now being inaugurated, because it would...effectively prevent inflation.

11 As Friedman (correspondence to the author, 1 September 2002) correctly points out, this is pure speculation. However, Friedman's response ('pure conjecture. Gives misleading impression') may also reveal a certain sensitivity to this possibility. Friedman was criticised for his wartime involvement in the introduction of income tax withheld at source. Murray Rothbard (1971, 3, 4) described him as the 'Establishment's Court Libertarian.... In many ways we have Milton Friedman to thank for the present monster Leviathan State in America.' His wife was also critical: 'Rose has repeatedly chided me over the years about the role I played in making possible the current overgrown government we both criticise. That is in jest, since withholding would have been introduced had I been involved or not. The most I accept blame for is helping to make it more efficient than it otherwise might have been.' However, Friedman felt that he had contributed towards a system that was 'too intrusive, too destructive of freedom' (Friedman and Friedman 1998, 123). Had he also contributed towards the establishment of the par value system, this would have been another blemish on his Chicagoan libertarian credentials.
12 The Stiglers first met while staying at the International House in Chicago; the Friedmans first met in Jacob Viner's Economics 301 (Stigler 1988, 28; Friedman and Friedman 1998, 1).
13 Friedman Archives, Correspondence, W. Allen Wallis file.
14 Homer Jones Papers, Box 2.
15 In 1965, Stigler organised Knight's eightieth birthday party. Ed Levi (11 November 1969) reported to Stigler that Knight did not want a memorial service after he died: 'He said he had one funeral here on his 80th birthday.' Knight died on 15 April 1972. On 24 May, at the memorial service that Knight had not wished for, Wallis explained that 'we are gathered not for him but for us'. George Stigler Papers, Box 10.
16 Burstein continued: Upon being told this Harberger exclaimed: 'then why cannot they understand each other'. Patinkin Papers, Box 2.
17 Eisenhower was President of Columbia prior to becoming US President. He recruited Burns as his CEA Chairman (Stigler 1988, 42–3).
18 Schultz apparently exerted an important influence on the Chicago department. When Friedman became AEA President-elect, Schultz (15 March 1965) promptly assessed the department's record relative to Harvard: 'Yesterday, running down the list of former presidents, I was suddenly struck that no one from Chicago had been president of the association prior to 1934...since then, with your election, there will have been seven, running Harvard a see-saw race since that date.' Schultz explained that he was looking forward to Friedman's 'presidential address which will become a classic!' Friedman Archives, Correspondence, Theodore Schultz file.

19 Friedman Archives, Correspondence, W. Allen Wallis file.
20 George Stigler Papers, Supplementary Box, Burns Correspondence.
21 There is no exact date on the letter, only 'Friday'. Friedman Archives, Correspondence, Aaron Director file.
22 George Stigler Papers, Supplementary Box, Friedman file.
23 Friedman Archives, Correspondence, George Stigler file.
24 Friedman Archives, Correspondence, W. Allen Wallis file.
25 Simons (1935, 1421) wrote of the 'strange human behavior induced latterly by the combination of economic depression and the California climate'.
26 George Stigler Papers, Box 9, Harry Johnson file.
27 George Stigler Papers, Box 8, Milton Friedman file.
28 In this instance, Friedman was referring to Johnson's review of Friedman and Schwartz (1963). Friedman considered replying 'preceded of course by some hypocritical drivel about how ungrateful it is for me to comment on a review so fulsome in its praise etc etc.... I should appreciate very much your judgement and advice, both on the intellectual issue and on the tactical one.' George Stigler Papers, Box 8, Milton Friedman file.
29 Burns Papers, Box B81, Money Supply 1970–71.
30 Burns Papers, Review of the Advice of the Academic Consultants. 24 January 1969, Box A10, Federal Reserve System (1).
31 Burns Papers, Box B60, Incomes Policy 1971.
32 Correspondence to the author, 27 October 2001.

15 Intellectuals

1 Correspondence to the author from Graeme Dorrance, 8 August 2001; see also Goodwin (1998, 6).
2 Correspondence to the author, 8 August 2001.
3 Thus Johnson may, in effect, have self-sabotaged his attempt to obtain a chair at the LSE in the late 1950s. In consequence, Johnson (possibly at Harberger's suggestion) sought and obtained a chair at Chicago.
4 Robbins was referring to an exchange of letters in *The Economist* between Friedman and Richard Kahn. Friedman Archives, Correspondence, Lionel Robbins file.
5 Friedman Archives, Correspondence, Lionel Robbins file.
6 Friedman Archives, Correspondence, Lionel Robbins file.
7 Friedman Archives, Correspondence, Lionel Robbins file.
8 After a brief visit to the LSE in autumn 1950, Friedman (15 January 1951) asked Stigler whether he should go or not: 'We spent a couple of days at the London School which we enjoyed no end. It's a real interesting place. Robbins wants to know if I would come over for part or all of next year if it could be arranged. Should I think of it seriously?' George Stigler Papers, Supplementary Box, Friedman file.
9 Friedman Archives, Correspondence, Lionel Robbins file.
10 Conversation with Graeme Dorrance, 19 October 2000. Friedman (15 November 1950) reported to Stigler that in a conversation he had just had in Paris, Robbins 'sounded terribly like an apologist for the labor government'. George Stigler Papers, Supplementary Box, Friedman file.

11 Friedman Archives, Correspondence, Lionel Robbins file.
12 Friedman Archives, Correspondence, Lionel Robbins file.
13 Friedman Archives, Correspondence, Lionel Robbins file.
14 Friedman Archives, Correspondence, Lionel Robbins file.
15 However, Powell was not quite a monetarist in 1957. In December 1957, three weeks after his resignation, Powell (1969 [1957], 189, 190) declared that 'What is clear is that our contemporary monetary system lends itself more readily than those of earlier periods to action by government [and others] which results in debasement of the currency.' Powell advocated 'restraint in public expenditure [and private consumption]'. When his speech was reprinted in 1969 brackets were put round 'and others' and around 'and private consumption' because they 'reflect a conventional view which…the author came to reject'. By September 1966, Powell (1969 [1966], 172, 174) attributed the entire blame for inflation on 'the real culprits, the politicians' and denied that trade unions could cause rising prices.
16 Powell (1969 [1968], 289) declared that 'As I look ahead, I am filled with foreboding. Like the Romans, I seem to see "the river Tiber foaming with much blood".' Powell continued: 'those whom the gods wish to destroy they first make mad. We must be mad, literally mad' (cited by Wilson 1974, 663). In 1972, Powell 'with the appearance of a madman' horrified Mont Pelerin members by opposing a mark of respect for the Israeli athletes who had just been massacred at the Munich Olympics (Friedman and Friedman 1998, 335).
17 In 1980, Heath used a radio broadcast to launch 'a vitriolic and libellous attack' on the Thatcher advisers including Friedman (Friedman and Friedman 1998, 390–1). In 1978, the Institute of Economic Affairs arranged for Friedman to dine with Mrs Thatcher. The meeting was apparently very productive (Cockett 1995, 173–4).
18 Friedman Archives, Correspondence, John Kenneth Galbraith file.
19 Burns Papers, Box B23, CEA 1970.
20 Friedman Archives, Correspondence, Kenneth Arrow file.
21 Rose Friedman (21 December 1972) sent Burns a letter saying how 'comforting it's been to talk to you', indicating how personal closeness could coexist with intense intellectual disagreements. Burns Papers, Container K 12(1), Friedman file.
22 Friedman Archives, Correspondence, Kenneth Arrow file.
23 George Stigler Papers, Supplementary Box, Friedman file. Stigler (1988, 169) speculated that Samuelson (together with Solow and Tobin who also received offers from Chicago) declined 'largely because they felt they would be immersed in an alien intellectual environment'.
24 This appears to be a retrospective reconstruction rather than Samuelson's actual reply to the offer.
25 George Stigler Papers, Supplementary Box, Friedman file.
26 During the 1968 campus protests, Friedman's lectures were interrupted. Rudi Dornbusch (2000) recalled that Friedman informed the invaders that they were 'interfering with the freedom and choice to learn; moreover, not having registered, they were not even free to stay quietly. Amazingly, in hindsight, the protesters left, and our insular clique went on experiencing the quantity theory of money.'

27 Friedman (correspondence to the author, 13 February 2001) denies there was any truth about this oral tradition with respect to the Second World War, although the suggestion may have been made with respect to the Korean War. Stigler (1988, 61) received a note from Tjalling Koopmans asking whether he was the author of the oral tradition which asserted that use of the price mechanism was the optimal evacuation process for Manhattan in the event of a bomb attack.

16 US Senators

1 Friedman Archives, Correspondence, Paul Douglas file.
2 George Stigler Papers, Box 8, Milton Friedman file.
3 Douglas (1966, 325, 338) doubted that flexible exchange rates would be adopted in 'either the immediate or intermediate future' because it appeared 'too dangerous to adopt'.
4 Friedman Archives, Correspondence, Paul Douglas file.
5 Friedman Archives, Correspondence, Barry Goldwater file.
6 Friedman Archives, Correspondence, Barry Goldwater file.
7 Friedman Archives, Correspondence, Barry Goldwater file.
8 Friedman Archives, Correspondence, Barry Goldwater file.
9 Friedman Archives, Correspondence, Barry Goldwater file.
10 George Stigler Papers, Box 12, Robbins file.
11 Friedman Archives, Correspondence, Barry Goldwater file.
12 Friedman Archives, Correspondence, Barry Goldwater file.
13 For example, Goldwater (9 November 1978) sent Friedman a telegram: 'Would appreciate receiving information as soon as possible on what the economic effects would be if this country went back on the gold standard and what your suggestions would be in taking that step. My interest is wrapped around a speech I am doing on gold.' Sometimes (for example, 10 February 1978), Goldwater would simply send Friedman a copy of a speech made by the Senator along with the request that 'I would appreciate having your comments on this speech, and thanks for your cooperation.' Friedman Archives, Correspondence, Barry Goldwater file.
14 Burns Papers, Box B23, CEA 1972.
15 Friedman Archives, Correspondence, Barry Goldwater file.
16 Friedman sent a blind carbon copy of his letter to Edward C. Banfield, a professor of politics at Chicago and a close personal friend (Friedman Archives, Correspondence, Barry Goldwater file; Friedman and Friedman 1998, 185). Reviewing *Capitalism and Freedom,* Banfield (1962, 401) wrote that 'Once in the clutch of Friedman's logic, the most reluctant reader will find it difficult, if not impossible, to escape his conclusions.' Had he been reviewing the book for a journal other than the *National Review,* Banfield would have sought to 'try to entice the reader into his clutch'. Banfield headed Nixon's 1968 Task Force on Urban Affairs and by 1972, his *The Unheavenly City: the Nature and Future of Our Urban Crisis* (1970) had sold 100,000 copies and was closely associated with the revival of the libertarian right (Nash 1976, 329, 432, n. 51).

17 Friedman advised Goldwater on a variety of levels. In *The Conscience of a Conservative*, Goldwater (1960, 68, 72) stated that 'Socialism-through-Welfarism poses a far greater danger to freedom than Socialism-through-Nationalisation precisely because it is more difficult to combat.' The antidote, Goldwater argued, was that 'the government must begin to *withdraw* from a whole series of programs that are outside its constitutional mandate – from social welfare programs' and a host of 'other activities that can be better performed by lower levels of government or by private institutions or by individuals'. During the 1964 New Hampshire primary this led to a newspaper headline 'Goldwater to Destroy Social Security'; a headline which was reproduced and sent to every social security recipient in the state by Rockefeller supporters (Goldwater 1979, 167–8). During the Presidential election campaign, social security was the issue on which the Democrats 'chose to hook and hang' Goldwater (White 1965, 360). The Friedmans remained 'glued to the radio' during the Republican convention in July 1964 (Friedman and Friedman 1998, 368). On 11 October 1964, three weeks before the final poll, Friedman sought to minimise the damage to Goldwater's candidacy. In 'The Goldwater View of Economics', Friedman (1964, 135) explained that Goldwater 'recognises that the Federal Government must stand by in case of need to assure that the floor is truly there and truly universal. That, in his view, is the prime purpose of Social Security.' Shortly before his retirement Goldwater (7 April 1975) wrote to Friedman explaining that he had been pondering about his political legacy, and not wishing to 'sort of fade away' had come to the conclusion that 'it is time that I advocate the end to Social Security'. Friedman (19 May 1975) advised Goldwater that it 'would not be wise to undertake that particular crusade as your final parting shot in the public arena'. Friedman Archives, Correspondence, Barry Goldwater file.

18 Friedman Archives, Correspondence, Barry Goldwater file. Friedman's influence extended to Congressman Barry Goldwater Jr. (14 March 1973) who wrote to Friedman asking for help 'with a presentation of arguments against the creation of a Consumer Protection Agency...you seem to have a simplistic way of explaining these truths...the time spent on this request might very well educate a disciple and help the understanding of the concept by one political editor'. Friedman Archives, Correspondence, Barry Goldwater Jr. file.

17 The International Policemen

1 Not only were the Bretton Woods veterans among the first of the international jetsetters, they also floated on the 'gilded surface of Washington'. Jacobsson, in his capacity as IMF Managing Director, 'could have gone to several cocktail parties each evening and always had a choice of dinner parties'. He loved dancing and insisted that the IMF annual meeting should always end with a formal dance. He also 'liked to have ladies around' and expected husbands to take as a compliment the attention he paid to their wives. In these social gatherings, judgements were made about the 'quality' of the people invited. It took Jacobsson three years to 'get the Christmas

party the way he wanted' (Jacobsson 1979, 314, 316, 327, 330). He objected that the New York Fed only served iced water, but not wine, with lunch (Coombs 1976, 23).

2 These threats may have partially succeeded. Nixon's speechwriter was convinced that for Volcker the Bretton Woods Agreement was 'sacrosanct' (Safire 1975, 518). Certainly, Volcker decided that when he needed a precise calculation of the extent of the 'fundamental disequilibrium' of the dollar in 1970, it was unsafe to discuss the matter with anyone except a socially gauche economist who would remain 'quiet'. He was persuaded of the overriding importance of maintaining an international 'framework for cooperation, both institutional and personal' (Volcker and Gyohten 1992, 72, 78).

3 In a speech on the occasion of Friedman's retirement from Chicago, Stigler stated that he had never known Friedman

> to lose an argument, although in one or two cases I dream that I almost got a draw. Let me advise you on how to conduct yourself if you ever have the misfortune to debate with Milton. He will begin by asking you to grant, say, three assumptions: 1. $2 is better than $1; 2. the law of diminishing returns; 3. Individuals do not have complete and accurate knowledge of the future. My fundamental advice is: *do not grant these assumptions*. If you do, you will find yourself led, by irresistible logic, to conclusions such as these: 1. The Federal Reserve Board should be abolished; 2. The Board of Governors of the Federal Reserve Board should be put on Social Security; 3. Social Security should be abolished.

George Stigler Papers, Box 8, Friedman file.

4 When in London, Jacobsson would first call on the Swedish Ambassador to collect the gossip, then spend three hours extemporising with the Governor of the Bank of England. Then he would ask: 'Do you think I should go and visit the Prime Minister?' He was often surrounded by obsequiousness. He courted and flattered the press, who responded in kind (Jacobsson 1979, 387, 388, 395).

5 He appeared to be especially impressed with the fact that the British contingent were a 'collection of lords and past and future knights!'

6 Stigler (1954, 14) had used this analogy to denigrate another Chicago opponent: 'Galbraith cannot persuade us that we should turn our economic problems over to Santa.' Earlier, von Mises (1949) complained that the Keynesian emphasis on aggregate expenditure was 'the Santa Claus fable raised by Lord Keynes to the dignity of an economic doctrine and enthusiastically endorsed by all those who expect personal gain from government spending'.

7 Since 1959, Friedman had been campaigning for the 'Dutch auction' method of auctioning government securities, and with Shultz as Secretary of the Treasury, Friedman was 'able to persuade them to experiment with Dutch auctions' until Simon became Secretary: 'Personalities do matter. If George Shultz had remained treasury secretary, I am persuaded that the method of auctioning securities would long ago have been drastically reformed' (Friedman and Friedman 1998, 376, 386).

18 US Treasury Secretaries

1 Halm thought that the IMF Executive Directors were offering only 'a rather feeble excuse' for the preservation of the existing system.
2 Friedman Archives, Correspondence, David Kennedy file.
3 Friedman dates this meeting with the 'newly appointed secretary of the treasury' as 'mid-1970' but this must refer to either late 1970 or early 1971.
4 Telex from Schweitzer to Herrn Kurt-Georg Kiesinger, Box S123 Monetary Crisis Not Resulting in General Revaluation, 1968–July 1971, IMF Archives.
5 Burns Papers, Box B34, Exchange Rates 1970.
6 Southard, Memorandum for files, Subject: Currency Crisis – Informal Talks with Executive Directors, May 7, 1971, IMF Archives.
7 Burns Papers, Box B65, IMF 1971 (2).
8 For two weeks after the NEP, the Japanese attempted to maintain the old yen–dollar rate by adding $4 billion to its reserves. On 28 August 1971, the Bank of Japan surrendered and allowed the yen to float (James 1996, 221).
9 Minutes of Executive Board Meeting, 71/38, 5 May 1971, Box S123 Monetary Crisis Not Resulting in General Revaluation, 1968–July 1971, IMF Archives,
10 'The Role of the Fund in the Quest for Financial Stability', Box S123, Monetary Crisis Not Resulting in General Revaluation, 1968–July 1971, IMF Archives.
11 Polak to Schweitzer, confidential memorandum, Subject: Issues for Discussion with Secretary Connally, 5 April 1971, Box S123, Monetary Crisis Not Resulting in General Revaluation, 1968–July 1971, IMF Archives.
12 Treasury Press Release, 28 May 1971, Box S123, Monetary Crisis Not Resulting in General Revaluation, 1968–July 1971, IMF Archives.
13 Burns Papers, Box B100, Treasury April–July 1971.
14 Dale, memorandum to members of the Executive Board, 9 August, 1971, Subject: Report of the Joint Economic Committee, Subcommittee on International Exchange and Payments, Box S123, Monetary Crisis: Resulting From US Economic Measures (General) August 1–16 1971, IMF Archives.
15 Burns Papers, Box B65, IMF 1971 (2).
16 Southard, Memorandum for Files, Subject: U.S. Dollar: Events of August 15, 1971, Box S123, Monetary Crisis: Resulting From US Economic Measures (General) August 1–16 1971, IMF Archives.
17 Burns Papers, Box B65, IMF 1971 (2).
18 Southard, Memorandum for files, Subject: Dollar Crisis: Meetings with Mr Ossola, August 22–23, 1971, Box S123, Monetary Crisis, August 17–31, 1971, IMF Archives.
19 National Broadcasting Company, An Interview with Dr. Pierre-Paul Schweitzer, Box S123, Monetary Crisis, August 17–31 1971, IMF Archives.
20 Schweitzer, Recorded Interview by the BBC, August 24 1971, Box S123, Monetary Crisis, August 17–31 1971, IMF Archives.
21 Schweitzer, Memorandum, Subject: Internal Security in the Fund under Present Conditions, Box S123, August 17–31, 1971, IMF Archives.
22 Southard, Memorandum for files, Subject: Dollar Crisis: Conversation with Under Secretary Volcker, Box S123, Monetary Crisis: Resulting From US Economic Measures (General) September 1971, IMF Archives.

23 Letter, Southard to Burns, 12 November 1971, Box S123, Monetary Crisis: Resulting From US Economic Measures (General) November 1971–, IMF Archives.
24 Polak, Confidential Memorandum to the files, Subject: Visit by Mr. Paul Volcker to the Managing Director, November 15, 1971, November 16, 1971, Box S123, Monetary Crisis: Resulting From US Economic Measures (General) November 1971–, IMF Archives.
25 Southard, Memorandum for files, Subject: Dollar Crisis: Conversation with Under Secretary Volcker, September 7, 1971, Box S123, Monetary Crisis: Resulting From US Economic Measures (General) September 1971, IMF Archives.
26 Polak, Confidential Memorandum to the files, Subject: Visit by Mr. Paul Volcker to the Managing Director, November 15, 1971, November 16, 1971, Box S123, Monetary Crisis: Resulting From US Economic Measures (General) November 1971–, IMF Archives.
27 *New York Times* press cutting, Box S123, Monetary Crisis: Resulting From US Economic Measures (General) August 1–16 1971, IMF Archives.
28 Friedman Archives, Correspondence, John Connally file.
29 Friedman (21 February 1989) reminded Fed Chairman, Alan Greenspan, of 'The standing invitation to "Paradise"', his Californian Sea Ranch: 'Pardon my plain speaking, but Washington is corrupting. It is hard in the midst of it to keep oneself free from the prevailing clichés.' Greenspan (13 January 1989) replied: 'Thanks for the standing invitation to "Paradise". I hope to take you and Rose up on it, at which time we can debate the deficit.' Friedman Archives, Correspondence, Alan Greenspan file.
30 Friedman Archives, Correspondence, John Connally file.
31 Burns Papers, Box B24, CIEP (1).
32 Friedman advised him not to take the job on the grounds that 'if we go to floating rates the job is not necessary, and if we don't it's impossible' (correspondence from Friedman to the author, 22 August 2002).
33 Friedman Archives, Correspondence, John Connally file.
34 Friedman Archives, Correspondence, Homer Jones file.
35 Nixon was also apprehensive about George Wallace splitting the right-wing vote by running as a third-party candidate. On 13 January 1972, the Wallace threat was neutralised when he announced he was entering the Democrat primaries. The day before, the IRS announced that it was dropping its investigation into his brother (Ambrose 1989, 455, 500, 542).
36 Various people in the Fed were not so pleased with either Shultz or Friedman. Joseph Coyne (9 April 1974), Assistant to the Board, wrote to Friedman underlining the first sentence of this quotation from his *Newsweek* column: 'The underlined portion of the above quotation about the Federal Reserve is of concern, and we would appreciate if you would provide us with evidence that you may have relating to this statement.' Burns Papers, Container K 12 (2), Friedman file.
37 Parts of the academic world, such as Harvard and the Massachusetts Institute of Technology (MIT), appeared on Nixon's list of enemies. Nixon instructed Shultz (then OMB Director) to cancel all funding for MIT: 'All money stops by Friday. I don't want a nickel to go to MIT' (cited by Summers 2001, 17). Two days after Shultz was appointed Treasury Secretary,

Nixon told Haldeman: 'I want those funds cut off for that MIT.... Slice them.' Archibald Cox was appointed as Watergate Special Prosecutor in May 1973, and rapidly became the premier villain in Nixon's eyes. Kissinger informed Nixon that Cox, his Harvard colleague, was 'a fanatic liberal Democrat and all his associates are fanatics'. President Kennedy's former Special Assistant for National Security, William McGeorge Bundy, also of Harvard, apparently claimed that the Kennedy administration did not undertake any wire-tapping. On 1 June 1973, Nixon told Kissinger that the list of those who had been tapped by Bobby Kennedy would be released 'next Thursday...Monday'. In the meantime, Nixon wanted Kissinger to 'leak it to someone.... Be sure McGeorge Bundy knows this is coming out.' Nixon instructed his Secretary of State to inform his 'liberal friends' that 'this whole business of tapping, they have, they have opened it up, they have really opened it up, because Bobby Kennedy – '. Nixon saw in his opponents a mirror image of himself self-interestedly pursuing Alger Hiss. He hoped that by threatening their self-interest he could persuade Kissinger's 'liberal friends' to call off or restrict the Watergate investigation: 'remember on this tap business, it's gonna catch some of your friends, incidentally. Cause I know some of the names...they want a brutal fight, they're gonna get one. And they're gonna get it Goddamned soon' (Kutler 1997, 39–40, 561–2, 610).

38 Vice President Agnew made several highly provocative speeches about the university community, and the administration generated unparalleled hostilities from American campuses. When Nixon welcomed home the first American prisoners of war from Vietnam, Agnew compared them to 'those sniveling Ivy Leaguers' (Ambrose 1991, 65). Shultz appeared 'groggy' after watching on television the National Guard kill four students at Kent State University (Safire 1975, 191). In contrast, Nixon expressed no sympathy to the families of the dead students (Ambrose 1989, 351).

39 Nixon appointed Johnnie Walters as IRS Commissioner: 'hand-picked for his presumed loyalty to Nixonian ideals' (Chester *et al.* 1973, 87). Within the White House an 'enemies list' was compiled of people who 'had been targeted for IRS and other government harassment'. John Dean, the President's counsel, forced Walters to take the 'enemies list' to Shultz so as to begin the harassment. Shultz refused and told Walters to do nothing with the lists (Price 1977, 232; Safire 1975, 249). Nixon instructed Shultz to 'clean the house' at the IRS, in part, because there were 'too many Jews' and to assault Ford, Brookings and other foundations that 'had been used for left wing purposes' (Ambrose 1991, 19). Ehrlichman told Nixon that Shultz was 'just touchy as hell about cooperating with us on this sort of thing'. Nixon was becoming impatient, and wanted the IRS to harass George McGovern, his 1972 Presidential opponent. Nixon reflected that 'Everyone thinks Shultz is an honest, decent man.' Haldeman asked, 'is there a way to cause him to do it externally, so that it isn't his initiative?...Can we get an external tip that gives him a rationale for doing it?' Nixon complained that 'George has got a fantasy. What is George's – what's he trying to do, say that you can't play politics with IRS?' There may have been some surreptitious assistance. According to Richard Reeves (2001, 520–1) in August 1972, it took three days for Haldeman to get hold of the tax returns of a prominent McGovern contributor, Henry Himmelman.

According to Haig, in June 1973 someone in the Treasury alerted him to a forthcoming IRS audit of Nixon's friend Bebe Rebozo. But it was never enough. Haldeman spoke about getting 'loyalists in various positions that were sensitive'. Dean explained that the IRS bureaucrats were all Democrats and would not hand over the files (Kutler 1997, 113, 115, 119, 591–2).

40 Nixon (15 September 1972) told Bob Haldeman that with respect to the IRS 'The whole Goddamn bunch is to go out. And if he doesn't do it, he's out as Secretary of the Treasury.' Shultz 'didn't get to be Secretary of the Treasury because he had nice blue eyes. It was a goddamn favor to get him the job' (Ambrose 1989, 588, 611; Kutler 1997, 119; Woodward and Bernstein 1976, 97).

41 In March 1973, Nixon (1978, 993) had been ordered by the IRS to pay $400,000 in back taxes, and he was accused of spending $17 million of public funds on his private property.

42 On the day he was fired, the Watergate Special Prosecutor, Archibald Cox, invoked the integrity of Shultz's office to resist Nixon's order to abstain from seeking more White House tapes: 'You remember when Andrew Jackson wanted to take the deposits from the Bank of America and his Secretary of the Treasury wouldn't do it. He fired him and then he appointed a new Secretary of the Treasury, and he wouldn't do it, and he fired him. And finally he got a third who would' (cited by Woodward and Bernstein 1976, 75).

43 At a Cost of Living Council press conference (13 June 1973) Shultz was asked: 'How do you reconcile this action [Phase IV] with all the economic garbage that you and Mr Stein gave against the freeze during the past few weeks? Are all of those economic arguments inoperative now?'

44 Stein (1995, 103) tried to persuade Nixon of the validity of Heraclitus' remark about not being able to 'step into the same river twice'. Nixon, anxious to stem the tide of Watergate, retorted 'Yes, you can, if it's frozen.'

45 Shultz's disillusionment with the administration was likely to have been more wide-ranging. Certainly he did not resign for another year, and Nixon (1978, 908) recalled that Shultz wished to resign in part because he was 'disillusioned by my handling of Watergate'.

46 Friedman's private office, Correspondence, George Shultz file, not yet processed into the Archives.

47 Friedman's private office, Correspondence, George Shultz file, not yet processed into the Archives.

48 Friedman's private office, Correspondence, George Shultz file, not yet processed into the Archives.

49 Friedman's private office, Correspondence, George Shultz file, not yet processed into the Archives.

50 On 26 July 1971, a group of prominent conservatives, including William Buckley, Jr, publicly 'suspended their support' for the Nixon administration, mainly in opposition to the prevailing social and foreign policy (Nash 1976, 337).

51 'How wrong can you be!!' was Friedman's scribbled comment on this passage.

52 Friedman's private office, Correspondence, George Shultz file, not yet processed into the Archives.

53 Friedman's private office, Correspondence, George Shultz file, not yet processed into the Archives.

54 William Simon Archives, Correspondence, F file.
55 William Simon Archives, Correspondence, F file.
56 William Simon Archives, Correspondence, F file.

19 Chairmen of the Federal Reserve System

1 Friedman Archives, Correspondence, Lionel Robbins file.
2 Friedman Archives, Correspondence, Alan Greenspan file.
3 In a letter to Homer Jones, Friedman (22 July 1969) expressed concern that 'the Fed has tightened the [monetary] screw another notch'. He dissented from Jones's proposal that M1 should grow by 3 per cent per annum on the grounds that this would lead to

> a rate of decline of about 1 per cent per year in prices. I would have no objection to that as a really long-term objective, but compared to the recent rate of growth of prices of 5 per cent, it seems to me a greater shift than is feasible without a politically unacceptable recession. I would readily grant that the best way to get back on a non-inflationary course might really be to have a severe recession, but it just seems to me to be ruled out by political considerations.

Friedman Archives, Correspondence, Homer Jones file.
4 Jones was also responsible for launching Stigler's academic career – by declining a post at Iowa State College in 1936, thus allowing Stigler (1988, 38–9) to take the position. Had Jones taken the position, Stigler believes he might have become a Seattle real estate dealer.

5 As of the moment, the most likely candidate, I think, still remains Arthur Burns. In my opinion, he would be absolutely first-rate and far away the best of anybody I can think of. However, this may not develop, and if it does not, we ought to be doing what you are doing here – trying to think up possible alternatives. We will obviously not be able to determine the matter, but at least we can see to it that names are considered (Friedman to Jones 22 July 1969).

Friedman Archives, Correspondence, Homer Jones file.
6 Shultz (4 February 1970) sent the ballad to Burns and Burns (11 March 1970) replied: 'I hope that you remain in good voice because I want to have a recording of the ballad before too long.' Burns Papers, Container K 32.
7 Burns Papers, Box A1, AFL-CIO.
8 Johnson replied: 'I have asked [CEA] Chairman Ackley to review your article and report to me on its contents.' Burns Papers, Box N41, Presidential, Incoming, L.B. Johnson.
9 'Nixon and Burns Spar Amiably at Swearing-In Rites'. Freedom and Union, March 1970: 7.
10 One of these 'critics' was strategically located within the Fed – in the Burns papers there is a copy of this article with a highly critical handwritten commentary including 'B.S'. Burns Papers, Container K 12 (3).

11 Burns Papers, Box A9, Economy General (2).
12 Burns Papers, Box A9, Economy General (2).
13 'Nixon and Burns Spar Amiably at Swearing-In Rites'. Freedom and Union, March 1970: 7.
14 This statement before the House Subcommittee on Domestic Monetary Policy was made on 6 February 1975. Later, Burns (1978 [11 May 1977], 473) praised the Bundesbank for initiating the system of monetary targets in December 1974, explaining that such 'growth targets provide a meaningful framework for fostering monetary discipline'.
15 Friedman (15 July 1965) wrote to Stigler about the 'distorted sense of values' revealed by his decision to work on the second Friedman and Schwartz (1970) volume rather than 'lolling in Windermere and enjoying the company of you and Chick.... One reason I am pushing ahead on this is that I am anxious to get this volume done so I can be free of the commitments I've let myself drift into and cut my link with the Bureau.' George Stigler Papers, Box 8, Friedman file. Chick Stigler died at the Stiglers' summer cottage in August 1970 (Stigler 1988, 29).
16 Friedman Archives, Correspondence, Arthur Burns file.
17 For understandable reasons, Burns (26 February 1947) was keen to minimise the potential damage inflicted on the National Bureau as a consequence of this dispute: 'I do not wish to close this letter without making it perfectly clear that if any member of the National Bureau staff, including myself, can be of service to you at any time, I hope you will not hesitate to call us.' Friedman Archives, Correspondence, Arthur Burns file.
18 Burns Papers, Container K 12 (2), Friedman file.
19 Burns Papers, Container K 12 (2), Friedman file.
20 Burns Papers, Container K 12 (2), Friedman file.
21 Burns papers, Container K 12 (2), Friedman file.
22 Friedman continued: 'Best personal regards to you and Helen. Vermont has been beautiful in its mantle of white, especially these past few days when we have enjoyed bright sunshine.' Burns Papers, Container K 12 (2), Friedman file.
23 Friedman Archives, Correspondence, Homer Jones file.
24 Friedman Archives, Correspondence, Arthur Burns file.
25 Friedman Archives, Correspondence, Homer Jones file. The letter actually referred to 'Frank Marsh' but since it was 'Dictated but not read' this presumably is a reference to Morris, the President of the Federal Reserve Bank of Boston. This Bank had recently organised conferences on *Controlling Monetary Aggregates* and the *International Adjustment Mechanism* and in June 1970 held a conference on State and Local Government Finances.

20 Within the White House

1 Rinfret-Boston Associates confidential Memorandum, dated 28 December 1972. Burns Papers, Container K 29 (2), Rinfret file.
2 Rinfret-Boston Associates confidential Memorandum, dated 28 December 1972. Burns Papers, Container K 29 (2), Rinfret file.
3 Friedman published his famous 'Social Responsibility of Business' essay in the *New York Times Magazine* on 13 September 1970, after Nixon's statement.

4 He was referring to his wartime experiences in the Treasury.
5 Neither advocate agrees with Safire's recollection. Friedman scribbled 'Nonsense' in the margin alongside this sentence in an earlier draft. Rinfret (correspondence to the author, 16 September 1999) denies that he would have exchanged unpleasantries in front of the President, but indicates that in private he would have been felt no such inhibition in combating Friedman. Either Safire has exaggerated the heat, or time has cooled the memory for both Friedman and Rinfret.
6 Friedman's private office, Correspondence, George Shultz file, not yet processed into the Archives.
7 George Stigler Papers, Box 10.
8 Friedman (27 July 1960) was optimistic about Nixon's chances in 1960 because, as he explained to Stigler, the Democratic Party

> platform is too transparent a fraud for even the gullible U.S. public – I take that back, since I think the public is far more sensible + less gullible than our academic confreres – to swallow. The Johnson nomination was as clever as hell + would have been a master stroke without the platform but will not the combination make the sheer cynicism + expediency of it all crystal clear?

Friedman also estimated that the expected recession would be sufficiently delayed to prevent much damage to Nixon's cause. George Stigler Papers, Supplementary Box, Friedman file.
9 Friedman Archives, Correspondence, W. Allen Wallis file.
10 Jones, who worked for the Federal Reserve Bank of St Louis, was informed by Friedman (7 July 1970) that 'Nothing has done so much to produce at least a small chance of sanity in monetary policy as what you have been doing in St. Louis.' Later, Friedman (10 September 1971) discussed with Jones an upcoming vacancy on the Federal Reserve Board: 'In preparing for this, would you scratch ahead about people who in your opinion would be good replacements.' Friedman Archives, Correspondence, Homer Jones file.
11 Friedman Archives, Correspondence, Alan Greenspan file.
12 Friedman Archives, Correspondence, Alan Greenspan file. In 1957, Friedman also failed to persuade CEA Chairman Raymond Saulnier that moral suasion was not an appropriate method of restraining inflation (De Marchi 1975, 116; Burck 1971, 120).

21 Secretary Shultz

1 Burns Papers, Box B90, Prices and Wages.
2 Burns Papers, Box B90, Prices and Wages.
3 Burns Papers, Box B90, Prices and Wages.
4 Fed memorandum, 29 November 1971, Burns Papers, Box B85, OMB April 26–December 31 1971.
5 Burns Papers, Box B100, Treasury, November–December 1970.
6 In this instance, a conflict between the Executive Office of the President and the Treasury over the introduction of a value added tax.

7 Burns Papers, Box B67, IMF Committee of Twenty Papers June 12–13 1974 Briefing Book.
8 Burns Papers, Box B74, International Monetary Reform Issues, Treasury.
9 Burns Papers, Box B40, FRB General 1974–6.
10 Burns Papers, Box B90, Prices and Wages.
11 Burns Papers, Box B64, IMF May–August 1972.
12 'I believe that the wider application of incomes policy – supported by a careful adaptation of the fiscal and monetary instruments – could prove useful in the present circumstances.' To achieve 'progress…countries will need to take inspiration from the principles of cooperation and high purpose that guided our predecessors in the conference at Bretton Woods'.
13 Correspondence to the author, 20 September 1999. Shultz (1995, 8) was involved with the proposal which became the 1986 Tax Reform Act: 'As secretary of state, after talking it over with Milton Friedman – a source of wise and practical counsel over many years – I suggested the idea…to Ronald Reagan in December 1982.'
14 Burns Papers, IMF Press release No. 77, 29 September 1972, Box B66.
15 As Nixon opened the 1972 IMF meeting, Liddy, Howard Hunt and the five Watergate burglars were indicted on Federal charges (25 of the 'Watergate alumni' subsequently went to jail).
16 Nixon (1978, 1057) later acknowledged that it was this 'smoking gun' that ultimately made his Presidency untenable.
17 Burns Papers, H.M. Treasury Press Office, Box B74, International Monetary Reform 1972 Miscellaneous (1).
18 Burns Papers, Box B74, International Monetary Reform Issues Treasury August 1972.
19 Burns Papers, Box N41, Presidential, Outgoing, R.M. Nixon.
20 Burns Papers, Box B24, CIEP (1).
21 White House Press Secretary Press Release 11 January 1973. Burns Papers, Box B101, Treasury January–February 1973.
22 On 7 February 1973, the US Senate voted 70–0 to establish a select committee to investigate Watergate. Nixon was shocked to hear that the proceedings would be televised (Kutler 1997, 211).
23 Burns Papers, Treasury Press Release, Box B101, Treasury January–February 1973.
24 Burns Papers, Box B101, Treasury March–April 1973.
25 Burns Papers, Box B67, IMF 1974 Committee of Twenty Briefing Book.
26 'OFFICIAL USE ONLY – LIMDIS Suggested Talking Points and Background on Guidelines for Floating'. Burns Papers, Box B67, IMF Committee of Twenty June 12–13 1974 Briefing Book.
27 Henceforth (from early 1973), *The Times* became openly committed to monetarism (Congdon 1978, 5).

22 Secretary Simon

1 Burns Papers, Box B62, International Economic Summits Rambouillet November 1975 (1).

23 Conclusion

1 Solomon (14 June 1971) wrote a confidential memo for Volcker on 'U.S. Objectives for Greater Exchange Rate Flexibility' in which he stated that 'There is no danger of competitive revaluations.' Burns Papers, Box E6, Background International Monetary Situation June 1970 to June 1971. On 23 December 1972, the newly elected Australian Labour government revalued the Australian dollar by 7.05 per cent (Schedvin 1992, 485). On 26 December 1972, Burns received a memo from Sydney Key explaining that this had come 'as a surprise'. Burns Papers, Box B34, Exchange Rates 1971–5.

2 Correspondence to the author, 24 September 1999.

Bibliography

Acheson, A.L.K. Chant, J. and Prachowny, M. (eds) 1972. *Bretton Woods Revisited*. London: Macmillan – now Palgrave Macmillan.

Ackley, G. 1966. 'The Contribution of Guidelines'. In G.P. Shultz and R.Z. Aliber (eds), *Guidelines: Informal Controls and the Market Place*. Chicago: University of Chicago Press.

Aldcroft, D.H. and Oliver, M.J. 1998. *Exchange Rate Regimes in the Twentieth Century*. Cheltenham: Edward Elgar.

Alogoskoufis, G. 1992. 'Monetary Accommodation, Exchange Rate Regimes and Inflation Persistence'. *Economic Journal*, May, 102: 461–80.

Ambrose, S.E. 1989. *Nixon: the Triumph of a Politician 1962–72*. New York: Simon and Schuster.

—— 1991. *Nixon: Vol. 3 Ruin and Recovery 1973–1990*. New York: Simon and Schuster.

—— 1994. 'Introduction'. In H.R. Haldeman, *The Haldeman Diaries: Inside the Nixon White House*. New York: G.P. Putnam's Sons.

Anderson, M. 1990. *Revolution: the Reagan Legacy*. Hoover Institution Press: Stanford, California.

—— 1993. 'The All-Volunteer Armed Force'. In L. Friedman and W.F. Levantrosser (eds), *Cold War Patriot and Statesman: Richard M. Nixon*. London: Greenwood.

Angell, J.W. 1961. 'The Reorganisation of the International Monetary System: an Alternative Proposal'. *Economic Journal*, December, LXXI(284): 691–708.

Arndt, H.W. and Corden, W.M. (eds) 1963. *The Australian Economy: a Volume of Readings*. Melbourne: F.W. Cheshire.

Banfield, E.C. 1962. 'Freedom and the Market'. *National Review*, November: 401–3.

—— 1970. *The Unheavenly City: the Nature and Future of Our Urban Crisis*. Boston: Little Brown.

Barber, W. 1987. 'The Career of Alvin H. Hansen in the 1920s and 1930s: a Case Study in Intellectual Transformation'. *History of Political Economy*, Summer: 191–205.

Baxter, M. and Stockman, A.C. 1989. 'Business Cycles and the Exchange Rate Regime: Some International Evidence'. *Journal of Monetary Economics*, 23: 377–400.

Becker, G. 1993. 'George Joseph Stigler: January 17, 1911–December 1, 1991'. *Journal of Political Economy*, 101(5), October: 761–7.

Bernstein, E.M. 1965. 'International Monetary Mechanism Discussion'. *American Economic Association Papers and Proceedings*, May: 181–6.

—— 1972. 'The Evolution of the International Monetary Fund'. In A.L.K. Acheson, *et al.* (eds), *Bretton Woods Revisited*. London: Macmillan – now Palgrave Macmillan.

—— 1996. 'The Making and Remaking of the Bretton Woods Institutions'. In O. Kirshner (ed.), *The Bretton Woods–GATT System: Retrospect and Prospect after Fifty Years*. London: M.E. Sharpe.

Bernstein, E.M., Cooper, R.N., Islam, N., Kindleberger, C., Machlup, F., Roosa, R., Triffin, R. and Williamson, J. 1976. *Reflections on Jamaica*. Essays in International Finance, No. 115. Princeton University.

Beveridge, W. *et al.* 1932. *Tariffs: the Case Examined*. By a committee of economists under the chairmanship of Sir William Beveridge. London: Longmans, Green.

Bhagwati, J. and Johnson, H.G. 1960. 'Some Controversies in the Theory of International Trade'. *Economic Journal*, 70, March: 74–93.

—— 1961. 'Some Controversies in the Theory of International Trade: a Rejoinder'. *Economic Journal*, 71, June: 427–30.

Blaug, M. 1985. *Great Economists since Keynes*. New York: Harvester.

Blessing, K. 1970. 'Commentary'. In W. McChesney Martin *et al.*, *Towards a World Central Bank*. Basle, Switzerland: Per Jacobsson Foundation.

Blumenthal. S. 1986. *The Rise of the Counter-establishment from Conservative Ideology to Political Power*. New York: Times.

Bordo, M.D. and Eichengreen, B. (eds) 1993. *A Retrospective on the Bretton Woods System: Lessons for International Monetary Reform*. Chicago: University of Chicago Press.

Bordo, M.D. and James, H. 2002. 'Haberler versus Nurkse: the Case for Floating Exchange Rates as an Alternative to Bretton Woods'. The Adam Klug Memorial Lecture. In W. Young and A. Arnon (eds), *The Open Economy Macromodel: Past, Present and Future*. Boston: Kluwer.

Bordo, M.D. and Jonung, L. 1996. *Monetary Regimes, Inflation and Monetary Reform*. Stockholm: Stockholm School of Economics Reprint Series, No. 156.

Brandon, H. 1973. *The Retreat of American Power*. New York: Doubleday.

Breit, W. and Spencer, R.W. (eds) 1986. *Lives of the Laureates*. Cambridge: MIT Press.

Brittan, S. 1964. *The Treasury under the Tories 1951–64*. England: Penguin.

—— 1970. *The Price of Economic Freedom: a Guide to Flexible Rates*. London: Macmillan – now Palgrave Macmillan.

Burck, G. 1971. 'Union Power and the New Inflation'. *Fortune*, February: 65–120.

Burgess, W.R. 1964. 'Concluding Remarks'. In *Economic Growth and Monetary Stability*. Basle, Switzerland: Per Jacobsson Foundation.

Burns, A.F. 1946. *Economic Research and the Keynesian Thinking of our Time*. Twenty-sixth annual report of the NBER. NBER: New York.

—— 1947. 'Keynesian Economics Once Again'. *Review of Economic Statistics*, November, 29: 252–68.

—— 1969. *The Business Cycle in a Changing World*. New York: National Bureau of Economic Research.

—— 1972. 'Some Essentials of International Monetary Reform'. *Federal Reserve Bulletin*, June: 545–9.

—— 1978. *Reflections of an Economic Policy Maker. Speeches and Congressional Statements 1969–1978*. Washington: American Enterprise Institute.

—— 1979. 'The Anguish of Central Banking'. In A.F. Burns *et al. The Anguish of Central Banking*. Belgrade: Per Jacobsson Foundation.

Burns, A.F. Cirovic, M. and Polak, J.J. 1979. *The Anguish of Central Banking*. Belgrade: Per Jacobsson Foundation.

Burns, A. and Mitchell, W. 1946. *Measuring Business Cycles*. New York: National Bureau of Economic Research.

Callaghan, J. 1987. *Time and Chance*. London: Collins.
Campos, R. 1996. 'Fifty Years of Bretton Woods'. In O. Kirshner (ed.), *The Bretton Woods–GATT System: Retrospect and Prospect after Fifty Years*. London: M.E. Sharpe.
Carli, G. 1967. 'An Italian Viewpoint'. *Banking,* May: 56.
Caves, R. 1963. 'Flexible Exchange Rates'. *American Economic Review,* May, 1: 120–9.
Chambers, H. 1943. 'International Economic Relations – Discussion'. *American Economic Review,* March, XXXIII(1): 448–54.
Chester, L, McCrystal, C, Aris, S. and Shawcross, W. 1973. *Watergate: the Full Inside Story*. Sydney: Angus and Robertson.
Claassen, E. and Salin, P. (eds) 1976. *Recent Issues in International Monetary Economics*. Amsterdam: North-Holland.
Coase, R. 1983. In E.W. Kitch (ed.), 'The Fire of Truth: a Remembrance of Law and Economics at Chicago, 1932–1970'. *Journal of Law and Economics,* XXVI, April, 163–234.
—— 1998. Aaron Director. In P. Newman (ed.), *The New Palgrave Dictionary of Law and Economics*. London: Macmillan – now Palgrave Macmillan.
Cockett, R. 1995. *Thinking the Unthinkable: Think Tanks and the Economic Counter-Revolution, 1931–1983*. London: HarperCollins.
Colander, D.C. and Landreth, H. (eds) 1996. *The Coming of Keynesianism to America: Conversations with the Founders of Keynesian Economics*. Cheltenham: Edward Elgar.
Colson, C. 1976. *Born Again*. London: Hodder and Stoughton.
Congdon, T. 1978. *Monetarism: an Essay in Definition*. London: Centre for Policy Studies.
Coombs, C.A. 1976. *The Arena of International Finance*. New York: John Wiley.
Cosgrave, P. 1989. *The Lives of Enoch Powell*. London: Bodley Head.
Coyne, J. 1949. 'A Method of Combining a Free Exchange Rate with the Present System of Exchange Control in Canada'. Bank of Canada memorandum.
Crawford, K.G. 1939. 'From Pump-Priming to Pumping'. *Nation,* May 27, 148: 606–7.
Dam, K. 1982. *The Rules of the Game*. Chicago: University of Chicago Press.
Darby, M.R. and Lothian, J.R. 1988. 'International Transmissions Afloat'. In NBER Conference volume in Honour of Anna J. Schwartz.
Davenport, J. 1967. 'The Radical Economics of Milton Friedman'. *Fortune,* 1 June: 130–54.
Dean, J. 1976. *Blind Ambition*. New York: Simon and Schuster.
De Marchi, N. 1975. 'The First Nixon Administration: Prelude to Controls'. In C.D. Goodwin (ed.), *Exhortation and Controls: the Search for a Wage–Price Policy 1945–1971*. Washington, DC: The Brookings Institution.
De Vries, G.M. 1969. 'The Par Value System and Fluctuating Exchange Rates'. In G.M. de Vries and J.K. Horsefield (eds), *The International Monetary Fund 1945–1965: Twenty Years of International Monetary Cooperation*. Vol. 2: *Analysis*. Washington, DC: IMF.
—— 1976a. *The International Monetary Fund 1966–1971: the System under Stress*. Vol. I: *Narrative*. Washington, DC: IMF.
—— 1976b. *The International Monetary Fund 1966–1971: the System under Stress*. Vol. II: *Documents*. Washington, DC: IMF.
—— 1985a. *The International Monetary Fund 1972–1978: Cooperation on Trial*. Vol. I: *Narrative and Analysis*. Washington, DC: IMF.

—— 1985b. *The International Monetary Fund 1972–1978: Cooperation on Trial.* Vol. III: *Documents*. Washington, DC: IMF.
—— 1987. *Balance of Payments Adjustment, 1945 to 1986: the IMF Experience.* Washington, DC: IMF.
—— 1996. 'Bretton Woods Fifty Years Later: a View from the International Monetary Fund'. In O. Kirshner (ed.), *The Bretton Woods–GATT System: Retrospect and Prospect after Fifty Years*. London: M.E. Sharpe.
De Vries, G.M. and Horsefield, J.K. (eds) 1969. *The International Monetary Fund 1945–1965: Twenty Years of International Monetary Cooperation*. Vol. 2: *Analysis*. Washington, DC: IMF.
Diamond, R. 1972. *Nixon: the Third Year of His Presidency*. Washington: Congressional Quarterly.
Dornbusch, R. 1993. 'Comment'. In M.D. Bordo and B. Eichengreen (eds), *A Retrospective on the Bretton Woods System: Lessons for International Monetary Reform*. Chicago: University of Chicago Press.
—— 2000. 'The Original Chicago Boys'. *Financial Post*, 11 December: C12.
Douglas, P. 1951. *US Congressional Record – Senate*. 82nd Congress, 1st Session, February 22: 1648–82.
—— 1966. *America in the Market Place: Trade, Tariffs and the Balance of Payments*. New York: Holt, Rinehart and Winston.
Douglas, P. and Powell, J.E. 1968. *How Big Should Government Be?* Washington: American Enterprise Institute.
Dreyer, J.S. (ed.) 1978. *Breadth and Depth in Economics: Fritz Machlup – the Man and His Ideas*. Toronto: Lexington.
Eatwell J., Milgate M. and Newman P. (eds) 1987. *The New Palgrave Dictionary of Economics*. London: Macmillan – now Palgrave Macmillan.
Eckes, A.E. 1975. *A Search for Solvency: Bretton Woods and the International Monetary System, 1941–1971*. London: University of Texas Press.
Ehrlichman, J. 1982. *Witness to Power: the Nixon Years*. New York: Simon and Schuster.
Eichengreen, B. 1993. 'Epilogue: Three Perspectives on the Bretton Woods System'. In M.D. Bordo and B. Eichengreen (eds), *A Retrospective on the Bretton Woods System: Lessons for International Monetary Reform*. Chicago: University of Chicago Press.
Ellis, H.S. (ed.) 1948. *A Survey of Contemporary Economics*. Homewood, Ill.: Richard D. Irwin.
—— 1949. 'Research as Seen in *A Survey of Contemporary Economics*'. *American Economic Review Papers and Proceedings*, 39(3), May: 427–39.
Emminger, O. 1973. *Inflation and the International Monetary System*. The 1993 Per Jacobsson Lecture. Washington, DC: Per Jacobsson Foundation.
—— 1976. *On the Way to a New International Monetary Order*. Washington, DC: American Enterprise Institute for Public Policy Research.
—— 1977. *The D-Mark in the Conflict between Internal and External Equilibrium, 1948–75*. Essays in International Finance, No. 122. Princeton University.
—— 1978a. 'The International Monetary Arena Seen from Two Different Angles'. *Journal of Monetary Economics*, April, 4: 397–403.
—— 1978b. 'International Monetary Reform – Design and Reality'. In J.S. Dreyer (ed.), *Breadth and Depth in Economics: Fritz Machlup – the Man and His Ideas*. Toronto: Lexington.

Evans, R. and Novak, R. 1971. *Nixon in the White House*. London: Davis-Poynter.
Federal Reserve Bank of Boston. 1970. *The International Adjustment Mechanism*. Boston, Mass.: Federal Reserve Bank of Boston.
Fellner, W. 1966. 'On Limited Exchange Rate Flexibility'. In W. Fellner *et al.* (eds), *Maintaining and Restoring Balance in International Payments*. Princeton: Princeton University Press.
Fellner, W. Friedman, M. Johnson, H.G. and Machlup, F. 1967. 'Strong Dollar Seen in Free Markets'. Letter to the editor. *New York Times*, Sunday 26 November.
Fellner, W., Machlup, F. and Triffin, R. 1966. 'Introduction'. In W. Fellner *et al.* (eds), *Maintaining and Restoring Balance in International Payments*. Princeton: Princeton University Press.
Fellner, W., Machlup, F., Triffin, R. *et al.* 1966. *Maintaining and Restoring Balance in International Payments*. Princeton: Princeton University Press.
Fisher, A. 1949. *The Case for Freedom*. London: Runnymede.
—— 1974. *Must History Repeat Itself?* Enfield, Middlesex: Churchill Press.
Fisher, I. 1922. *The Purchasing Power of Money*. New York: Macmillan – now Palgrave Macmillan.
Fleming, J.M. 1962. 'Domestic Financial Policies under Fixed and Floating Exchange Rates'. *International Monetary Fund Staff Papers*, 9: 369–79.
—— 1974. *Reflections on the International Monetary Reform*. Princeton, NJ: International Finance Section, Princeton University.
Ford, G. 1979. *A Time to Heal*. New York: Harper and Row.
Frere, M. 1964. *Economic Growth and Monetary Stability*. Basle, Switzerland: Per Jacobsson Foundation.
Friedman, L. and Levantrosser, W.F. (eds) 1993. *Cold War Patriot and Statesman: Richard M. Nixon*. London: Greenwood.
Friedman, M. 1948. 'Why Not Devalue Canadian Dollar? Here are views of U.S. and Canadian Economists'. *Toronto Financial Post*, May 22: 22.
—— 1953. *Essays in Positive Economics*. Chicago: University of Chicago Press.
—— (ed.) 1956. *Studies in the Quantity Theory of Money*. Chicago: University of Chicago Press.
—— 1962a. *Capitalism and Freedom*. Chicago: University of Chicago Press.
—— 1962b. *Price Theory: a Provisional Text*. Chicago: Aldine.
—— 1964. 'The Goldwater View of Economics'. *The New York Magazine*, October 11: 35, 133–7.
—— 1965. 'International Monetary Mechanism Discussion'. *American Economic Association Papers and Proceedings*, May: 178–81.
—— 1966. 'What Price Guideposts?' In G.P. Shultz and R.Z. Aliber (eds), *Guidelines: Informal Controls and the Market Place*. Chicago: University of Chicago Press.
—— 1967. In M. Friedman and R.V. Roosa, *The Balance of Payments: Free versus Fixed Exchange Rates*. Washington: American Enterprise Institute for Public Policy Research.
—— 1968a. *Dollars and Deficits: Inflation, Monetary Policy and the Balance of Payments*. Englewood, NJ: Prentice Hall.
—— 1968b. 'The Role of Monetary Policy'. *American Economic Review*, LVIII(1), March: 1–17.
—— 1968c. 'Floating Dollars'. Letter to the editor. *Wall Street Journal*, 8 May.

—— 1968d. Complete Transcript of National Education Television's Great Decisions 1968: 'The Dollar in Danger'.
—— 1969a. Epilogue. For French translation of *Dollars and Deficits*. Mimeo, 27 July.
—— 1969b. 'Reply'. In M. Friedman and W.W. Heller, *Monetary versus Fiscal Policy: a Dialogue*. New York: W.W. Norton.
—— 1969c. 'Round Table on Exchange Rate Policy'. *American Economic Association Papers and Proceedings*, May, LIX(2): 364–6.
—— 1970. 'The International Adjustment Mechanism'. In Federal Reserve Bank of Boston, *The International Adjustment Mechanism*. Boston, Mass.: Federal Reserve Bank of Boston.
—— 1971. 'The Need for Futures Markets in Currencies'. Prepared for the Chicago Mercantile Exchange, 20 December.
—— 1972a. *Money and Economic Development*. New York: Praeger.
—— 1972b. *An Economist's Protest*. Glen Ridge, NJ: Thomas Horton.
—— 1972c. 'Have Fiscal and/or Monetary Policies Failed?' *American Economic Review*, May: 11–18.
—— 1972d. 'Three Views on Nixonomics and Where it Leads'. *Newsweek*, January 31: 74–5.
—— 1974a. 'Schools at Chicago'. *University of Chicago Magazine*, 67: 11–16.
—— 1974b. 'Exchange Rates: How Flexible Should They Be?' In W.E. Mitchell *et al.* (eds), *Readings in Macroeconomics*. New York: McGraw-Hill.
—— 1974c. 'The President's New Economic Program: Domestic Wage and Price Controls'. In W.E. Mitchell *et al.* (eds), *Readings in Macroeconomics*. New York: McGraw-Hill.
—— 1975. *There's No Such Thing as a Free Lunch*. Open Court: LaSalle.
—— 1977. *From Galbraith to Economic Freedom*. London: Institute of Economic Affairs.
—— 1978. 'Preface'. In W.E. Simon, *A Time for Truth*. Sydney: McGraw-Hill.
—— 1986. 'Milton Friedman'. In W. Breit and R.W. Spencer (eds), *Lives of the Laureates*. Cambridge: MIT Press.
—— 1987. 'Simon Newcomb'. In J. Eatwell *et al.* (eds), *The New Palgrave Dictionary of Economics*. London: Macmillan – now Palgrave Macmillan.
—— 1988a. 'Introduction'. In L. Melamed (ed.), *The Merits of Flexible Exchange Rates: an Anthology*. Fairfax, Va: George Mason University Press.
—— 1988b. 'A Proposal for Resolving U.S. Balance of Payments Problems'. In L. Melamed (ed.), *The Merits of Flexible Exchange Rates: an Anthology*. Fairfax, Va: George Mason University Press.
—— 2000. 'Friedman versus Mundell on Exchange Rates'. *National Post On Line*, 11 December.
—— 2003a. 'The Quantity Theory of Money – a Restatement'. In R. Leeson (ed.), *Keynes, Chicago and Friedman*. London: Chatto and Pickering.
—— 2003b. 'Comment on the Critics'. In R. Leeson (ed.), *Keynes, Chicago and Friedman*. London: Chatto and Pickering.
Friedman, M. and Friedman, R. 1962. *Capitalism and Freedom*. Chicago: University of Chicago Press.
—— 1982. *Capitalism and Freedom*, 2nd edn. Chicago: University of Chicago Press.
—— 1980. *Free to Choose*. Penguin: Middlesex.

—— 1998. *Two Lucky People: Memoirs*. Chicago: University of Chicago Press.
Friedman, M. and Heller, W.W. 1969. *Monetary versus Fiscal Policy: a Dialogue*. New York: W.W. Norton.
Friedman, M., Meltzer, L., Harbison, F.H., Mints, L.W., Schultz, T.W. and Lewis, H.G. 1951. 'Statement: the Failure of the Present Monetary Policy'. *US Congressional Record – Senate*. 82nd Congress 1st Session, 22 February: 1681–2.
Friedman, M. and Roosa, R.V. 1967. *The Balance of Payments: Free versus Fixed Exchange Rates*. Washington: American Enterprise Institute for Public Policy Research.
Friedman, M. and Schwartz, A. 1963. *A Monetary History of the United States, 1867–1960*. Princeton: Princeton University Press for the National Bureau of Economic Research.
—— 1970. *Monetary Statistics of the United States*. New York: Columbia University Press for the National Bureau of Economic Research.
Friedman, R. 1998. 'Tribute on the Quad'. *Hoover Digest*, 4: 1–9.
Frost, D. 1978. *'I Gave Them a Sword': Behind the Scenes of the Nixon Interviews*. London: Macmillan – now Palgrave Macmillan.
Galbraith, J.K. 1949. 'In defence of laissez-faire'. *New York Times Book Review*, October 30: 45.
—— 1951. 'The Strategy of Direct Controls in Economic Mobilisation'. *Review of Economics and Statistics*, February: 12–17.
—— 1952. *A Theory of Price Control*. Cambridge: Harvard University Press.
—— 1964. 'The Balance of Payments: a Political and Administrative View'. *Review of Economics and Statistics*, 46: 115–22.
—— 1971. *Economics, Peace and Laughter*. Middlesex: Penguin.
—— 1973. 'Power and the Useful Economist'. *American Economic Review*, March, 63(1): 1–11.
—— 1977. *The Age of Uncertainty*. London: André Deutsch.
—— 1981. *A Life in Our Time: Memoirs*. Boston: Houghton Mifflin.
—— 1987. *A History of Economics: the Past as the Present*. London: Hamish Hamilton.
—— 1996. 'John Kenneth Galbraith'. In D.C. Colander and H. Landreth (eds), *The Coming of Keynesianism to America: Conversations with the Founders of Keynesian Economics*. Cheltenham: Edward Elgar.
Gannon, J.P. 1975. 'Monetary Accord at Meeting Next Month Held Unlikely by U.S. Treasury Official'. *Wall Street Journal*, 22 May.
Gardner, R.N. 1956. *Sterling–Dollar Diplomacy*. Oxford: Clarendon.
Gideonse, H. 1937. 'Introduction by the Editor'. In B.W. Lewis, *Price and Production Control in British Industry*. University of Chicago Public Policy Pamphlet No. 25.
Giscard d'Estaing, Valéry. 1969. The International Monetary Order. In R. Mundell and A. Swoboda (eds), *Monetary Problems of the International Economy*. Chicago: University of Chicago Press.
Gold, J. 1969. 'The Institution and the Code of Conduct'. In G.M. de Vries and J.K. Horsefield (eds), *The International Monetary Fund 1945–1965. Twenty Years of International Monetary Cooperation*. Vol. 2: *Analysis*. Washington, DC: IMF.
Goldwater, B. 1960. *The Conscience of a Conservative*. New York: Macfadden.
—— 1970. *The Conscience of a Majority*. Englewood Cliffs, NJ: Prentice Hall.

——1979. *With No Apologies: the Personal and Political Memoirs of United States Senator Barry M. Goldwater*. New York: William Morrow.

—— 1988. *Goldwater*. With Jack Cassidy. New York: Doubleday.

Gomez, R. 1964. *Economic Growth and Monetary Stability*. Basle, Switzerland: Per Jacobsson Foundation.

Goodwin, C.D. (ed.) 1975. *Exhortation and Controls: the Search for a Wage–Price Policy 1945–1971*. Washington, DC: The Brookings Institution.

—— 1998. 'Some Reflections on Editing *History of Political Economy*'. *History of Economics Review*, Winter, 27: 6–11.

Gordon, D. 1948. 'Why Not Devalue the Canadian Dollar? Here are views of U.S. and Canadian Economists'. *Toronto Financial Post*, 22 May: 22.

Gordon, H.S. 1961. 'The Bank of Canada in a System of Responsible Government'. *Canadian Journal of Economics and Political Science*, XXVII(1), November: 1–22.

Gordon, M. 1943. 'International Economic Relations – Discussion'. *American Economic Review*, March XXXIII(1): 446–8.

Goulden, J.C. 1972. *Meany*. New York: Atheneum.

Gowa, J. 1983. *Closing the Gold Window: Domestic Politics and the End of Bretton Woods*. London: Cornell University Press.

Graham, F.D. 1940. 'The Achilles Heel in Monetary Standards'. *American Economic Review*, March: 16–32.

—— 1954. *Fundamentals of International Monetary Policy*. Essays in International Finance, No. 2. Princeton University.

Graham, J. 1969. 'President Nixon Faces an Urgent Need for Powerful Magic. *Financial Times*, 8 April.

Greenspan, A. 1974. 'Economic Policy Problems for 1975'. Remarks before the National Economists' Club, 2 December.

—— 1988. 'Excerpts from the Council of Economic Advisers' Report to the President, 1975, 1976, 1977'. In L. Melamed (ed.), *The Merits of Flexible Exchange Rates: an Anthology*. Fairfax, Va: George Mason University Press.

Gruebel, H. (ed.) 1963. *World Monetary Reform: Plans and Issues*. Stanford: Stanford UP.

Haberler, G. 1937. *Prosperity and Depression: a Theoretical Analysis of Cyclical Movements*. Geneva: League of Nations.

—— 1945. 'The Choice of Exchange Rates after the War'. *American Economic Review*, June, 35(3): 308–18.

—— 1949. 'The Market for Foreign Exchange and the Stability of Balance of Payments: a Theoretical Analysis'. *Kyklos*, III: 193–218.

—— 1961. 'Domestic Economic Policies and the United States Balance of Payments'. In S.E. Harris (ed.), *The Dollar in Crisis*. New York: Harcourt Brace and World.

—— 1966. 'Adjustment, Employment and Growth'. In W. Fellner *et al.* (eds), *Maintaining and Restoring Balance in International Payments*. Princeton: Princeton University Press.

—— 1969a. 'Taxes on Imports and Subsidies on Exports as a Tool of Adjustment'. In R. Mundell and A. Swoboda (eds), *Monetary Problems of the International Economy*. Chicago: University of Chicago Press.

—— 1969b. *Money in the International Economy*. London: Institute of Economic Affairs.

—— 1969c. 'Round Table on Exchange Rate Policy'. *American Economic Association Papers and Proceedings*, May: 357–60.
—— 1974. 'U.S. Balance of Payments Policy and the International Monetary System'. Reprinted in W.E. Mitchell *et al.* (eds), *Readings in Macroeconomics*. New York: McGraw-Hill.
—— 1978. 'The Problem of Adjustment and Liquidity under a Regime of Widespread Floating'. In J.S. Dreyer (ed.), *Breadth and Depth in Economics: Fritz Machlup – the Man and His Ideas*. Toronto: Lexington.
—— 1988. 'The International Monetary System and Proposals for International Policy Coordination'. In L. Melamed (ed.), *The Merits of Flexible Exchange Rates: an Anthology*. Fairfax, Va: George Mason University Press.
Haberler, G. and Willett, T. 1971. *A Strategy for U.S. Balance of Payments Policy*. Washington: AEI.
Haig, A. 1992. *Inner Circles: How America Changed the World: a Memoir*. New York: Warner.
Haldeman, H.R. 1994. *The Haldeman Diaries: Inside the Nixon White House*. Edited by Steven Ambrose. New York: G.P. Putnam's Sons.
Halm, G. 1965. 'The "Band" Proposal: the Limit of Permissible Exchange Rate Variation'. Special Papers in International Economics, No. 6, Dept of Economics, Princeton University, NJ.
—— 1969. *Towards Limited Exchange-Rate Flexibility*. Princeton Essays in International Finance, Princeton University, NJ.
—— (ed.) 1970. *Approaches to Greater Flexibility of Exchange Rates: the Burgenstock Papers*. Princeton: Princeton University Press.
—— 1971. *The International Monetary Fund and the Flexibility of Exchange Rates*. Princeton Essays in International Finance, Princeton University, NJ.
Hamilton, E.J., Rees, A. and Johnson, H.G. (eds) 1962. *Landmarks in Political Economy*. Chicago: University of Chicago.
Hammond, J.D. 1996. *Theory and Measurement: Causality Issues in Milton Friedman's Monetary Economics*. Cambridge: CUP.
Hansen, A.H. 1936. 'The International Monetary Situation'. *Yale Review*, 26, September: 26–36.
—— 1939. 'Economic Progress and Declining Population Growth'. *American Economic Review*, 29(1), March: 1–15.
—— 1946. 'Notes on Mints' Paper on Monetary Policy'. *Review of Economic Statistics*, November: 69–74.
—— 1947. 'Dr Burns on Keynesian Economics'. *Review of Economic Statistics*, 29, November: 247–52.
—— 1948. 'Fundamental Disequilibrium'. In S.E. Harris (ed.), *Foreign Economic Policy for the United States*. Cambridge, Mass.: Harvard University Press.
—— 1962. 'Comment of a Keynesian'. *New Republic*, 20 October: 28–9.
—— 1966. 'Keynes after Thirty Years (with Special Reference to the United States)'. *Weltwirtschaftliches Archiv*, 97(2): 213–31.
Hansen, A.H. and Kindleberger, C.P. 1942. 'The Economic Tasks of the Post-war World'. *Foreign Affairs*, 21: 466–76.
Harbison, F.H. and Mooney, J.D. (eds) 1966. *Critical Issues in Employment Policy*. Industrial Relations Section: Princeton University Press.
Hardy, C.O. 1940. *Wartime Control of Prices*. Washington: Brookings Institution.

Harris, S.E. (ed.) 1948. *Foreign Economic Policy for the United States*. Cambridge, Mass.: Harvard University Press.
—— 1948. 'Introduction'. In S.E. Harris (ed.), *Foreign Economic Policy for the United States*. Cambridge, Mass.: Harvard University Press.
—— (ed.) 1961. *The Dollar in Crisis*. New York: Harcourt Brace and World.
Harrod, R.F. 1933. *International Economics*. London: Nisbet.
—— 1951. *The Life of John Maynard Keynes*. London: Macmillan – now Palgrave Macmillan.
Hartwell, R.M. 1995. *A History of the Mont Pelerin Society*. Indianapolis: Liberty Fund.
Hawtrey, R. 1946. *Bretton Woods For Better or Worse*. Longmans: London.
Hayek, F.A. 1931. *Prices and Production*. London: Routledge.
—— 1967. *Studies in Philosophy, Politics and Economics*. London: Routledge and Kegan Paul.
—— 1978. 'Foreword'. In W.E. Simon, *A Time for Truth*. Sydney: McGraw-Hill.
Heller, W. 1967. *New Dimensions in Political Economy*. New York: W.W. Norton.
—— 1969. 'Is Monetary Policy Being Oversold?' In M. Friedman and W. Heller, *Monetary versus Fiscal Policy: a Dialogue*. New York: W.W. Norton.
Hicks, J. 1959. *Essays in World Economics*. Oxford: Clarendon.
Hinshaw, R. (ed.) 1967. *Monetary Reform and the Price of Gold*. Baltimore: Johns Hopkins Press.
HMSO. 1959. *Committee on the Working of the Monetary System (Radcliffe Committee). Report*. London: HMSO.
Horsefield, J.K. 1969a. *The International Monetary Fund 1945–1965: Twenty Years of International Monetary Cooperation*. Vol. I: *Chronicle*. Washington, DC: IMF.
—— 1969b. *The International Monetary Fund 1945–1965: Twenty Years of International Monetary Cooperation*. Vol. III: *Documents*. Washington, DC: IMF.
Hoover Digest. 2000. No. 3. www.hoover.stanford.edu/publications/digest/default.html
Houthakker, H. 1962. 'Exchange Rate Adjustment'. In *Factors Affecting the United States Balance of Payments*. Joint Economic Committee, Congress of the United States. Washington: US Government Printing Office.
—— 1978. 'The Breakdown of Bretton Woods'. In W. Sichel (ed.), *Economic Advice and Executive Policy Recommendations from Past Members of the Council of Economic Advisers*. New York: Praeger.
Howe, G. 1991. 'The 364 Economists: Ten Years On'. *Fiscal Studies*, 13: 92–107.
International Monetary Fund. 1964. *Annual Report*. Washington, DC: IMF.
—— 1970. *The Role of Exchange Rates in the Adjustment of International Payments: a Report by the Executive Directors*. Washington, DC: IMF.
—— 1974. *International Monetary Reform: Documents of the Committee of Twenty*. Washington, DC: IMF.
—— 1975. *IMF Survey*. Annual Meeting Issue, September 15: 257–80.
Irwin, D.A. 1996. *Against the Tide: an Intellectual History of Free Trade*. Princeton, NJ: Princeton University Press.
Jacobsson, E.E. 1979. *A Life for Sound Money: Per Jacobsson His Biography*. Oxford: Clarendon.
Jacobsson, P. 1959. *Towards a Modern Monetary Standard*. University of London: Athlone Press.
Jacoby, N.H. (ed.) 1964. *United States Monetary Policy*. New York: Praeger.

James, H. 1996. *International Monetary Co-operation since Bretton Woods*. IMF, Washington, DC: Oxford University Press.

Johnson, H.G. 1951. 'The Taxonomic Approach to Economic Policy'. *Economic Journal*, December: 812–32.

—— 1969. 'The Case for Flexible Exchange Rates, 1969'. In H.G. Johnson and J.E. Nash, *UK and Floating Exchange Rates: a Debate on the Theoretical and Practical Significance*. London: IEA.

—— 1970. Commentary. In W. McChesney Martin *et al.*, *Towards a World Central Bank*. Basle: Per Jacobsson Foundation.

—— 1976. 'The Future of Floating Rates'. In E. Claassen and P. Salin (eds), *Recent Issues in International Monetary Economics*. Amsterdam: North-Holland.

—— 1977. 'The Monetary Approach to the Balance of Payments'. *Journal of International Economics*, August, 7: 220–74.

—— 2003. 'The Keynesian Revolution and the Monetarist Counter-Revolution'. In R. Leeson (ed.), *Keynes, Chicago and Friedman*. London: Chatto and Pickering.

Johnson, H.G. and Nash, J.E. 1969. *UK and Floating Exchange Rates: a Debate on the Theoretical and Practical Significance*. London: IEA.

Johnson, H.G. and Swoboda, A.K. (eds) 1973. *The Economics of Common Currencies*. London: George Allen and Unwin.

Johnson, H.G., Wonnacott, P. and Shibata H. 1968. *Harmonization of National Economic Policies under Free Trade*. Toronto: Published for the Private Planning Association of Canada by University of Toronto Press.

Kahn, R.F. 1952. 'Monetary Policy and the Balance of Payments'. *Political Quarterly*, July–September: 250–61.

Keegan, W. 1984. *Mrs Thatcher's Economic Experiment*. London: Penguin.

Kenen, P. 1969. 'The Theory of Optimum Currency Areas: an Eclectic View'. In R. Mundell and A. Swoboda (eds), *Monetary Problems of the International Economy*. Chicago: University of Chicago Press.

Keynes, J.M. 1936. *The General Theory of Employment, Interest and Money*. London: Macmillan – now Palgrave Macmillan.

—— 1972–89. *Collected Writings*. London: Macmillan – now Palgrave Macmillan.

Kindleberger, C.P. 1937. *International Short-term Capital Movements*. New York: Columbia University Press.

—— 1962. *Foreign Trade and the National Economy*. New Haven: Yale University Press.

—— 1965. *Balance of Payments Deficits and the International Market for Liquidity*. Princeton: Princeton University.

—— 1966a. *International Monetary Arrangements*. Lecture delivered at the University of Queensland, St Lucia, 25 July 1966. St Lucia: University of Queensland Press.

—— 1966b. *Europe and the Dollar*. Cambridge, Mass.: MIT Press.

—— 1967. *The Politics of International Money and World Language*. Princeton, NJ: International Finance Section, Dept. of Economics, Princeton University. Essays in International Finance No. 61.

—— 1968. *International Economics*, 4th edn. Homewood, Ill.: R.D. Irwin.

—— 1970a. 'The Case for Fixed Exchange Rates, 1969'. In Federal Reserve Bank of Boston, *The International Adjustment Mechanism*. Boston, Mass.: Federal Reserve Bank of Boston.

—— 1970b. *Power and Money; the Economics of International Politics and the Politics of International Economics*. New York: Basic Books.
—— 1973. *The World in Depression 1929–1939*. London: Allen Lane.
—— 1976. 'The Exchange-Stability Issue at Rambouillet and Jamaica'. In E.M. Bernstein *et al.*, *Reflections on Jamaica*. Essays in International Finance No. 115, Princeton University.
—— 1985. *Keynesianism vs. Monetarism and Other Essays in Financial History*. London: George Allen and Unwin.
—— 1986. 'International Public Goods without International Government'. *American Economic Review*, March: 1–13.
—— 1987. *Marshall Plan Days*. Boston: Allen & Unwin.
—— 1991. *The Life of an Economist*. Oxford: Basil Blackwell.
Kirshner, O. (ed.) 1996. *The Bretton Woods–GATT System: Retrospect and Prospect after Fifty Years*. London: M.E. Sharpe.
Kissinger, H. 1979. *The White House Years*. London: Weidenfeld and Nicolson.
—— 1982. *Years of Upheaval*. Boston: Little, Brown.
Kitch, E.W. 1983. 'The Fire of Truth: a Remembrance of Law and Economics at Chicago, 1932–1970'. *Journal of Law and Economics*, XXVI, April: 163–234.
Knight, F. 1935. *The Ethics of Competition and Other Essays*. New York: Book for Libraries Press.
—— 1954–55. 'Schumpeter's History of Economics'. *Southern Economic Journal*, 21: 261–72.
Koopmans, T.C. 1947. 'Measurement without Theory'. *Review of Economics Statistics*, August: 161–72.
—— 1949. 'Reply to Rutledge Vining'. *Review of Economics and Statistics*, 31: 86–91.
Kraft, J. 1962. 'Economics of the New Frontier'. *New Republic*, 20 October: 12–13.
Krause, C. 1972. 'Shultz Says Martin Cost U.S. Jobs'. *Washington Post*, 21 February.
Krause, L. 1971. *Sequel to Bretton Woods: a Proposal to Reform the World Monetary System*. Washington, DC: Brookings Institution.
Kutler, S.I. 1997. *Abuse of Power: the New Nixon Tapes*. New York: Simon and Schuster.
Laffer, A. 1973. 'Two Arguments for Fixed Rates'. In H.G. Johnson and A.K. Swoboda (eds), *The Economics of Common Currencies*. London: George Allen and Unwin.
Latham, E. 1966. *The Meaning of McCarthyism*. Boston: D.C. Heath.
The League of Nations. 1944. *International Currency Experience: Lessons of the Inter-War Period*. Princeton, NJ: League of Nations Publications.
Leeson, R. 2000. *The Eclipse of Keynesianism: the Political Economy of the Chicago Counter-Revolution*. New York: Palgrave Macmillan.
—— Forthcoming. *The Political Economy of the Inflation–Unemployment Trade-Off*. Cambridge: Cambridge University Press.
—— (ed.) 2003. *Keynes, Chicago and Friedman*. London: Chatto and Pickering. Two volumes.
Lennep, J. 1966. 'Foreword'. In W. Fellner *et al.* (eds), *Maintaining and Restoring Balance in International Payments*. Princeton: Princeton University Press.
Leube, K.R. 1986. 'George J. Stigler: a Biographical Introduction'. In G. Stigler, *The Essence of Stigler*. Stanford, Calif.: Hoover Institution Press.
Lewis, B.W. 1937. *Price and Production Control in British Industry*. University of Chicago Public Policy Pamphlet No. 25.

Liddy, G.G. 1980. *Will*. Glasgow: Collins.

McChesney Martin, W. 1970. 'Towards a World Central Bank'. In W. McChesney Martin *et al.*, *Towards a Central Bank*. Basle: Per Jacobsson Foundation.

McChesney Martin, W., Blessing, K, Machado Gomez, A., and Johnson, H. 1970. *Towards a World Central Bank*. Basle, Switzerland: Per Jacobsson Foundation.

Machlup, F. 1964. *Plans for the Reform of the International Monetary System*. International Finance Section, Princeton University.

—— 1966a. 'In Search of Guides for Policy'. In W. Fellner *et al.* (eds), *Maintaining and Restoring Balance in International Payments*. Princeton: Princeton University Press.

—— 1966b. 'Preface'. In W. Fellner *et al.* (eds), *Maintaining and Restoring Balance in International Payments*. Princeton: Princeton University Press.

—— 1970. 'The Forward Exchange Market: Misunderstandings between Practitioners and Economists'. In G. Halm (ed.), *Approaches to Greater Flexibility of Exchange Rates: the Burgenstock Papers*. Princeton: Princeton University Press.

—— 1976. 'Between Outline and Outcome the Reform was Lost'. In E.M. Bernstein *et al.*, *Reflections on Jamaica*. Essays in International Finance No. 115, Princeton University.

Machlup, F., Malkeil, B.G. *et al.* 1964. *International Monetary Arrangements: the Problem of Choice. Report on the Deliberations of an International Study Group of 32 Economists*. International Finance Section, Princeton University.

McKinnon, R.I. 1963. 'Optimal Currency Areas'. *American Economic Review*, 53, September: 717–24.

—— 2002. 'Optimal Currency Areas and Key Currencies'. In W. Young and A. Arnon (eds), *The Open Economy Macromodel: Past, Present and Future*. Boston: Kluwer.

McMahon, C. 1964. *Sterling in the Sixties*. London: Oxford University Press.

McQuillan, L.J. 2000. *The Case against the IMF*. Hoover Essays in Public Policy, Stanford, Calif.

Maisel, S.J. 1973. *Managing the Dollar*. New York: W.W. Norton.

Malkeil, B.G. 1978. 'Fritz Machlup as Teacher'. In J.S. Dreyer (ed.), *Breadth and Depth in Economics: Fritz Machlup – the Man and His Ideas*. Toronto: Lexington.

Malkin, L. 1971. A Practical Politician at the Fed. *Fortune*, May: 148–264.

Manchester, W. 1975. *The Glory and the Dream: a Narrative History of America 1932–72*. London: Michael Joseph.

Marsh, D.M. 1970. 'Canada's Experience with a Floating Exchange, 1950–62'. In G. Halm (ed.), *Approaches to Greater Flexibility of Exchange Rates: the Burgenstock Papers*. Princeton: Princeton University Press.

Marshall, A. 1922. *Principles of Economics*, 8th edn. London: Macmillan – now Palgrave Macmillan.

—— 1926. *Official Papers of Alfred Marshall*. London: Macmillan for the Royal Economic Society.

Mayer, M. 1981. *The Fate of the Dollar*. New York: Signet.

Mayer, T. 1999. *Monetary Policy and the Great Inflation in the United States: the Federal Reserve and the Failure of Macroeconomic Policy, 1965–1979*. Cheltenham: Edward Elgar.

Meade, J.E. 1948a. 'Financial Policy and the Balance of Payments'. *Economica*, n.s. 15 (2): 101–15.

—— 1948b. 'Bretton Woods, Havana and United Kingdom Balance of Payments'. *Lloyds Bank Review*, January: 1–18.
—— 1949. *Planning and the Price Mechanism: the Liberal Socialist Solution*. New York: Macmillan – now Palgrave Macmillan.
—— 1951. *The Theory of International Economic Policy*. Vol. I *The Balance of Payments*. Oxford: Oxford University Press.
—— 1955. 'The Case for Variable Exchange Rates'. *Three Banks Review*, September, 27: 3–27.
—— 1963. 'The Future of International Payments'. In H. Gruebel (ed.), *World Monetary Reform: Plans and Issues*. Stanford: Stanford University Press.
—— 1964. 'The International Monetary Mechanism'. *Three Banks Review*, September, 63: 3–25.
—— 1966. 'Exchange Rate Flexibility'. *Three Banks Review*, June: 3–27.
—— 1967. 'Gold and Reform: Other Views'. In R. Hinshaw (ed.), *Monetary Reform and the Price of Gold*. Baltimore: Johns Hopkins Press.
Meany, G. 1973. *A Modern Trade Policy for the Seventies*. Washington, DC: American Federation of Labor and Congress of Industrial Organizations.
Meier, G.M. 1982. *Problems of a World Monetary Order*. New York: Oxford University Press.
Melamed, L. 1988a. 'Foreword'. In L. Melamed (ed.), *The Merits of Flexible Exchange Rates: an Anthology*. Fairfax, Va: George Mason University Press.
—— 1988b. 'The International Monetary Market'. In L. Melamed (ed.), *The Merits of Flexible Exchange Rates: an Anthology*. Fairfax, Va: George Mason University Press.
—— (ed.) 1988c. *The Merits of Flexible Exchange Rates: an Anthology*. Fairfax, Va: George Mason University Press.
Meyer, M. 1981. *The Fate of the Dollar*. New York: Signet.
Middleton, R. 2002. 'Struggling with the Impossible: Sterling, the Balance of Payments and British Economic Policy, 1949–72'. In W. Young and A. Arnon (eds), *The Open Economy Macromodel: Past, Present and Future*. Boston: Kluwer.
Mises, L. von. 1949. *Human Action*. New Haven: Yale University Press.
Mitchell, W.E. Hand, J.H. and Walter, I. (eds) 1974. *Readings in Macroeconomics*. New York: McGraw-Hill.
Mints, L. 1950. *Monetary Policy for a Competitive Society*. New York: McGraw-Hill.
Moggridge, D. 1992. *Maynard Keynes: an Economist's Biography*. London: Routledge.
Morse, J. 1972. 'Commentary'. In H. Wallich *et al.*, *The Monetary Crisis of 1971 – the Lessons to be Learned*. Washington, DC: Per Jacobsson Foundation.
—— 1974. 'Nature of Monetary System's Evolution Assessed in Address by Jeremy Morse'. *IMF Survey*, 17 June: 186–9.
Muirhead, B. 1999. *Against the Odds: the Public Life and Times of Louis Rasminsky*. Toronto: University of Toronto Press.
Mundell, R. 1963. 'A Theory of Optimum Currency Areas'. *American Economic Review*, 51, November: 509–17.
—— 1969. 'Opening Remarks'. In R. Mundell and A. Swoboda (eds), *Monetary Problems of the International Economy*. Chicago: University of Chicago Press.
—— 1973a. 'Uncommon Arguments for Common Currencies'. In H.G. Johnson and A.K. Swoboda (eds), *The Economics of Common Currencies*. London: George Allen and Unwin.

—— 1973b. 'A Plan for a European Currency'. In H.G. Johnson and A.K. Swoboda (eds), *The Economics of Common Currencies*. London: George Allen and Unwin.
—— 2001. Notes on the Development of the International Macroeconomic Model. Presented to 'The Open Economy Macromodel: Past, Present and Future', Israel.
Mundell, R. and Swoboda, A. (eds) 1969. *Monetary Problems of the International Economy*. Chicago: University of Chicago Press.
Nash, G.H. 1976. *The Conservative Intellectual Movement in America since 1945*. New York: Basic Books.
Navasky, V.S. 1967. 'Galbraith on Galbraith'. *New York Times*, 25 June: 2–39.
Newman, P. (ed.) 1998. *The New Palgrave Dictionary of Law and Economics*. London: Macmillan – now Palgrave Macmillan.
Nixon, R.M. 1962. *Six Crises*. London: W.H. Allen.
—— 1972. 'Opening Address to Annual Meeting of the Board of Governors of the Fund, Bank, IFC and IDA'. Press release No. 3.
—— 1978. *The Memoirs of Richard Nixon*. Sydney: Macmillan – now Palgrave Macmillan.
—— 1980. *The Real War*. New York: Warner.
—— 1987. *In Memorandum: Arthur Burns 1904–1987*. Washington, DC: Board of Governors Federal Reserve Board.
Nourse, E. 1940. 'Director's Preface'. In C.O. Hardy, *Wartime Control of Prices*. Washington, DC: Brookings Institution.
Nurkse, R. 1945. *Conditions of International Monetary Equilibrium*. Essays in International Finance, No. 4, Princeton.
Oudes, B. (ed.) 1989. *From the President: Richard Nixon's Secret Files*. New York: Harper and Row.
Parkin, M. 1977. 'The Transition from Fixed Exchange Rates to Money Supply Targets'. *Journal of Money, Credit, and Banking*, IX(1), February: 228–42.
Parsons, M.H. 1970. 'Stabilising the Present International Payments System'. In Federal Reserve Bank of Boston, *The International Adjustment Mechanism*. Boston: Federal Reserve Bank of Boston.
Parsons, W. 1989. *The Power of the Financial Press*. Aldershot, England: Edward Elgar.
Patel, I.G. 1972. 'Commentary'. In H. Wallich *et al.*, *The Monetary Crisis of 1971 – the Lessons to be Learned*. Washington, DC: Per Jacobsson Foundation.
Patinkin, D. 1971. 'Keynesian Economics versus the Quantity Theory'. *Bulletin Bank Markazi Iran*, 55, May/June: 6–14.
—— 1981. *Essays on and in the Chicago Tradition*. Durham, NC: Duke University Press.
—— 2003. 'The Chicago Tradition, the Quantity Theory and Friedman'. In R. Leeson (ed.), *Keynes, Chicago and Friedman*. London: Chatto and Pickering.
Pepper, G.T. and Oliver, M.J. 2001. *Monetarism under Thatcher: Lessons for the Future*. Cheltenham, UK: Edward Elgar.
Pitchford, J.D. 1990. *Australia's Foreign Debt: Myths and Realities*. Sydney: Allen & Unwin.
Plumptre, A.F.W. 1970. *Exchange Rate Policy: Experience with Canada's Floating Rate*. Essays in International Finance, No. 81. Princeton: Princeton University.
—— 1977. *Three Decades of Decision: Canada and the World Monetary System, 1944–75*. Toronto: McClelland and Stewart.

Polak, J.J. 1979. 'The Evolution of the International Monetary System'. In A.F. Burns *et al.*, *The Anguish of Central Banking*. Belgrade: Per Jacobsson Foundation.
—— 1995. 'Fifty Years of Exchange Rate Research and Policy at the International Monetary Fund'. *IMF Staff Papers*, 42(4), December: 734–61.
—— 2002. 'The Two Monetary Approaches to the Balance of Payments: Keynesian and Johnsonian'. In W. Young and A. Arnon (eds), *The Open Economy Macromodel: Part, Present and Future*. Boston: Kluwer.
Powell, J. 1999. *A History of the Canadian Dollar*. Ottawa: Bank of Canada.
Powell, J.E. 1967. *Exchange Rates and Liquidity*. London: Institute of Economic Affairs.
—— 1969. *Freedom and Reality*. Edited by John Wood. Kingswood, Surrey: Elliott Right Way Books.
—— 1970. *Income Tax at 4/3 in the Pound*. Edited by Anthony Lejeune. London: Tom Stacey.
Powers, R.G. 1995. *Not without Honor: the History of American Anticommunism*. New York: Free Press.
Price, R. 1977. *With Nixon*. New York: Viking.
Rampa, G. Stella, L. and Thirlwall, A.P. (eds) 1998. *Economic Dynamics, Trade and Growth: Essays in Harrodian Themes*. London: Macmillan – now Palgrave Macmillan.
Ranelagh, J. 1991. *Thatcher's People*. London: HarperCollins.
Rather, D. and Gates, G.P. 1974. *The Palace Guard*. New York: Harper and Row.
Reagon, R. 1990. *An American Life*. London: Random.
Reder, M. 1982. 'Chicago Economics: Permanence and Change'. *Journal of Economic Literature*, XX, March: 1–38.
—— 1987. The Chicago School. In J. Eatwell *et al.* (eds), *The New Palgrave Dictionary of Economics*. London: Macmillan – now Palgrave Macmillan.
Rees-Mogg, W. 1977. *Democracy and the Value of Money: the Theory of Money from Locke to Keynes*. London: IEA.
Reeves, R. 1993. *President Kennedy Profile of Power*. New York: Simon and Schuster.
—— 2001. *President Nixon Alone in the White House*. New York: Simon and Schuster.
Reichley, A.J. 1981. *Conservatives in an Age of Change: the Nixon and Ford Administrations*. Washington: Brookings Institution.
Reisman, S. 1996. 'The Birth of a World Trading System: ITO and GATT'. In O. Kirshner (ed.), *The Bretton Woods–GATT System: Retrospect and Prospect after Fifty Years*. London: M.E. Sharpe.
Report of the Task Force on US Balance of Payments Policies. 1968a. Prepared for the New Haven Symposium.
Report of the Task Force on US Balance of Payments Policies. 1968b. *Final Report*.
Robbins, L. 1951. *The Balance of Payments*. London: University of London Athlone Press.
—— 1967. 'Issues and Alternatives'. In R. Hinshaw (ed.), *Monetary Reform and the Price of Gold*. Baltimore: Johns Hopkins Press.
—— 1968. 'The International Monetary Problem'. *Journal of Political Economy*, July/August, 76(4): 664–77.
—— 1971. *Autobiography of an Economist*. London: Macmillan – now Palgrave Macmillan.

—— 1976. *Political Economy Past and Present: a Review of Leading Theories of Economic Policy*. London: Macmillan – now Palgrave Macmillan.
Robinson, A. 1981. *George Meany and His Times: a Biography*. New York: Simon and Schuster.
Robinson, J. 1966. *The New Mercantilism: an Inaugural Lecture*. Cambridge: Cambridge University Press.
—— 1969. *Introduction to the Theory of Employment*, 2nd edn. London: Macmillan – now Palgrave Macmillan.
Roosa, R. 1961. 'The Central Bank in a Market Economy'. *Fortune*, March: 124–81.
—— 1962. 'Assuring the Free World's Liquidity'. In *Factors Affecting the United States Balance of Payments*. Joint Economic Committee Congress of the United States. Washington: US Government Printing Office.
—— 1967a. *The Dollar and World Liquidity*. New York: Random House.
—— 1967b. In M. Friedman and R. Roosa, *The Balance of Payments: Free versus Fixed Exchange Rates*. Washington: American Enterprise Institute for Public Policy Research.
—— 1970. 'Currency Parities in the Second Decade of Convertibility. In G. Halm (ed.), *Approaches to Greater Flexibility of Exchange Rates: the Burgenstock Papers*. Princeton: Princeton University Press.
—— 1976. 'Some Questions Remaining'. In E.M. Bernstein *et al.*, *Reflections on Jamaica*. Essays in International Finance, No. 115. Princeton University.
Rothbard, M.N. 1971. 'Milton Friedman Unravelled'. *The Individualist*, February: 3–7.
Rowen, H. 1970. 'Burns Pressing Hard for "Incomes Policy"'. *Washington Post*, 15 November.
—— 1971. 'One Thing about Nixon's Policy – It Certainly Isn't Any Secret'. *Washington Post*, 7 March.
—— 1973. 'Floating on a Sea of Crisis'. *Washington Post*, 8 March.
—— 1975. 'Arthur Burns Goes Public'. *Washington Post*, 22 May.
Safire, W. 1975. *Before the Fall: an Inside View of the Pre-Watergate White House*. New York: Belmont.
Salvatore, D. 1993. *International Economics*, 4th edn. New York: Macmillan – now Palgrave Macmillan.
Samuels, W. and Medema, S.G. 1990. *Gardiner C. Means Institutionalist and Post Keynesian*. New York: M.E. Sharp.
Samuelson, P.A. 1948. 'Disparity in Postwar Exchange Rates'. In S.E. Harris (ed.), *Foreign Economic Policy for the United States*. Cambridge, Mass.: Harvard University Press.
—— 1958. *Economics: an Introductory Analysis*, 4th edn. London: McGraw-Hill.
—— 1968. Complete Transcript of National Education Television's Great Decisions 1968: 'The Dollar in Danger'.
—— 1974. 'The President's New Economic Program: Domestic Wage and Price Controls'. In W.E. Mitchell *et al.* (eds), *Readings in Macroeconomics*. New York: McGraw-Hill.
Sargent, T. and Wallace, N. 1976. 'Rational Expectations and the Theory of Economic Policy'. *Journal of Monetary Economics*, 2 (2), April: 169–83.
Scammell, W.M. 1983. *The International Economy since 1945*. New York: St Martin's Press – now Palgrave Macmillan.

Schedvin, C.B. 1992. *In Reserve: Central Banking in Australia, 1945–75*. Sydney: Allen and Unwin.
Schlesinger, A.M. Jr 1965. *A Thousand Days: John F. Kennedy in the White House*. London: Mayflower-Dell.
Schwartz, A.J. 1987. *Money in Historical Perspective*. Chicago: University of Chicago Press.
Schweitzer, P-P. 1971. 'The Role of the Fund in the Quest for Financial Stability'. Address to the Stuttgart Chamber of Industry and Commerce, 28 April.
—— 1972a. 'A Report on the Fund'. In A.L.K. Acheson *et al.* (eds), *Bretton Woods Revisited*. London: Macmillan – now Palgrave Macmillan.
—— 1972b. 'Statement. Twenty Seventh Annual Report of the Executive Directors to the Board of Governors of the Fund'. Press release No. 2.
—— 1976. 'Political Aspects of Managing the International Monetary System'. *International Affairs*, April: 208–18.
Scitovsky, T. 1966. 'Alternative Measures for Restoring Balance'. In W. Fellner *et al.* (eds), *Maintaining and Restoring Balance in International Payments*. Princeton: Princeton University Press.
Selden, R.T. 1962. 'Stable Monetary Growth'. In L.B. Yeager (ed.), *In Search of a Monetary Constitution*. Cambridge, Mass.: Harvard UP.
Shapiro, E. 1970. 'Discussion'. In Federal Reserve Bank of Boston, *The International Adjustment Mechanism*. Boston: Federal Reserve Bank of Boston.
Shultz, G.P. 1971. 'Prescription for Economic Policy: "Steady As You Go"'. Address before the Economic Club of Chicago, 22 April.
—— 1972a. 'A Sketch of a World Monetary System'. Mimeo.
—— 1972b. Statement at the Joint Annual Discussion of the Board of Governors. September 26. Press release No. 21.
—— 1993. *Turmoil and Triumph: My Years as Secretary of State*. New York: Charles Scribner's Sons.
—— 1995. 'Economics in Action: Ideas, Institutions and Policies'. *American Economic Review*, 85(2), May: 1–8.
Shultz, G.P. and Aliber, R.Z. (eds) 1966. *Guidelines: Informal Controls and the Market Place*. Chicago: University of Chicago Press.
Shultz, G.P. and Dam, K.W. 1977a. *Economic Policy beyond the Headlines*. New York: W.W. Norton.
Shultz, G.P. and Dam, K.W. 1977b. 'Reflections on Wage and Price Controls'. *Industrial and Labor Relations Review*, 31: 139–51.
Shultz, G.P. Simon, W.E. and Wriston, J.B. 1998. *Who Needs the IMF?* http://www.imfsite.org/abolish/needsshultz.html
Sichel, W. (ed.) 1978. *Economic Advice and Executive Policy Recommendations from Past Members of the Council of Economic Advisers*. New York: Praeger.
Silberman, H.L. 1971. 'Introducing the Potomac Papers: the Rise of the Revolutionary Establishment'. *Finance*, September: 8–15.
Silk, L. 1976. *The Economists*. New York: Avon.
Simon, W.E. 1978. *A Time for Truth*. Sydney: McGraw-Hill.
Simons, H. 1934. 'Money and the New Deal: Review of Pasvolsky's *Current Monetary Issues*'. *New Republic*, 21 February: 53–4.
Simons, H.C. 1935. 'Depression Economics'. *The Christian Century*, November 6: 1421.
—— 1948. *Economic Policy for a Free Society*. Chicago: University of Chicago Press.

—— 1962. 'Rules versus Authorities in Monetary Policy'. In E.J. Hamilton *et al.* (eds), *Landmarks in Political Economy*. Chicago: University of Chicago.

Skidelsky, R. 1983. *John Maynard Keynes: Hopes Betrayed, 1883–1920*. London: Macmillan – now Palgrave Macmillan.

—— 1992. *John Maynard Keynes: the Economist as Saviour, 1920–1937*. London: Macmillan – now Palgrave Macmillan.

Smith, D. 1987. *The Rise and Fall of Monetarism*. London: Penguin.

Smithies, B. and Fiddick, P. 1969. *Enoch Powell on Immigration: an Analysis*. London: Sphere.

Soddy, F. 1934. *The Role of Money*. London: George Routledge.

—— 1943. *The Arch-Enemy of Economic Freedom*. Oxford: Knapp, Enstone.

Sohmen, E. 1957. 'Demand Elasticities and the Foreign Exchange Market'. *Journal of Political Economy*, 65, October: 431–6.

—— 1961a. 'Notes on Some Controversies in the Theory of International Trade: a Comment'. *Economic Journal*, 71, June: 423–6.

—— 1961b. *Flexible Exchange Rates*. Chicago: University of Chicago Press.

Solomon, R. 1982. *The International Monetary System, 1945–1981*. New York: Harper and Row.

Solow, R. 1966a. 'The Wage–Price Issue and the Guidelines'. In F.H. Harbison and J.D. Mooney (eds), *Critical Issues in Employment Policy*. Industrial Relations Section: Princeton University Press.

—— 1966b. 'The Case against the Case against the Guidelines'. In G.P. Shultz and R.Z. Aliber (eds), *Guidelines: Informal Controls and the Market Place*. Chicago: University of Chicago Press.

—— 1970. Statement. In *Hearings before the Joint Economic Committee Congress of the United States*, Part 2. Washington: US Government Printing Office.

Southard, F.A. 1979. *The Evolution of the International Monetary Fund*. Essays in International Finance, No. 135. Princeton: Princeton University.

Stein, H. 1969. *The Fiscal Revolution in America*. Chicago: University of Chicago Press.

—— 1995. *On the Other Hand…Essays on Economics, Economists, and Politics*. Washington, DC: AEI Press.

Stigler, G. 1954. 'The Economist Plays with Blocs'. *American Economic Association Papers and Proceedings*, May: 7–14.

—— 1963. *The Intellectual and the Market Place*. London: Free Press.

—— 1966a. 'Report'. In G.P. Shultz and R.Z. Aliber (eds), *Guidelines: Informal Controls and the Market Place*. Chicago: University of Chicago Press.

—— 1966b. *The Theory of Price*. London: Macmillan – now Palgrave Macmillan.

—— 1967. 'The Changing Problem of Oligopoly'. *Il Politico*, 32: 355–61.

—— 1986. *The Essence of Stigler*. Edited by Kurt Leube and Thomas Gale Moore. Stanford, Calif.: Hoover Institution Press.

—— 1987. *The Theory of Price*. New York: Macmillan – now Palgrave Macmillan.

—— 1988. *Memoirs of an Unregulated Economist*. New York: Basic Books.

Summers, A. 2001. *The Arrogance of Power: the Secret World of Richard Nixon*. London: Phoenix.

Swan, T. 1963. 'Longer-run Problems of the Balance of Payments'. In H.W. Arndt and W.M. Corden (eds), *The Australian Economy: a Volume of Readings*. Melbourne: F.W. Cheshire.

Tavlas, G.S. 1977. 'The Chicago Tradition Revisited: Some Neglected Monetary Contributions: Senator Paul Douglas (1892–1976)'. *Journal of Money Credit and Banking*, 9, November: 529–38.

Taylor, J. 2000. 'An Interview with Milton Friedman'. *Macroeconomic Dynamics*, 5: 101–31.

Thirlwall, A. (ed.) 1976. *Keynes and International Monetary Relations*. London: Macmillan – now Palgrave Macmillan.

Triffin, R. 1948. 'Exchange Controls and Equilibrium'. In S.E. Harris (ed.), *Foreign Economic Policy for the United States*. Cambridge, Mass.: Harvard University Press.

—— 1957. *Europe and the Money Muddle: From Bilateralism to Near-Convertibility*. New Haven: Yale University Press.

—— 1963. 'After the Gold Exchange Standard'. In H. Gruebel (ed.), *World Monetary Reform: Plans and Issues*. Stanford: Stanford University Press.

—— 1968. *Our International Monetary System*. New York: Random House.

—— 1970. 'Discussion'. In Federal Reserve Bank of Boston, *The International Adjustment Mechanism*. Boston: Federal Reserve Bank of Boston.

—— 1976. 'Jamaica: "Major Reform" or Fiasco?' In E.M. Bernstein *et al.*, *Reflections on Jamaica*. Essays in International Finance, No. 115. Princeton University.

—— 1978. 'The Impact of the Bellagio Group on International Monetary Reform'. In J.S. Dreyer (ed.), *Breadth and Depth in Economics: Fritz Machlup – the Man and this Ideas*. Toronto: Lexington.

Viner, J. 1942. 'Inflation – Menace or Bogey?' *Yale Review*, 31: 684–702.

—— 1964. *Problems of Monetary Control*. Essays in International Finance, No. 45. Princeton University, Department of Economics.

Vining, R. 1949. 'Koopmans on the Choice of Variable to be Studied and of Methods of Measurement'. *Review of Economics and Statistics*, 31(2), May: 77–86, 92–4.

Volcker, P. 1978–79. 'The Political Economy of the Dollar'. *Federal Reserve Bank of New York Quarterly Review*, Winter: 1–12.

—— 1990. *The Triumph of Central Banking*. The 1990 Per Jacobsson Lecture. Washington, DC: Per Jacobsson Foundation.

Volcker, P. and Gyohten, T. 1992. *Changing Fortunes: the World's Money and the Threat to American Leadership*. New York: Times.

Wallich, H. 1972. 'Commentary'. In H. Wallich *et al.*, *The Monetary Crisis of 1971 – the Lessons to be Learned*. Washington, DC: Per Jacobsson Foundation.

Wallich, H. and Axilrod, S.H. 1964. 'Postwar United States Monetary Policy Appraised'. In N.H. Jacoby (ed.), *United States Monetary Policy*. New York: Praeger.

Wallich, H., Morse, J. and Patel, I.G. 1972. *The Monetary Crisis of 1971 – the Lessons to be Learned*. Washington, DC: Per Jacobsson Foundation.

Wallis, W.A. 1942. 'How to Ration Consumers' Goods and Control Their Prices'. *American Economic Review*, September: 501–12.

—— 1976. *An Overgoverned Society*. London: Free Press.

Walters, A. 1989. 'A Life Philosophy'. *American Economist*, 33: 18–24.

Weinberger, C. 1990. *Fighting for Peace: Seven Critical Years in the Pentagon*. New York: Warner.

Wells, W.C. 1994. *Economist in an Uncertain World: Arthur F. Burns and the Federal Reserve, 1970–78*. New York: Columbia University Press.
White, T.H. 1965. *The Making of the President 1964*. New York: Signet.
Williamson, J. 1977. *The Failure of World Monetary Reform*. London: Nelson.
—— 1978. 'Machlup and International Monetary Reform'. In J.S. Dreyer (ed.), *Breadth and Depth in Economics: Fritz Machlup – the Man and His Ideas*. Toronto: Lexington.
—— 1987. *Political Economy and International Money: Selected Essays of John Williamson*. Edited by Chris Milner. New York: New York University Press.
Wilson, H. 1971. *The Labour Government, 1964–1970*. Middlesex: Penguin.
Witteveen, H.J. 1975. 'Annual Address of the Managing Director'. *IMF Survey* Annual Meeting Issue, 15 September: 259–62.
Wittner, L.S. 1978. *Cold War America from Hiroshima to Watergate*. New York: Holt, Rinehart and Winston.
Wolf-Heidegger, G. 1964. 'Opening Remarks'. In *Economic Growth and Monetary Stability*. Basle, Switzerland: Per Jacobsson Foundation.
Woodward, B. and Bernstein, C. 1976. *The Final Days*. London: Coronet.
Woolley, J.T. 1984. *Monetary Politics: the Federal Reserve and the Politics of Monetary Policy*. Cambridge: Cambridge University Press.
Working Party No. 3. 1966. *The Balance of Payments Adjustment Process*. Economic Policy Committee of the OECD.
Yeager, L.B. 1976. *International Monetary Relations: Theory, History and Policy*, 2nd edn. New York: Harper and Row.
Young, W. 1998. 'Harrod and Haberler beyond the Trade Cycle: Exchanges on International Liquidity, Gold, Trade, Inflation, Monetarism and Friedman, 1961–1971'. In G. Rampa *et al.* (eds), *Economic Dynamics, Trade and Growth: Essays in Harrodian Themes*. London: Macmillan – now Palgrave Macmillan.
Young, W. and Arnon, A. (eds) 2002. *The Open Economy Macromodel: Past, Present and Future*. Boston: Kluwer.

Index